THE
REBIRTH
OF AFRICAN
ORTHODOXY

THE REBIRTH OF AFRICAN ORTHODOXY

RETURN TO FOUNDATIONS

THOMAS C. ODEN

Abingdon Press
Nashville

THE REBIRTH OF AFRICAN ORTHODOXY:
RETURN TO FOUNDATIONS

Copyright © 2016 by Thomas C. Oden

All rights reserved.

No part of this work may be reproduced or transmitted in any form or by any means, electronic or mechanical, including photocopying and recording, or by any information storage or retrieval system, except as may be expressly permitted by the 1976 Copyright Act or in writing from the publisher. Requests for permission can be addressed to Permissions, The United Methodist Publishing House, 2222 Rosa L. Parks Blvd., P.O. Box 280988, Nashville, TN, 37228-0988 or e-mailed to permissions@umpublishing.org.

Library of Congress Cataloging-in-Publication Data has been requested.

ISBN 978-1-5018-1909-4

Scripture quotations unless noted otherwise are taken from the Common English Bible. Copyright © 2011 by the Common English Bible. All rights reserved. Used by permission. www.CommonEnglishBible.com.

Scripture quotations marked NIV are taken from the Holy Bible, NEW INTERNATIONAL VERSION®. Copyright © 1973, 1978, 1984 by International Bible Society. All rights reserved throughout the world. Used by permission of International Bible Society.

Scripture quotations marked KJV are from The Authorized (King James) Version. Rights in the Authorized Version in the United Kingdom are vested in the Crown. Reproduced by permission of the Crown's patentee, Cambridge University Press.

Scripture quotations marked "NKJV™" are taken from the New King James Version®. Copyright © 1982 by Thomas Nelson, Inc. Used by permission. All rights reserved.

Scripture quotations marked *THE MESSAGE* are taken from *THE MESSAGE*. Copyright © by Eugene H. Peterson 1993, 1994, 1995, 1996, 2000, 2001, 2002. Used by permission of NavPress Publishing Group.

CONTENTS

LIST OF ABBREVIATIONS ix

PART ONE: AFRICA'S GIFT

SEMINAR 1: RETURN TO THE FOUNTAIN 3
   A. REDISCOVERING THE EARLIEST AFRICAN BIBLICAL INTERPRETERS 4
   B. CLASSIC CHRISTIANITY IN AFRICA 9

SEMINAR 2: THE AWAKENING OF A GIANT 15
   A. ATHANASIUS AND FRIENDS 15
   B. HISTORICAL PERSPECTIVE: A TURNAROUND IS OCCURRING 23
   C. THE HIGH COST OF MODERN LIVING 26

SEMINAR 3: AFRICA'S GIFT TO GLOBAL CHRISTIANITY 31
   A. THE HUNGER FOR ROOTS 31
   B. ORTHODOX PRACTICE AS A SOCIOLOGICAL SKILL 34
   C. ORTHODOX JEWS AND ORTHODOX CHRISTIANS 38

SEMINAR 4: ORTHODOX REMEMBERING 43
   A. REMEMBERING THAT WHICH IS MOST WORTHY OF MEMORY 43
   B. RETURNING TO THE FOUNTAIN 45
   C. POLITICAL WINNERS? 49

CONTENTS

SEMINAR 5: WHY ORTHODOXY PERSISTS 53
  A. NINE REASONS ORTHODOXY SURVIVES 53
  B. GOING DEEPER: THE KERNEL OF TENACITY 62

SEMINAR 6: ONE FAITH: CONCORD AS THE GIFT OF THE SPIRIT 69
  A. HOW AFRICAN ORTHODOXY IS STILL NURTURING GLOBAL CHRISTIANITY 69
  B. DIVERGING VIEWS OF CHRISTIAN UNITY 75
  C. THE UNITING WORK OF THE SPIRIT 77

PART TWO: SIGNS OF NEW LIFE

SEMINAR 7: THE NEW BIRTH OF AFRICAN ORTHODOXY 83
  A. ORDINARY LIVES ARE BEING REVITALIZED ONE BY ONE 83
  B. HOW MY ROAD TO ORTHODOXY LED THROUGH AFRICA 85

SEMINAR 8: RECLAIMING THE SACRED TEXTS 91
  A. LISTENING TO SCRIPTURE THROUGH THE COMMUNITY OF BELIEVERS 91
  B. THE CHURCH'S BOOK 94
  C. FOLLOWING THE WORD IN ORDER TO HEAR IT 99
  D. TOWARD A WIDER CROSS-CULTURAL CONSENSUS 101

SEMINAR 9: CONSENSUS RECOGNITION 109
  A. LEARNING TO TRUST 109
  B. DISCERNING THE POWER OF THE CONSENSUS 114
  C. LEARNING TO SAY NO 118
  D. HONING A CRITICAL ORTHODOXY 120
  E. RECOGNIZING ANCIENT BOUNDARY STONES 122
  F. REGAINING EQUILIBRIUM 124
  G. RECENTERING FAITH 128
  H. CUTTING THROUGH THE RHETORIC 132

SEMINAR 10: REDISCOVERING CLASSIC ECUMENICAL
METHOD   135
   A. AN AID TO REMEMBERING   135
   B. FOUR HISTORIC PROTOTYPES OF CRISES OF CONFIDENCE
      IN GENERAL CONSENT   142
   C. THE APOSTOLIC MODEL OF RIGHT REMEMBERING   150
   D. TREASURES OLD AND NEW   153
   E. CONCLUDING IMPERATIVES   156

BIBLIOGRAPHY OF ORTHODOX AFRICAN WRITERS:
CLASSIC AND CONTEMPORARY   159
   A. PRIMARY SOURCES: CLASSIC AFRICAN CHRISTIAN
      THEOLOGIANS AND KEY TEXTS BEFORE 700 AD   160
   B. THE AFRICAN DESERT MOTHERS   163
   C. THE AFRICAN DESERT FATHERS   165
   D. CONTEMPORARY ORTHODOX AFRICAN THEOLOGIANS
      AND WRITERS   167

LIST OF ABBREVIATIONS

ACCS	Ancient Christian Commentary on Scripture
AD	Anno Domini, Latin for "year of our Lord," the number of years since the time of Jesus Christ.
AF	*The Apostolic Fathers.* Edited by J. N. Sparks. New York: Thomas Nelson, 1978.
ANF	*Ante-Nicene Fathers.* 10 vols. Edited by A. Roberts and J. Donaldson. 1885–1896. Reprint. Grand Rapids: Eerdmans, 1979. References include book (in Roman numerals) and chapter or section number (usually in Arabic numerals), followed by volume and page number.
BC	Before Christ
CB	The Church's Bible, General Series Editor Robert Wilkin, Grand Rapids, Eerdmans, 2003ff.
CC	*Creeds of the Churches.* Edited by John Leith. Richmond, VA: John Knox Press, 1979.
CEB	Common English Bible, CEB Study Bible with Apocrypha, Nashville, Abingdon, 2013.
FC	The Fathers of the Church: A New Translation. 127 vols. to date. Edited by R. J. Deferrari. Washington, DC: Catholic Univ. Press, 1947–.
FEF	*The Faith of the Early Fathers.* 3 vols. Edited by William A. Jurgens. Collegeville, MN: Liturgical Press, 1970 ff.

LIST OF ABBREVIATIONS

IDC	International Data Corporation
JJW	*The Journal of the Reverend John Wesley.* 8 vols. Edited by Nehemiah Curnock. London: Epworth, 1909–1916.
JWO	*John Wesley.* Edited by Albert C. Outler. LPT. New York: Oxford Univ. Press, 1964.
KJV	King James Version of the Bible, 1611.
LCM	"Letter to the Rev. Dr. Conyers Middleton"
LJW	*The Letters of John Wesley*, ed. John Telford, 8 vols. London: Epworth Press, 1931.
NIV	New International Version of the Bible
NPNF	Nicene and Post-Nicene Fathers
SCD	*Sources of Catholic Dogma (Enchiridion Symbolorum).* Edited by Henry Denzinger and translated by Roy J. Deferrari. New York: Herder, 1954.
SCG	Saint Thomas Aquinas. *Summa Contra Gentiles.* 5 vols. Edited by Anton Pegis. Garden City, NY: Image Books, 1955–1957.
WCC	World Council of Churches

PART ONE
AFRICA'S GIFT

SEMINAR 1
RETURN TO THE FOUNTAIN

Classic African Christian teaching in the patristic period (100–750 AD) preceded modern colonialism by over a thousand years. Many young African women and men are now reexamining these lost roots. They are hungry for accurate information on their brilliant Christian ancestors.

Here are ten sessions of a seminar in which the rebirth of African orthodoxy is examined in terms of its hopes, methods, and conclusions.

A seminar hinges on a regular session reading that forms the basis of a probing discussion where all voices are respected. This dialogue could be held among students or laypersons, friends, or even family members—anyone who has caught the vision of early African Christianity and wants to test its feasibility. It may be led by an educator or pastor or parent or skeptic who might wish to explore the consequences of these ten introductory reflections. Aware that learning in many parts of Africa is a social process shared in a community and not simply by an individual reading a book, this plan of study is designed more for interaction than individual reflection.

The sessions can be completed in a weekend retreat or weekly sessions or any time frame, but preferably in no more than a semester. The two parts of the course could be done in a laid-back way in five days with a half day for each seminar topic; or more concentrated in two intensive days by preparing entirely beforehand through reading all ten introductions before meeting. The ten seminars are made available free in digital form to African seminarians through the Kindle eBook loan program funded by the United Methodist Publishing House and Discipleship Ministries, a UMC agency.

These discussions could occur anywhere within global Christianity, but are focused primarily on Africa and Africans living either on the continent or in the vast African diaspora. Investigators from any nation or ethnicity can enter the sacred archive of this treasured African library (see Bibliography Part A). Both lay and professional persons have equal claim to this heritage.

Nothing in this study requires confession or consent; it is rather *about* classic Christian confession and consent while leaving it to each conscience as to how to respond. The seminar permits ample room for debate, comparison of perspectives, and further refinement. These sessions can be taken independently of my two previous books *How Africa Shaped the Christian Mind* and *The African Memory of Mark*, though both books will be useful for any who wish to read further about the rebirth of African orthodoxy.

Although this topic is best experienced in a dialogue, it is possible to read all these seminar introductions as a single book. If you do not have seminar partners, you can do it alone.

The original *Rebirth of Orthodoxy* was written primarily for a North American audience.[1] After it was translated into Arabic in Egypt and Amharic in Ethiopia, the need for an international edition was clear. Then a persistent request came from sub-Saharan Africans that it be translated into other languages of Africa. This required a complete overhaul focusing on the rebirth of African orthodoxy.

The metaphor of "returning" in the subtitle refers to educators, theologians, pastors, and lay readers who are coming home to early African Christian sources. Many have wandered far away. They seek sufficient reasons to return to ancient African writers.

A. REDISCOVERING THE EARLIEST AFRICAN BIBLICAL INTERPRETERS

The leading indicator of the rebirth of African orthodoxy is the widespread study of the earliest African Christian writers. African orthodoxy is reappearing as a distinct genre of investigation because its earliest texts are enjoyed by countless Africans and many around the world.

Consensual orthodoxy is preferred to the term generic orthodoxy. Generic refers to that which is commonly held in a group or class. But generic is a thin adjective far less descriptive of the active voluntary consent given to the apostolic witness over twenty centuries. This form of "African orthodoxy" already exists as a fact of our time. (See Bibliography.) It is a palpable movement of confession and renewal within the divided churches as an answer to the hunger for roots within chaotic modern culture. It is an emerging global reality. The work of the Holy Spirit is deepening the spiritual unity of the international community of baptized believers. Documenting the evidences for African orthodoxy is what we are about in this book.

---

1. This work is a sequel to *The Rebirth of Orthodoxy: Signs of New Life in Christianity* (San Francisco: HarperCollins, 2003). Conditions have changed since 2003, with the study of orthodoxy now stimulated by numerous translation projects that have made many of the early African texts more available and digitally accessible.

AFRICA'S ROLE IN THE GLOBAL CONSENSUS FORMED EARLY FROM APOSTOLIC TEACHING

In recent years a flurry of activity has centered on the wonder of reading the Bible alongside its earliest interpreters. This has had special importance for Africans.

The most active stimulant for the recovery of African orthodoxy is the translation and interpretation of early African ways of reading scripture. This field is called the history of exegesis, from the Greek term for interpretation (ἐξήγησις, *exegesis*). Patristic[2] exegesis is part of the history of biblical study that was initiated in the earliest Christian centuries. Where the word "patristic" occurs, read as patristic/matristic, since numerous women were participants in the interpretation of early Christian scriptures—Macrina, Amma Theodora, Paula, Marcela, Melania the Elder, Fabiola, Eustochium, and others (see Bibliography Part B). Africa's role in early exegesis has been immense.

An extraordinary effort is underway to reclaim the earliest African commentators on scripture.[3] The study of the early African church fathers and mothers is an active subsection of contemporary biblical and historical investigations. The most robust work is being done by young African biblical scholars.

When Bible study is guided by the first African interpreters of scripture, it comes alive with personal testimony, moral intensity, and worthwhile insight. It burns from within. By contrast, when Bible study is guided exclusively by modern Euro-American biblical interpreters it is typically imprinted by western values. African students of the Bible easily recognize the difference.

Modern African theology has been plagued by an unwanted and unneeded dependency upon modern western ideas. This has occurred after a century in which the most ancient African Christian ideas and achievements have been largely ignored, even demeaned.

In the modern period Africans often sought education, approval, and a personal legitimacy from western elites. Not so today. They are more often looking for ancient African wisdom uncontaminated by skewed modern western ideologies.

AN UNEXPECTED OUTCOME OF THE ANCIENT CHRISTIAN COMMENTARY ON SCRIPTURE

Over one third of entries in the Ancient Christian Commentary on Scripture came out of Africa. This can be verified by comparing references from primary

---

2. See Kevin Madigan and Carolyn Osiek, eds., *Ordained Women in the Early Church* (Baltimore, Maryland: The Johns Hopkins University Press, 2005).

3. InterVarsity Press is publishing a series on Ancient Christian Texts which includes volumes by Origen and Cyril of Alexandria, and The Institute of Classical Christian Studies is publishing a two-volume work on patristic sources from Africa ordered verse by verse. The Ancient Christian Commentary on Scripture contains thousands of references to text sources from Africa.

sources. Though less than 10 percent of Christians lived in patristic Africa, they contributed more than 30 percent of the stored wisdom of the church fathers and mothers on understanding the Bible.

A major involvement in this journey for me has been the project for which I have been personally responsible as General Editor—the Ancient Christian Commentary on Scripture (ACCS). This vast twenty-year effort stands as primary scholarly evidence of the rebirth of orthodoxy. Its preparation began in 1990 and by 2010 the intensive study of patristic exegesis was complete.

The ACCS is the work of an international team of Catholic, Protestant, and Orthodox scholars, translators, and editors who reconstructed for the first time in centuries a massive (twenty-nine-volume) classic patristic commentary on the whole of scripture. These early voices echo today from the languages of Africa written in the third to the seventh centuries, especially in Greek, Coptic, Latin, and Ge'ez.

So many of the best of these earliest interpreters come from the African continent. In 2003 The Church's Bible (CB) edited by Robert Wilkin began its first volume. These two series (ACCS and CB) have drawn many global evangelical and Catholic voices into the discussion. They did not go unnoticed in Africa.

The Ancient Christian Commentary on Scripture is similar to the chains (*catena*) of patristic recollections that conveyed the thoughts of the first Christian commentators. The catena writers of the fifth century and following were very selective in remembering those comments most worthy of being written down in a collection. A comment did not enter the catena without having been used, valued, and transmitted by ardent readers over several generations. That was a powerful winnowing process that tended to keep the finest, and arrange them verse by verse. They became classic arguments for all subsequent Bible readers to consider, and the primitive template of the modern commentary.

THE EARLY INTERPRETERS OF THE CHRISTIAN SCRIPTURES

Now we have accessible an abundance of powerful primary texts from early Africa about biblical passages as they were viewed by Cyprian, Origen, Tertullian, and Clement, as well as the leading Patriarchs Dionysius, Peter, Alexander, Athanasius, and Cyprian—all Africans, born on African soil. Together they form a huge collection of profound reflections and homilies on scripture. I spent almost two decades of my life editing all the volumes of this general patristic commentary before I firmly grasped that so many of such high quality and influence came from Africa. That recognition elicited the Center for Early African Christianity.

Virtually every verse of scripture has been examined by Africans writing earlier than 750 AD. The observations, debates, musings, and deliberations of early African Christian minds may now be scrutinized through the whole range of scripture and taught to a newly receptive African audience. The high intellectual quality of these African writers is evident.

Origen and Cyprian set the patterns for early Bible commentaries that became exemplary precedents for Bible study in Jerusalem, Caesarea, Antioch, and Rome. The Cappadocian commentators (Basil the Great, Gregory Nyssa, Gregory of Nazianzus, as well as John Chrysostom) depended heavily on African sources. Later the major European commentators such as Ambrose, Jerome, Leo I, and Gregory the Great stood on the shoulders of the Africans and Cappadocians.

This body of scriptural interpretation shows evidence of an emerging worldwide, consensual approach to the study of Scripture. It now is obtainable in both print and digital forms so that any who wish to think with the best minds of the early church can do so. They can see these minds at work on a particular passage of scripture.

THE WHOLE CANON OF SCRIPTURE DEFINED AND SYSTEMATICALLY RESEARCHED IN AFRICA

The canon of scripture itself was explicitly defined for eastern and western Christianity in Africa. The biblical canon is the church's book that lists the writings of the first witnesses to be read in church. A canon is a list of writings that advise Christians of all cultures on which writings from the apostolic beginnings have been most widely received as reliable. The canon of holy writ, received by the faithful of all times around the world, remains the crucial criterion for orthodox doctrine, polity, ethics, and social teaching. The Hebrew Bible is always included in the Christian canon.

These lists existed in many parts of world Christianity in the third and fourth centuries, but none of these lists was regarded as acceptable by virtually all parties. It was not until the Egyptian Patriarch Athanasius wrote his Paschal letter of Easter 367 that a list was provided that in due time became most widely received by worshipping communities of the East and West, later including many Protestants. The prevailing western canon harks back to the Synod of Hippo Regius in North Africa (393), whose acts were confirmed by the Councils of Carthage in 397 and 419 under the authority of St. Augustine.

The three commonly held criteria for books being included in the New Testament canon were:

1. all agreed that they must be of apostolic origin based upon preaching of the first generation of witnesses;

2. they must have received worldwide consent by major Christian communities of the ancient world; and

3. they must be approved for public reading in church when gathered for Holy Communion at the Lord's Table.

These were the books of the Hebrew Bible and the New Testament that remain of unparalleled interest to believers everywhere, and nowhere more attentively than in Africa.

Thus African Christianity as represented by the ancient churches of Alexandria and Carthage played a major role not only in defining the canon of scripture but in interpreting it in a way that became a model for liturgy and scripture study in the later major patriarchates of Antioch, Jerusalem, and Rome. Antiochene historical interpretation relied heavily on Alexandrian models of plain sense, moral, spiritual interpretation, even while amplifying them and correcting their limitations.

THE PERSISTENCE OF AFRICAN WRITERS AMONG THE EARLIEST COMMENTATORS ON SCRIPTURE

Serious readers of scripture have long wished that these early commentaries might be accurately recovered, translated, and thoughtfully examined. This longing had largely been ignored by the last two hundred years of Enlightenment-period biblical scholarship, which has instead focused attention on European rational, empirical, historical, literary, and critical methods.

Now, for the first time in recent centuries, these earliest layers of classic African Christian readings of biblical texts are widely available in common-language translation for pastors, teachers, parents, and lay leaders. The Institute for Classical Christian Studies Press is publishing a multivolume African Library that will bring many of these biblical and doctrinal sources together.

Virtually no portion of Hebrew and Christian scripture was neglected in the investigation of these early Christian writers. In Africa especially they studied the Bible with deep thoughtfulness, carefully comparing text with text, often memorizing large portions of holy writ, especially the psalms, canticles, and New Testament Gospels and Letters.

The African writer Didymus the Blind (c. 313–398), for example, was a biblical scholar in the Church of Alexandria whose famous Catechetical School he directed for almost half a century. Due to his blindness since childhood, Didymus had to memorize the Scriptures by having others read them to him. Despite his impaired vision, his memory was so powerful that he mastered the scriptures as well as the liberal arts. His work *On the Trinity* is an ordered recollection of scriptures harvested from his prodigious memory.

Today African believers are asking how they might grasp the meaning of their sacred texts by utilizing the great minds of the ancient African tradition. Since the times of Cyprian and Origen these interpretations have illuminated world Christians in the deeper study of scripture.

The Holy Spirit has a history. A decisive portion of that history occurred on the African continent. Whenever this history is systematically forgotten, it is a blessed task to remember it, and to do so accurately. A sustained effort is required to recover hard-won achievements disregarded over time.

THE INSPIRING VOICES OF ORTHODOX WOMEN IN THE FORMATION OF THE CONSENSUS

There are many others who speak in the same voice as these most widely acknowledged consensual teachers. These include the faithful women of the early church whom the Holy Spirit inspired to create and sustain the ecumenical consensus. Among them are names of women previously cited—Macrina the Younger, Paula, Marcela, Melania the Elder, Eustochium—as well as Olympia, Amma Sarah, and Amma Theodora, and later holy women such as Teresa of Ávila, Catherine of Siena, and Hildegard of Bingen who were named Doctors of the Church in the Latin tradition. None of the more generally acknowledged Doctors of the Church have led the ensuing tradition to rebellion against the classic consensual teaching, including Phoebe Palmer, who followed the "old religion" and quoted the ancient Christian writers. Many of the above women were charged with the spiritual formation of women, but all had a wide following among all the faithful. If the criterion for holy teachers of the church at the time of Vincent of Lérins (fl. 430s AD) is pertinent here, as we will discuss in the last chapter, there were many women saints and martyrs, some living ascetic lives and others in marriages with families.

Countless orthodox women over two millennia have articulated and followed the classic Christian consensus. Obviously no male father of the church could have ever existed without a mother, and among patristic writers the most notable mothers are Monica, mother of Augustine, and Macrina the Elder, Emmelia the revered grandmother of three influential theologians: Basil the Great, Gregory of Nyssa, and Peter of Sebaste.

Moreover, without the Virgin Mary there would be no incarnate Lord, no Mediator between God and humanity, no human element in the divine human reconciliation.

B. CLASSIC CHRISTIANITY IN AFRICA

African Christians look back to the longest uninterrupted memory of the coming of Jesus, since Mark, who wrote the earliest Gospel, was the first sent to Africa, likely in the 40s or 50s AD. The Ethiopian eunuch was the first sub-Saharan African to be baptized (Acts 8:38). This occurred before either Paul was baptized by Ananius (Acts 9:17-18) or Cornelius by Peter (Acts 10:44-48). The date was about 34 AD.

In no generation since Mark has Africa lacked an apostolic witness. Thus the depth, longevity, and continuity of African orthodoxy make it exceptionally strong in tested judgment. Many doctrinal boundaries (concerning Arius, Montanus, Pelagius,

Donatus, and others) were first established in Africa before they became ecumenical consensus in Europe and Asia.

DEFINING CLASSIC CONSENSUAL CHRISTIANITY

By *orthodox* (lowercase) I mean ancient scriptural teaching as understood by its most consensual classic interpreters in the earliest Christian centuries, from 150 to 750 AD. If African writers ever had a golden period it would be this one, especially in the generations before Nicea (325).

For Jews orthodoxy means accurate rabbinic reading of the Law and Prophets. For Christians it means correct teaching of the central core of the history of Israel as viewed in the light of its first witnesses, and as they were consensually explained on behalf of all believers of all times, commonly called classical Christian teaching.

By *consensual*[4] I mean the teaching duly confirmed by a process of general consent of the faithful over two millennia. For Jews this means the Talmud, Midrash, and commentaries. For Christians this means the teaching of the same time period, confirmed by the ecumenical councils that have been widely acknowledged and received as reliable by the faithful worldwide. The similar term "Classic Christianity" is the unified teaching that has remained faithful to the biblical witness as received by Christian believers of all cultures, languages, and times.

Consensus here means the harmony of voices celebrating the apostolic testimony. This harmonic assent is being spoken and sung in hundreds of languages and thousands of cultural mutations without changing its core testimony. It is also different from a current political consensus because it lives through many political cultures without abandoning its apostolic identity.

C. S. Lewis called it "mere Christianity." Christian orthodoxy bears the good news of the coming of the incarnate Lord who died for our sins. This testimony has been consensually received and faithfully transmitted for two millennia. It is ancient ecumenical teaching, as distinguished from modern ecumenical dialogue.

The intellectual seedbed in which these consensus teachings were initially hammered out was North Africa. In Africa conflict was so intense over varied interpretations of the apostles that it required councils to settle them. These African Councils contributed decisively to early Christian doctrinal definition.

Consensual orthodoxy refers to all Christians of all places and languages who confess with one heart to the teaching of the apostles. Thus the consensual orthodoxy to which we refer is inclusive of Coptic Orthodoxy, Ethiopian Orthodoxy, Catholic teaching, and Protestant and charismatic forms of orthodoxy that affirm Jesus Christ as Lord, only Son of God the Father through the power of the Spirit according to the scriptures. All who from the heart truly confess the Apostles' Creed and its equivalents are orthodox. Those who follow the decisions of the earliest Ecumenical Councils (Nicea, Constantinople, and Ephesus) hold orthodox beliefs common to all

---

4. That which conveys the ecumenical consensus.

African Christianity. Wherever these convictions are held in the heart by faith, which is something different from intellectual assent alone, there orthodox Christianity is coming to life. This circle includes most Protestant, Pentecostal, and African Instituted Church traditions who confess the same faith today.

African orthodoxy is not different in basic Christian teaching from global orthodoxy, but it is significantly rooted in and shaped out of indigenous African experience. African orthodoxy today is the same faith as that confessed by Athanasius and Augustine more than seventeen centuries ago.

EARLY AFRICAN ORTHODOX FAITH

The phrase "early African orthodoxy" is the form of classic Christian consensual teaching that was first planted in Africa by Africans from Mark to Clement to Tertullian to Cyprian to Augustine to Cyril the Great—all African born, all affirming the same core faith.

Early African orthodox faith is in accord with both the ancient faith of African Christians and the present faith of countless African Catholics, Copts, Pentecostals, charismatics, African Independent Churches, and many Protestant believers of Spirit-led scriptural teaching. The task ahead is to show how all of these voices at some level sing in harmony in the one body of Christ.

Uppercase *Orthodoxy* (spelled with a capital O) refers to the faith confessed by the great historical traditions of Coptic Orthodox, Ethiopian Orthodox, and Eastern Orthodox churches (such as Greek, Syrian, and Armenian), which have had such great influence in early African Christianity. While the "capital O Orthodox" faithful are orthodox in teaching, lowercase orthodox teaching is not limited to the particular Orthodox traditions of the East, since it was conceived as worldwide from the times of the Acts of the Apostles.

The Patriarchs of Alexandria, Antioch, and Rome honored and recognized each other and sought consensus. The One, Holy, Catholic, Apostolic Church has from the outset aspired to speak in one voice. Western orthodox Christian teaching shares much in common with Eastern Orthodoxy. Both depend heavily on early African teaching. That which is commonly confessed between them is orthodox in faith. Thus there are Protestants, including Lutheran, Reformed, Baptist, Anglican, Methodist, Pentecostal, and Charismatic believers, who share the common core of faith held by all who confess the faith of the apostles. This does not settle all questions of church order and sacramental life, but it does touch their common core.

What we call here "lowercase orthodox faith" is commonly shared by all Eastern Orthodox Church traditions, Coptic traditions, Roman Catholics, and those who confess the faith of the apostles. Core essential teachings are shared by Catholics and Orthodox and Protestants on scriptural authority, triune teaching, and the Lordship of Christ.[5] The official statements of concord between Roman Catholics and Eastern Orthodox and Coptic Orthodox show that such a classic Christian consensus exists.[6] The orthodox faith in these pages refers to that faith confessed and embodied by all who hold to the faith of the apostles.

THE INTELLECTUAL GIFTS OF EARLY AFRICA TO WORLD CHRISTIANITY

The good news took especially powerful forms in Africa. It was distinguished by its highly intelligent minds and courageous moral actions.

In the first three Christian centuries the intellectual power of its teachers was emulated and followed by Christians throughout Europe and the Near East. Patterns of prayer, community life, acts of mercy, and consensus formation developed early in Africa in ways that were favorably received by the global body of Christians.

The special gift of African orthodoxy lies in how early it appeared with unequaled moral power and intellectual genius in the third century. A whole book could be devoted to each of the following points, here summarized:

1. The City of Alexandria harbored the best library in the ancient world, a tradition of critical acumen, and world-class scholars in abundance sufficient to provide the pattern for early Christian education, which morphed into the medieval universities and stimulated intellectual genius throughout the world church in the third century.

2. The fury of martyrdom hit Africa sooner and harder than elsewhere, and elicited a depth of faith in the face of suffering and death that was unsurpassed.

3. The movement to make durable decisions by general consent based on meticulous debate on sacred texts was more fully formed in Africa than anywhere else in the third century.

---

5. See T. Oden, *Classic Christianity*, for detailed analysis of the continuity of the core of these teachings.

6. In 1988 the Coptic Orthodox joined with the Catholic Church in this statement, which calmed down a disagreement lasting 1537 years (between 451 and 1988): "We believe that our Lord, God and Saviour Jesus Christ, the Incarnate-Logos is perfect in His Divinity and perfect in His Humanity. He made His Humanity One with His Divinity without Mixture, nor Mingling, nor Confusion. His Divinity was not separated from His humanity even for a moment or twinkling of an eye." See also the Signed Christological Agreement signed by His All Holiness Ecumenical Patriarch Bartholomew I on "Eastern and Oriental Orthodox unity," http://www.zeitun-eg.net/members_contrib/EcumenicalPatriarchBartholomewIOnEOUnion.mp3. "Both families accept the first three Ecumenical Councils which constitute our common heritage." Add to these a long history of common agreements between the Pontifical Council for Promoting Christian Unity and other Christian bodies.

4. The most astute ways of connecting orthodoxy with philosophy were more advanced in Alexandria than in Athens and more in Carthage than in Rome. Many of the best professors in Roman schools, such as Tyconius, Marius Victorinus, Lactantius, and Augustine, were born and bred in Africa.

5. The brilliant minds of Cyprian, Julius Africanus, and Optatus prepared the way for later European leaders such as Leo, Benedict, and Gregory the Great.

6. Clement, Origen, and Athanasius forged pathways in scripture interpretation of both testaments for others to follow in the Middle East and Europe.

7. The movement of intellectual history at the time of the earliest Neo-Platonists Ammonius Saccas, Plotinus, Marius Victorinus, and Synesius progressed from the south to the north, not from Europe to the African continent as it has often been portrayed.

In *How Africa Shaped the Christian Mind*[7] I have laid out this evidence, which need not be repeated here.

TENACIOUS FAITH

Why has the vitality of early African Christianity been sustained even until today? Why has it been so durable despite such obstacles? Why has the memory of African Christian intellect and moral fiber penetrated almost every human culture since the good news was first heard by the Ethiopian eunuch? Is African Christianity today reawakening to listen once again to these intrepid guides?

These are questions that young Africans are determined to probe deeply. This book provides support for their efforts, giving reasons for this durability, not only for African believers but for the faithful everywhere.

This book expands the groundbreaking work of African theologians Kwame Bediako, Lamin Sanneh, and Tite Tienou,[8] as well as the work of the Center for Early African Christianity (earlyafricanchristianity.com) as they seek to renew the faith of the earliest centuries of African Christianity. We stand on their shoulders.

---

7. Thomas C. Oden, *How Africa Shaped the Christian Mind: Rediscovering the African Seedbed of Western Christianity* (Downers Grove, IL: IVP, 2007).

8. See Kwame Bediako, *Theology and Identity: The Impact of Culture upon Christian Thought in the Second Century and in Modern Africa* (Oxford: Regnum Books, 1992); Lamin Sanneh, *Disciples of All Nations: Pillars of World Christianity* (Studies in World Christianity) (New York: Oxford University Press, 2008), and Tite Tienou, *Theological Task of the Church in Africa* (Theological Perspectives in Africa) (Achimota, Ghana: Africa Christian Press, 1996). Sanneh and Tienou have served on the Board of the Center for Early African Christianity and the late Prof. Bediako was one of its earliest supporters and counselors.

SEMINAR 2

THE AWAKENING OF A GIANT

A. ATHANASIUS AND FRIENDS

THE CONTINENT AWAKENS

A half-billion Christians live in Africa. There are more Christian believers in Africa now than at any time in human history.

The Spirit has awakened faith in all of the cultures and centuries since the apostles. That awakening once grew with astonishing power in Africa. Now the children of that awakening are returning to their roots.

The faith of early Africa is being rediscovered. The modern habit is to want to improve on the old message. The orthodox habit is to allow ourselves to be improved by the old message.

The steadfast old faith is being roused anew to once again empower the renewal of human cultures. This is happening as powerfully in Africa today as anywhere. The faith so well expressed by early African Christian teaching is still celebrated and sung in African villages and cities. Even without being consciously aware of their African roots, many global Christians are daily singing and affirming classic teachings and visions first explored in Africa.

Worldwide believers today are hearing the same good news that Africa first received in the mission of Mark in the first century. That consensus on the essentials of faith has not disappeared. It is stronger than ever, now confirmed by millions worldwide.

These seminars celebrate the African contribution to the formation of the consensus of faith. It was immense. Among those most deeply moved by early African Christianity was John Wesley.

NEAREST THE FOUNTAIN

Protestants today may be surprised to find that the earliest African writers like Clement, Didymus, Macarius, and Athanasius were revered by John Wesley as "*the most authentic commentators on Scripture*, as being both *nearest the fountain*, and eminently endued with the Spirit by whom all Scripture was given. . . . I speak chiefly of those who wrote before the Council of Nice [Nicea]."[9] He especially valued early African communities dedicated to holy living through constant prayer, reading the Word, and Spirit-led worship. They became models for his own ministry in eighteenth-century England.[10]

The term *Antiquity*, as Wesley used it, referred to "the religion of the primitive church, of the whole church in the purest ages."[11] He often made special reference to the early African writers: "Tertullian, Origen,[12] Clemens Alexandrinus,[13] and Cyprian[14] . . . and Macarius[15]."

All but Macarius preceded the First Ecumenical Council of Nicea. Among later African writers he quoted Didymus the Blind and Augustine with appreciation.[16] Wesley thought that these early African teachers were especially helpful in "the explication of a doctrine that is not sufficiently explained, or for confirmation of a doctrine generally received."[17] Wesley thought the early Christian writers were exemplary models of reliable scripture interpretation: "The Scriptures are a complete rule of faith and practice; and they are clear in all necessary points. And yet their clearness does not prove that they need not be explained. . . .The esteeming *the writings of the first three centuries, not equally with, but next to, the Scriptures,* never carried any man yet into dangerous errors, nor probably ever will."[18]

---

9. That is, before 325 AD. John Wesley, *A Roman Catechism, with a Reply*, Preface, *Works*, X:87, italics added; cf. JJW 1:367.

10. Wesley's ministry found its way back to Africa under the leadership of Methodists Thomas Freeman in Ghana, Yorubaland, and Barnabas Shaw in Namaqualand, South Africa.

11. "On Laying the Foundation of the New Chapel," 1777, ii.3; 3:586; LJW 11:387.

12. LJW 2:91f., 101,105; 3:137, 4:176.

13. For other references to Clement of Alexandria, see LJW 2:327–28, 342, 387; 5:43; 6:129; cf. B9:31; B3:586; 4:402; JJW 5:197.

14. For Wesley's extensive references to Cyprian, see B2:461–62; 3:196–97, 450–51, 458–59, 469–70; LJW 1:277, 323; 2:320, 333–37, 361, 373, 387; B1:437; JWO 42L, 126, 195, 264, 309, 328; JJW 1:416; 2:263; 4:97.

15. For notes on the identity and view of "Macarius the Egyptian," see JWO ix, 9, 31, 119, 252, 274f.; JJW 1:254; LJW 2:387.

16. JWO 129.

17. *A Roman Catechism, with a Reply*, Preface, *Works*, X:87, italics added; cf. JJW 1:367.

18. LCM X:14, italics added.

THE AFRICAN PRECURSORS OF WESTERN EVANGELICAL TEACHING

Wesley published a multivolume Christian Library with a "Preface to the Epistles of the Apostolical Fathers" of the earliest Christian years, where he offered translations of the writings of the earliest exegetes, many African. They delivered "the pure doctrine of the Gospel; what Christ and his apostles taught, and what these holy men had themselves received from their own mouths."[19] The first two volumes began with the epistles of the pre-Nicene writers, *The Homilies of Macarius*, and *The Acts and Monuments of the Christian Martyrs*,[20] many from Africa.

In *Christian Martyrs*, Mr. Wesley related that

> The places where this persecution most raged, were Africa, Alexandria, and Cappadocia. The number of them that suffered was innumerable. Of whom the first was Leonides, the father of Origen, who was beheaded, with whom Origen his son, being then seventeen years old, should have suffered . . . had not his mother privily in the night conveyed away his clothes. Whereupon, more for shame to be seen, than for fear to die, he was constrained to remain at home. . . . After the death of his father, all his goods being confiscated, he, with his poor mother, and six brethren, were brought to such extreme poverty, that he sustained both himself and them by teaching a school; till at length he transferred his study only to the knowledge of the Scriptures, and other learning conducible to the same.[21]

Having "the advantage of living in the apostolic times, of hearing the holy Apostles and conversing with them," and having been chosen by them for leadership in the nascent church, we "cannot with any reason doubt of what they deliver . . . but ought to receive it, though not with equal veneration, yet with only little less regard than we do the sacred writings of those who were their masters and instructors" and "as worthy of a much greater respect than any composures which have been made since."[22]

THE TILT TOWARD THE GLOBAL SOUTH

The Pew Research Center recently reported that there are 173 million Christians in America. Compare that with the half-billion of the world's Christians that live in Africa. For every one American Christian there are 3000 Christians on the continent of Africa. In 2015 Pew estimated that 516,470,000 Christians live in sub-Saharan Africa.[23]

---

19. Christian Library J XIV:223.
20. Adapted largely from Fox's *Book of Martyrs*.
21. http://wesley.nnu.edu/john-wesley/a-christian-library/, vol. 2, Part 1.
22. Christian Library, J XIV:223–25.
23. www.pewforum.org/2011/12/19/global-christianity-regions/.

This leads scholars such as Philip Jenkins,[24] Andrew Walls,[25] and Jehu Hanciles[26] to conclude that the future of world Christianity lies in the Global South, not from where previously expected, either in Europe or North America. Over the past century the demographic and spiritual center of world Christianity has shifted from the West to the Global South.

African Christians are already having more impact on world Christianity than most imagine. That is most evident in the Anglican Church in Africa, which has boldly shown its determination to live without outside financial dependency in relation to the Church of England. The great continent is awakening to its own strengths and gifts. Africa has moved from a missionary-receiving continent to a missionary-sending continent.[27]

THE WESLEYAN CONNECTION IN AFRICA: AN ONGOING ISSUE

Further evidence of this shift is seen in the growing importance of Africa to the largest Protestant denomination within the American mainline Protestant tradition, The United Methodist Church, the community of faith in which I was baptized and am ordained. Currently, 25 percent of American mainline Protestants identify with the UMC, down slightly from 28 percent in 2007.

The UMC membership is global. As of 2012 there were 7.4 million United Methodists living in the U.S. About 4.2 million United Methodists live in Africa.[28] These figures are sometimes disputed, but it is clear that about 35–50 percent of all United Methodist members are living in Africa.[29] While Methodist church attendance has been dwindling in North America, in Africa it is burgeoning. Even as the U.S. Methodist Church is losing nearly 100,000 members annually, the African United Methodists are gaining 200,000 annually.

---

24. *The Next Christendom: The Coming of Global Christianity*, 3rd ed. (New York: Oxford University Press, 2011).

25. William R. Burrows, Mark R. Gornik, and Janice A. McLean, *Understanding World Christianity: The Vision and Work of Andrew F. Walls* (Maryknoll, NY: Orbis Books, 2011).

26. *Beyond Christendom: Globalization, African Migration, and the Transformation of the West* (Maryknoll, NY: Orbis Books, 2008).

27. See http://www.christianpost.com/news/united-methodist-church.

28. pewforum.org/2015/05/12/americas-changing-religious-landscape; cf. christianpost.com.

29. Out-of-date figures have reported 8.2 million UMC members in the USA, and 1.5 million in Africa, but those older figures have changed. While the African UMC membership grows exponentially, the USA UMC seems to decline gradually. Earlier WCC studies had reported 1,631,631 United Methodists in Africa as opposed to 8,219,563 in the USA (oikoumene.org/en/member-churches/united-methodist-church); but this balance has by now become almost even, with the scales tipping toward Africa.

The growth of United Methodism abroad, especially in Africa, is already coming to exercise increasing influence in the American church. A few years ago it would have been unimaginable to think that Africans might soon be sharing with powerful voices in the moral and spiritual decisions being made in the UMC. The demographics say that this African influence will be increasing. Already Africans are playing key decision-making roles in UMC policy in the General Conference. In Africa UMC churches are full. People walk for miles to hear their preaching. At the current rates, United Methodists in Africa may outnumber church members in the U.S. within a decade or so.[30]

Only recently is it dawning on many American Methodist leaders that so many members of their own church live in Africa. A more decisive change may occur when the African influence begins to reshape the seminaries in the West and abroad. With more than 15 indigenous seminaries started in Africa, the question of what happens in the thirteen U.S. seminaries may soon need to be rebalanced. It is likely that early African Christian wisdom will increasingly influence the curriculum of African seminaries, which currently are biblically evangelical, morally earnest, and service oriented.[31]

A PATH FROM PATRISTIC TO AFRICAN STUDIES

My life has been transformed by early African orthodox prayer, scripture study, and discipline. I myself have experienced the same return to foundations that is occurring so powerfully in Africa.

Nearly two decades of research that produced the shelf of volumes of The Ancient Christian Commentary on Scripture (IVP Books, 1997–2010) are now complete. Their completion left our research task force free to turn to African exegetes where they have found a rich heritage to embrace.

That research group[32] has redirected all of its efforts since 2007 to serve this information famine by making ancient African texts of the first millennium available to Africans in the third millennium.

It may seem ironic that people like me are finding their intellectual home in Africa. After over four decades of teaching in universities and seminaries in North America, my focus has shifted to early African Christianity. My vocation is to point gratefully to my own spiritual roots in classic Christianity. There the prevailing voices are from Africa.

---

30. http://juicyecumenism.com/2012/08/02/united-methodisms-u-s-spiral. Although currently Africans only exercise about 4 percent of church agency leadership, they comprise 35 to 50 percent of total church membership.

31. The current presence of African students in the thirteen official North American UM seminaries is growing, with advanced programs in World Christianity spreading and with patristic studies burgeoning.

32. Christopher Hall, Joel Elowsky, Michael Glerup, and myself.

The heartening reception of information daily provided by the Center for Early African Christianity[33] shows how great this appetite is, not only in the continent of Africa but among global Christians.[34] In the Center for Early African Christianity my colleagues in the Ancient Christian Commentary on Scripture are committed to showing how Africa shaped the Christian mind, to making available the texts of Africa that have clarified what global Christians have always consensually believed, and to demonstrating how Africans significantly formed that consensus. This reorientation has required me to make a complete renovation of my earlier work on *The Rebirth of Orthodoxy* (HarperCollins, 2003) in order to focus intently on the wisdom of early Africa.[35]

AFRICAN THEOLOGIES IN SEARCH OF ROOTS

There is a large body of literature on new proposals and new theologies from Africa. They vary widely in viewpoint. Some value the early African writers;[36] some ignore them.[37] This study encourages those who have ignored them to take a look at them and let them speak for themselves.

With the spread of international interests in Africa from the Portuguese in the 1500s to the spread of western, Arabic, and Chinese interests in the 2000s, indigenous African values became muted. Those who rightly call for transcending colonial models do well to consider the precolonial African writers before 1500 from Ethiopia to Algeria—Christian teaching from earliest African Christianity. Africans do not need to look far away for remedies when the best solutions are from Africa itself. As the Euro-American initiatives have diminished, the African-based influences have increased.

From western perspectives, human failures appear to be prevailing, but they are not the last word. For Christians in Africa there is reason to celebrate rather than despair.

This study does not focus on what is newest in African theology, nor does it exalt antiquity as a virtue, but rather joyfully returns to ancient Africa for relevant wisdom on the perennial truth of Christianity. The essentials of that classic Christian teaching

---

33. See earlyafricanchristianity.com.

34. More than 15,000 visitors per week.

35. After ten years in print, the rights for this book were reverted to the author. In the intervening years, the focus of research for the author and his ACCS colleagues turned increasingly to early African sources, where they have remained concentrated since 2007. Virtually every sentence of the previous work required reconceptualization. The earlier work provided the scaffolding for this book, which seeks to convey the same overarching vision specifically within contemporary Africa.

36. Kwame Bediako, *Theology and Identity: The Impact of Culture upon Christian Thought in the Second Century and in Modern Africa* (Oxford: Regnum Books, 1992).

37. Michael N. Jagessar and Anthony G. Reddie, eds., *Postcolonial Black British Theology* (Peterborough, U.K.: Epworth, 2007).

were carefully articulated in Africa in the years after the founding of the Catechetical School about 180 AD. The bibliography at the end of this book shows evidence that many African scholars today are respectfully turning to these early African sources.

THE HIGH-TECH OPPORTUNITY

Mobile online app platforms are now allowing African youth access to ancient African religious texts in a way never before imagined. Only a few years ago there were few smartphones in Africa, but now "Key African markets experienced massive growth in smartphones, the IDC said. Nigeria hit 135% [growth] followed by Kenya at 112%."[38] The impact of smartphone technology upon theological education is already huge. Information sources previously available only in paper are becoming available in digital form with inexpensive options to print.

Serving these information needs is the goal of the Center for Early African Christianity, whose mission was launched with *How Africa Shaped the Christian Mind* in 2007. Several corresponding Centers for the Study of Early African Christianity are already growing in Nairobi, Kenya; Cairo, Egypt; Pretoria and Johannesburg, South Africa; Accra, Ghana; and Bangui, Central African Republic, with others information.[39]

Low-cost electronic tablets are bringing classic Christian education to millions of African students. In seminaries and universities from Senegal to Zululand, grassroots teachers are introducing these new learning tools to bring the ancient voices alive. This is a meek, quiet, good-sense awakening. Africa has heard enough of revolutionary pretensions and hyped media occurrences that have often had disappointing consequences. Here the battlefield is the village school, the local church, the regional seminary, and the parent with a child.

Imagine a young girl in Uganda today sitting in a block mud-brick classroom with crate wires for windows and wooden benches formed into a circle. With rain tapping on the tin roof, she can bring into that room reliable information in her own heart language about early African Christian writers via a cellphone or tablet in her hand. The work of the Spirit in Africa today is utilizing new technologies to communicate ancient forms of African wisdom.

Technology cannot produce faith. Only the Spirit can do that. But the Spirit is free to use new technology to teach ancient African wisdom. This is a stunning opportunity of providence.

Blessed with digital technology, any African today can gain ready access to hundreds of ancient texts and current discussions of all matters concerning early African Christianity on a low-cost cell phone. From these mobile connections the young people of Africa can hear the stories of the saints of early Africa and be introduced

---

38. http://www.fin24.com/Tech/Mobile/Smartphones-hit-record-growth-in-Africa-20150428.

39. See earlyafricanchristianity.com for news and current information.

to the powerful minds of Tertullian and Origen. The obstacles of expensive paper distribution systems are overleapt by digital access.

ATHANASIUS AND AUGUSTINE: THE PROTOTYPICAL TEACHERS OF AFRICAN CHRISTIANITY

The core teaching of classic African Christianity is most aptly summarized by two of its leading interpreters: Athanasius best represents the Greek-Coptic tradition and Augustine the North African Latin western tradition. Athanasius and Augustine together offer the greatest storehouse of African orthodox faith and indeed of world Christianity in the patristic period.

This opinion can be tested by asking what other Christians theologian of that period might exceed them in holy living, intellectual virtuosity, and historic influence. Ambrose, Basil, Gregory Nazianzus, and Gregory Nyssa come to mind—all great Christian minds. All of these had read Athanasius. It is difficult to make the case that any one of them was more gifted and persuasive than either Athanasius or Augustine. And Origen may exceed either of them. This question cannot be settled here, but the fact that it would be difficult to make a contrary case underscores the thesis that the most prominent teachers of world Christianity in the early patristic period are arguably from Africa.

Their legacy is available to be received worldwide. Through them the best of African Christianity belongs to all Christians. The western Catholic and Eastern Orthodox traditions are here joined as one since both Athanasius and Augustine were valued as doctors of the ancient worldwide church. This faith "was revealed by the Lord, proclaimed by the apostles and guarded by the fathers."[40] The faith was passed from the Lord to the apostles to the church.

To pit scripture against tradition is futile since the tradition depends upon scripture. That dichotomy is contrary to the faith received everywhere. Those who lapse from this faith can scarcely embrace and hold fast to the name Christian, which refers to those whose lives are lived in Christ, who dwell together in the living body of Christ as a single, universal body of the faithful.

Three Egyptian Patriarchs had great weight in the maturing of the ancient ecumenical consensus: Dionysius the Great, Athanasius, and Cyril the Great. Three early Catholic Popes were born in Africa: Pope Victor I (reigned c. 189 to 199), Pope Miltiades (reigned 311 to 314) and Pope Gelasius I (reigned 492 to 496). In those days the gap between the western Catholic and the Eastern Orthodox traditions had not widened and hardened as it did later.[41]

The African consensus is the single flowing wellspring to which African Christians are returning. Much later the magisterial Protestant confessional traditions (Lu-

---

40. Athanasius, Letter I to Serapion.

41. Compared to the centuries following Cyril the Great.

theran, Reformed, Anglican, Wesleyan, and most Pentecostal) affirmed the same or similar confessions of the three earliest Ecumenical Councils (of Nicea, Constantinople, and Ephesus) which the early Catholic and Orthodox jointly affirmed.

The unity of the body does not consist of the words of the Councils as such, but those who wish to hear this unity articulated in its classic form can find it in the Councils of Nicea, Constantinople, and Ephesus.

B. HISTORICAL PERSPECTIVE: A TURNAROUND IS OCCURRING

MOVING CONFIDENTLY BEYOND THE MODERN VISION OF THE FUTURE

The defenses of modern ideas have grown weary. Their shattered opportunities are strewn about in an exhausted landscape. The faithful have already paid their dues twice over to false, fleeting promises. Now believers are open to forgotten wisdom long ruled out by the narrowing expectations of modern choices.

A reversal is occurring in our time. The faithful have in fact outlived the collapse of the foundations of secular society. The modern outlook is disintegrating while communities of traditional faith are flourishing now more than ever. Especially in Africa.

We are witnessing an emerging resolve in worldwide Christianity to reclaim the classic spiritual disciplines: close study of scripture, daily prayer, regular observance in a worshipping community, doctrinal integrity, and moral accountability. These core affirmations of early African Christianity continued into Catholic, Orthodox, Reformed, and charismatic communities.

Turning from the illusions of modern life, the faithful are now quietly seeking out the spiritual disciplines of ancient Africa. This is the rebirth of African orthodoxy. This century promises to be a pivotal period of opportunity, recovery, and rebuilding.

Amid any declining culture, gracious gifts of providential guidance are being offered. Human folly is always being quietly curbed by divine grace.

This does not prevent the faithful from enjoying the technological gains of modern life. These can be celebrated while calmly recognizing that once-ruling modern vanities and misjudgments now face a deep crisis.

ENTERING THE SIXTH MILLENNIUM OF HUMAN CULTURE

Human cultures extend three millennia before the birth of Jesus, and two millennia after. We are entering the sixth millennium of civilly ordered human societies:

SIX THOUSAND YEARS OF HUMAN CIVILIZATIONS

Third millennium (3000–2000) BC: From Egyptian dynasties to the written law; from the wheel to writing	Second Millennium (2000–1000) BC: Abraham to David, Neolithic to the iron age	First Millennium (1000–0) BC: David to John the Baptist, iron age to messianic age
	The Pivot of History BIRTH OF CHRIST	
First Millennium AD: Paul to Augustine to the Cluniac reform of monasteries	Second Millennium AD: Medieval, Reformation, and Modern Times	Third Millennium AD: The Human Outlook after the Decline of Modern Times: Post-modern paleo-orthodoxy

In classic Christian perspective, the three millennia before Christ prepared the way for the coming of God in the flesh. The first millennium following spread the good news to most of the known world. The second millennium (1000–2000 AD) refined and reformed Christian presence in the world. In the third millennium a new post-secular turn is being made: Africa is resuming its earlier role of intellectual and moral leadership in global Christianity with the emergence of paleo-orthodoxy, the least likely expected outcome of the second millennium. Regardless of culture or skin color, Africa is an immense habitat of our Christian past.

The gains of modern life have been accompanied by a loss of wonder. The achievements of the end of the previous millennium have left humanity with a deep sense of moral rootlessness. God is giving us breathing time to rethink who we are in relation to our human past. This is a time for repentance and faith.

The crisis of this new epoch is not political but rather spiritual and moral. It is a crisis of courage, and more profoundly a crisis of faith. We have come to a major watershed in which everything seems in question: the family, the environment, sexuality, technology, economics, the future of freedom. But none is more decisive than the hunger for meaning. We wonder: How can children be nurtured today? Is life worth living? Is the human future worth tackling?

The western influence in Africa is fading. It is not completely gone, but it is numbed. Western ideas have lingered in some African knowledge elites dependent on the West, but with decreasing effect.

AVOIDING AFRO-CENTRIC EXAGGERATIONS

Afro-centrism must be rejected as an ideological bias contrary to the catholicity of the faith. Africa was the continent in which the concept of catholicity was first tested. Global vision is essential to catholicity. The aim of catholicity in Christian teaching is to reflect the wholeness of apostolic truth to the whole world, not simply the uniqueness of African Christianity to Africa.

The rediscovery of early African Christianity is derailed by adopting a chauvinistic Afro-centric bias. The gospel is not for or from Africans only. Classic African Christianity was attuned to a global citizenry. The notion that all Christian truth essentially emerges out of Africa is contrary to the inclusive teaching of early African Christianity. An exaggerated Afro-centrism tips the scales toward that imbalance. Early African Christianity was rooted uniquely in African soil while sharing fully in the ecumenical consensus.

THE OWL WITH BLINDERS

Georg Friedrich Hegel is often thought to be Europe's greatest philosopher. He wrote at an early point in his *History of Philosophy*: "At this point we leave Africa, not to mention it again. For it is no historical part of the World; it has no movement or development to exhibit. Historical movements in it—that is in its northern part—belong to the Asiatic or European World."[42] That is Euro-centrism.

Europe's leading interpreter of the history of ideas led an epoch of European historians into a misconceived idea of vast proportions: the intellectual unfruitfulness of Africa and the rational superiority of Europe. That misconception is based on ignorance of on-the-ground facts in Africa.[43]

In doing this Hegel closed his eyes to one third of the known world. This disaster has been persistently repeated by liberal historians such as Adolf von Harnack and Walter Bauer. More recently even such an eminent historian as Hugh Trevor Roper echoed the view that Africa had no history prior to European exploration and colonization. Such statements are typical of the dismissive attitude of modern historians who still see Augustine as an appendage of Rome and Athanasius as an echo of the Greeks.

Hegel used the metaphor of the owl of Minerva, which flies only at dusk after the day is over, as an analogy for philosophical inquiry, implying that philosophy can provide understanding of a stage of reality only after it has occurred.

Hegel's owl never flew over Africa, sadly, because he thought it did not exist intellectually.[44] African scholars are correcting this impaired vision.

---

42. Hegel, *The Philosophy of History* (New York: Dover, 1956), p. 99.

43. Ignoring the decisive ecumenical influence of African-born Origen, Athanasius, Augustine, and Cyril the Great.

44. Hegel, Preface, *The Philosophy of Right*.

Why has it taken so long for historians to rectify such a vast misconception? There are no easy excuses. The anatomy of the Hegelian misconception has never been fully investigated.[45]

The road ahead is intellectually rigorous. But it is amply supplied by grace. The providential moment of recognition is dawning.

C. THE HIGH COST OF MODERN LIVING

THREE WAYS TO TRY TO LIVE WITHOUT ROOTS

The modern intellectual and scientific elites in the west have sponsored a prevailing view of the world that admits no higher power than visible nature based on empirical testing, attempting desperately to rule out God and the unseen spiritual world. This false western ideology has cast a lengthy spell over African life. But western power and imagination have fallen into deep decline.

Those who remain most narrowly committed to the secular west have the least expectation that classic Christian teaching will ever be recovered. Meanwhile it is being recovered, more so in Africa than anywhere. But this recovery requires returning to the deepest wellsprings of the earliest forms of Christian faith. Those wellsprings once flowed most profusely in Africa.

Three fading western idea systems are closely associated with three of the leading shapers of the modern mind: Freud, Marx, and Nietzsche and their living descendants. They define the core of modernity. These are the foremost figures that have dominated the universities, media, and the information class.

The knowledge elites are those whose trade is in ideas, whose social location depends on thinking and writing. They have left their scars on Africa. But fortunately they have never been at home in Africa.

These normative western ideas have shorthand name-identifications borne out of much historical experience. The names are

1. Naturalism: forgetting the supernatural;

2. Statist utopianism: fantasizing that a just social order can remove sin; and

3. Moral relativism that seeks to exist without a moral compass.

In the pages ahead we will deal with these three declining western premises. Africans know that there is something better than these in their own historic memory: faith in God, realism about the human predicament, and moral clarity.

---

45. See T. Oden, *How Africa Shaped the Christian Mind* (Downers Grove, IL: IVP, 2007).

Under the captivity of modern western ideas, love has been reduced to sex, psychology to chemistry, politics to machinery, and persons to puppets.[46] These harmful ideas are today everywhere in crisis, even while still being worshipped by self-appointed gatekeepers in pop culture, politics, entertainment, and higher education.

THE AWKWARDNESS OF WESTERN MODERNITY IMPORTED INTO AFRICA

These three declining western intellectual movements have never fitted well into the varied cultures of Africa. Even in the West the psychoanalysis growing out of Sigmund Freud's work is no longer plausible as a reliable path to health. In Africa its key premises, such as oedipal conflict, psychosexual determinism, and transference, seem absurd. The fantasies of Karl Marx seeking violent revolution by the proletariat against property has created increasing poverty, dependency, and bloodshed as seen in Russia, China, and Cuba, and in parts of Africa where Marx's ideas lie in economic ruin. The key assumptions of Friedrich Nietzsche, such as the will to power, the *Übermensch,* and the death of God, appear implausible when placed in an African context.

These three worldviews have had a long run of respectability among western elites. They have imagined that they will continue on forever. That is a part of the modern mystique. But the seeds of their destruction are planted in their own deficient visions of human history.

One feature they share is that they imagined that all pre-modern truths are virtually worthless. Their arrogance is the slow corrosion that eventually brought them so quickly down. Where they have been practiced in Africa the outcomes have been disastrous.

They subdue all pre-modern wisdoms before they have had a chance to speak. They assume the ultimate inferiority of all pre-modern ideas and writings, and methods of investigation. The modern western elites have typically assumed that few if any pre-modern voices say anything worth hearing. They have carefully constructed defenses against taking seriously any ancient teaching.

But Africa has ancient teaching worth listening to, especially in an era of collapsing worldviews. The modern condition is not irreversible. It is a fertile field of promise.

These three ideologies have never been widely embraced in Africa. But they still hold many of Africa's elites in a prison of false ideas. It feels like they have spread doubt as to whether any wisdom of any past is worth heeding.

---

46. For more detailed reasoning about how this has happened see T. Oden, *Agenda for Theology* (San Francisco: Harper and Row, 1979); *Classic Christianity* (New York: HarperOne, 2009); and *A Change of Heart* (Downers Grove, IL: IVP, 2014).

THE DEMISE OF THE THREEFOLD THOUGHT FRAME OF THE MODERN WESTERN MIND

Modern western thought has passed over Africa like an angel of death.

1. The Marxism of the Soviet system is now a proven poverty-creator. Its influence is everywhere diminished except in despairing pockets of totalitarianism like Cuba and North Korea.

2. Sigmund Freud's daydream of sexual liberation has found it easier to make babies than parent them morally.

3. Nietzschean nihilism has elicited a trail of genocide.

These once-confident idea-systems are now unmasked as dated visions of the human possibility. None has succeeded in creating a sustainable culture.

Each of these ideological programs has colluded to support the others. They are now collapsing together like tottering dominoes: the command economies, the backfiring therapeutic experiments, the broken human remains of drug experimentation, and the exploding splinters of narcissism.

They have left behind an unfathomable pit of need. All their original exponents are dead, but they have left a deadly trail of misadventures that still plague western education, and which have had spillover effects in Africa.

These forms of secular advocacy have treated the liberal western Christian establishment as a wholly owned subsidiary. Knees buckle as the modern center fails to hold. The collapse is evident and far reaching. The Freudian project, the Marxist utopia, and the Nietzschean experiment are all spent. Do not confuse them with classic Christianity.

THE NEW BIRTH OF THE UNIVERSITY

In *How Africa Shaped the Christian Mind*, I set forth the evidence for how the African church gave birth to the idea of the university, which in time wound its way to Europe. Where did the idea of the university first emerge with plausibility?

The case for Alexandria is stronger than for the medieval universities of Paris, Bologna, Padua, or Damascus. Al-Azhar University in Cairo was founded in 970. Long before that, European higher education was taking place in monastic schools and cathedral schools and the scriptoria of the sixth century.

But these were all preceded by the magnificent library of Alexandria which drew the world's best minds, with lecture halls and seminars: all that is required to make a university. In the history of the university in Europe, the schools of late Roman antiquity and Byzantium were preceded by the Catechetical School of Alexandria, which was actively functioning by 190 AD, and which according to Coptic tradition had roots extending all the way back to Mark himself and his early successors.

All the elements of the modern university are found in third-century Alexandria—the liberal arts, the study of mathematics and science, the works of rhetoric and poetry, the study of history, and the greatest library in the world attracting the world's best scholars to Africa. Rome, Constantinople, Paris, and Oxford were substantially anticipated by the Alexandrian educators. The seeding of European higher education was developed in Africa.

For centuries preceding the formation of medieval higher education, classic Christian teaching of the sort found in Clement and Origen was the central archetype. Look as you may for this connection in modern histories of the university and you will find little mention of it. This disregard illustrates the European conceit toward the intellectual history of Africa.

THE WESTERN ACADEMIC STUDY OF RELIGION TODAY REFLECTS EXAGGERATED MODERN IDEOLOGIES

I taught for thirty-three years in a prominent graduate school in the New York area where many PhD students came from Africa as well as Asia. Did they get a deep immersion in early African Christianity? Almost none did, and only then with heavy western filtering.

The academic study of religion today proceeds largely without any reference to the worshipping community, or its historic liturgy, or its historic apostolic mission, or its classical texts. Moreover there is a fierce denial of classic Christianity as a source for the history of learning.

In the theological schools and seminaries associated with universities they founded, there is only grudging reference to the Christian sources of higher education. Most of the world's most distinguished universities had theological faculties before they had scientific faculties.

The most frequently chosen texts in theological education are easily identified by examining book selections for class use. The classic Christian teachers are hardly allowed to speak for themselves. They speak only through the secondary-source interpretations of modern writers. More often these are trendy ideologues that imagine that the critical study of religion begins with atheists like Rousseau, Feuerbach, Marx, and Freud. There are few Africans among them, and those who are have adopted the most western ideas. Classic Christianity thus has appeared to be systematically marginalized—but not for long.

The modern western ideological experiments can no longer regenerate themselves. Even their own moral certainties cannot be sustained to the third or fourth generation, and their resources for climbing out of this pit are exhausted. They flounder as if they still had authority.

The outrageous costs of higher education and the digital revolution are ending their dominance. Now cocooned universities are being forced to compete in the free market of ideas provided by mobile applications and computer technology. This technology ironically puts healthy classic Christian thinking at an unexpected advantage.

THE RETURN TO CLASSIC SOURCES

African Christian universities are giving new life to African Christianity. The faithful in Africa are renewing the very idea of the university by returning to their roots.

Global Christianity could give new life to the waning modern world through their thousands of colleges and universities worldwide. Africa can show the way for global Christianity to recover the educational institutions it has created. But not without finding their roots in early African Christianity.

What is happening globally amid this hazardous historical situation is a joyous return to sacred scripture and to the consensual guides of the formative period of its canon and early interpretation. The faithful are rediscovering how the Spirit is reawakening the worshipping communities, reclaiming them to ancient faith. They are repossessing their educational institutions.

Western knowledge elites have assumed that their ideas will stamp their genetic imprint on the next generation, and maybe on all future generations. Meanwhile providence has added a new wrinkle: now we see the brightest of the emerging African generation turning away from the empty days of uncritical secularization, and they are finding inexhaustible nourishment in their own early African storehouses of wisdom.[47]

The collapse of modern western morality is the seedbed in which the African faithful are growing in their awareness of Africa's gift to global Christianity. It is not a time for despair but a time for joy.

In the next section we will see why.

---

47. Kwame Bediako, *Christianity in Africa: The Renewal of a Non-Western Religion* (Edinburgh: Edinburgh Univ. Press; Maryknoll, N.Y.: Orbis Books, 1995); Lamin Sanneh, *Whose Religion Is Christianity? The Gospel Beyond the West* (Grand Rapids, MI: Eerdmans, 2003); Thabiti M. Anyabwile and Mark A. Noll, *The Decline of African American Theology: From Biblical Faith to Cultural Captivity* (Downers Grove, IL: IVP, 2007).

SEMINAR 3
AFRICA'S GIFT TO GLOBAL CHRISTIANITY

A. THE HUNGER FOR ROOTS

THE EARLIEST GENERATIONS OF CHRISTIAN BELIEF

Africa's gift to global Christianity is found in Africa's earliest interpreters of scripture.

Believers today are seeking to unpack and grasp the oldest layers of memory of the history of salvation as it was once understood worldwide. That happened with special power in ancient Africa.[48]

Africa's youth are once again embracing Africa's gift to world Christianity, which is early Christian wisdom as heard most clearly in the earliest Christian centuries. Those seeking a renewed sense of moral balance are turning to the recovery of the oldest and surest form of Christian belief.

This is happening most fruitfully on the African continent among its young generations, who have a passion for roots, a yearning for intellectual depth, an appetite for stable wisdom, and a taste for early African tradition that they know is more sound than declining materialistic ideologies.

African Christians of the earliest centuries learned to think from within the framework of the core of biblical faith found in the apostolic witness and its earliest interpreters. Among the most brilliant of these are those who lived in the Nile Valley and the Medjerda Valley in North Africa. That apostolic faith which has been commonly held from the beginning is shared by a great cloud of witnesses crossing every ethnic barrier. It already is a worldwide, multicultural, multigenerational reality. Its mission is continuing with the half-billion voices of African Christians. Their

---

48. Of the third and fourth centuries AD; See *How Africa Shaped the Christian Mind* (Downers Grove, IL: IVP, 2007).

grounding is not in the modern illusions of statism, self-obsession, or utopian socialism but in early African Christian faith and practice. When they are harassed they take heart from those great African intellects like Clement, Origen, Athanasius, and Augustine, who were similarly hassled.

THE LEAST LIKELY PREMISE

The demise of world Christianity is the least likely premise. Only under the old illusions of secularism could the false premise of the death of God appear to be credible.

Those who willingly subjugate themselves to passing fads should not be surprised when their gods are shown to have feet of clay. When idols die, the idolaters understandably mourn and rage. Meanwhile the grace-enabled community freely celebrates its exodus through and beyond modern trends.

African orthodoxy glories in the intricate providences of history. Each dying historical worldview is giving birth to new forms and refreshing occasions for living responsively in relation to grace. They are discovering that the first African Christians are the best teachers for today. What is happening before our eyes is a profound rediscovery of the texts, methods, and pastoral wisdom of seminal African Christians of the first millennium. There is a joyous return to the most frequently remembered African minds of the formative period of Christian scriptural interpretation.[49]

The earliest African Christians faced imprisonment, torture, and martyrdom without a loss of confidence in God. This is why many African parents are now reading to their children the stories of the African saints and heroes of the ten African persecutions.

These persecutions occurred mostly before 311 AD under Nero (64 AD), Domitian (c. 90–96), Trajan (98–117), Hadrian (117–138), Marcus Aurelius (161–181), Septimius Severus (202–211), Maximus the Thracian (235–238), Decius (249–251), Valerian (257–260), Diocletian (284–305), and Galerius (305–311). African Christians suffered mightily through imprisonment and harassment. Their deaths were remembered and their locations became oratories where cathedrals and churches were later built.

Meanwhile failed ideas continue to be propagated like sheets coming out of an old copy machine. They will persist for a short time in their fanatical preference for novelty and pretenses of originality, but they lose energy day by day. Global orthodoxy, however, has its eye upon the enduring truth that was so brilliantly grasped in ancient Africa.

---

49. Jehu Hanciles, *Beyond Christendom: Globalization, African Migration, and the Transformation of the West* (Maryknoll, NY: Orbis Books, 2008); Philip Jenkins, *The Next Christendom: The Coming of Global Christianity*, 3rd ed. (New York: Oxford University Press, 2011).

THE FAIRNESS REVOLUTION AND ITS MEANING FOR AFRICAN ORTHODOXY

In recent years many positive changes have occurred in efforts for human rights, equal opportunity, and freedom of religion. World Christianity has contributed mightily to the rising awareness of the status and role of women, although these changes are often credited to secularization without knowledge of their religious roots. The civil rights movement led by Rev. Dr. Martin Luther King, Jr., has awakened many to institutional racism and sought by legal and political and spiritual remedies to overcome it. The signs of the fairness revolution are everywhere.

But some initiatives intending to increase equality have resulted in deepening social stratification, entrenched poverty, and dependencies. They have reinforced the perennial human temptation to think that we are the only generation that has ever sought justice or equality.

Thus the whole human past has been downgraded and often demeaned by those who idealize progress narrowly defined. The Christian community looks toward the tested wisdom of previous generations, asking only that it might be treated with equal respect. An idea that is tested by many generations is stronger than one experienced by only one generation.

Since African orthodoxy listens to the voices of its apostolic ancestors, it has been belittled by modern self-righteousness, as if modern worldviews were naturally superior to all pre-modern worldviews. In this way the saints and thinkers of early African Christianity are dismissed even before they have a chance to make a case for Christian mercy, forgiveness, and justice in a fallen world.

Those who are given the gift of being born in this time of supposed greater equality and just treatment have often narrowed their range of historical vision to the last few years or months. They are frequently unaware of the history that they now deride. They have forgotten the courage and integrity of all who were born in pre-modern times. This includes the prophets, apostles, martyrs, and ancient consensual teachers of scripture. This trend is seen in downplaying the African martyrs as if their motives were tainted and their numbers were inconsequential. The actual martyrs who were innocent of ideas of conquest were committed to a global family of reconciliation.

As a result the modern worldview has itself become a means for self-justification. The temptation is to view our birth in this time as a legitimate claim to moral superiority. It is a modern version of a chosen people populated only by those more recently born. What a great achievement! By this means each later generation justifies itself simply by pretending superiority over all those born earlier. They have prevented themselves from knowing about the classic Christian teaching that we are justified not by works but by grace through faith.

The children of the secular egalitarian ideas are paying an extremely high price in family failure, adolescent suicide rates, and sexually transmitted diseases. A dependency population within a nanny state has become a new prison featuring poverty. Victimization has become a game. Women suffer more, not less, from divorce and economic instability. Family cohesion has diminished under the desire for individual independence. Any overarching attempt to celebrate the meaning of the whole of history is mistrusted. Religious claims of any sort are suspect as power moves. This unreasonable habit of dismissing any comprehensive human outlook is itself small-minded.

B. ORTHODOX PRACTICE AS A SOCIOLOGICAL SKILL

THE WORD ORTHODOXY

Our English word *orthodoxy* has a distinctly religious history. It is not one of those words borrowed from the pagan environment. Its meaning was hammered out in early Christian Africa through major debates over Gnostic, Marcionite, and Arian distortions. The very concept of orthodoxy emerged as early believers sought common clarity about what their scriptural texts meant based on their most trusted consensus interpreters in ways that have been received as plausible among believers of *all* different cultures, times, and places.

The Greek word *orthodox* was significantly shaped by the experience of Christians in Africa. The root word *orthodox* means straight opinion or right belief, in reference to the teaching of the apostles. There were varying opinions of who Jesus was, but there was a durable common understanding about what the apostles taught about who Jesus was as Son of God incarnate: God the Father revealing himself in his only-begotten Son through the Holy Spirit.

The view that Jesus was not really the eternal Son of God was first carefully debated in Africa, where the worshipping communities were forced to fend off attacks by Arius, a popular priest in Alexandria who taught that Jesus was not the eternal Son of God. The Christian world learned about what was heterodox (meaning other than the received consensus) by listening to Africans debating about whether Athanasius or Arius best represented the consensually received tradition that Jesus is the eternal Son of God. It was denied by Arius and affirmed by Athanasius. Though it continued to be debated, the orthodox tradition that was embraced after the Council of Nicea in 325 AD was that Athanasius was reading the apostolic testimony just as Christians everywhere had read it: "The Word became flesh" (John 1:14a).

One is orthodox who receives and confirms the classic Christian consensus that was established early and sustained durably. One is orthodox who adheres to the same apostolic faith that is everywhere and has always been confirmed by the original witnesses to Jesus's death and resurrection. Anyone can see by examining the Gnostic and Manichean texts that they were not received by believers of all times and places.

THE BASIS OF ORTHODOXY IS NOT AN IDEA BUT AN EVENT

This faith is not just about the idea of God becoming flesh. Rather it is about the reality of God who became flesh as an event in history. This faith lives in the hearts of a single community of worship worldwide. Believers of infinitely varied languages and cultures are united by faith in Jesus as the Son of God. That confession is the right way (*orthos doxa*, accurate opinion and correct way) of looking at the writings of the apostles and what they meant as received from generation to generation.

Those who deny that durable consensus are likely to be led astray by people who want to improve on the teaching of the apostles, and are therefore *hetero* (other than) *doxa*. There is a simple difference between heterodox and orthodox faith: one asserts a view not held worldwide by Christians of all times and places. The other receives what the church from the beginning has meant by the risen Son of God.

Orthodoxy is an aptitude of consent to faith. It can be viewed sociologically as a social process dedicated to the careful transmission of the tradition that holds that Jesus is Son of God. It states truth claims without apology, and seeks to guard those truth claims through the hazards of time. It is not afraid of conversation with any culture, but intends to remember God in the same way as that passed on by the apostles. The genius of faith is that it encounters each new culture confidently.

Secular orthodoxies exist in modernity, such as psychoanalytic orthodoxy, Maoist orthodoxy, and orthodox materialism. None of these movements have universal consent. Each of these orthodoxies has their own saints and canon and hierarchical tradition. They think out of exclusively modern premises without reference to pre-modern wisdom. Christians are not bound by modern ideologies. It is a simple matter for Christians to ask whether these views that claim to hold the right opinion of reality and religion are consistent with what the ancient Christian consensus has always held everywhere in all cultures.

CHRISTIAN ORTHODOXY AND MODERN CHAUVINISM

The term *orthodox* is used here to refer to the classic Christian way of remembering and reasoning. Classic Christian orthodoxy can be objectively investigated by recalling the texts of consensus definition that are embraced by both eastern and western Christianity as well as early African Christianity.

Africa was the first of the three known continents of the ancient world to make an intentional intellectual pursuit of right remembering by textual analysis. An experiment took place in the Nile Delta in a way that was widely adopted elsewhere. It was in Africa where precise distinctions were first made between apostolic teaching and Gnostic, Adoptionist, and Pelagian views of what the apostles meant. These were largely African debates before they became widespread debates. Their resolution in Africa was respected and widely accepted in the eastern and western churches as seen in Nicea.

Chauvinism means undue partiality or attachment to a group or place to which one belongs. *Male chauvinism* means excessive partiality to males as if they were naturally superior. The phrase "*modern chauvinism*"[50] points to an excessive loyalty toward whatever is perceived as the latest thing. It is the most stubborn vice of the modern western bent. Modern chauvinism is an undue attachment to modern worldviews so as to assume they are intrinsically superior, excluding pre-modern worldviews.

The modern chauvinists have focused obsessively on how Christian teaching must constantly be changing. This is a one-note song. The only note is about how much Christians have changed from one culture to another, ignoring the continuities so crucial to apostolic memory. They love to report every form of supposed change while refusing to listen for the durable consensus. African believers are turning back that recent western tide and seeking a wider and deeper historical consensus on truth.[51]

CONSCIENCE AND SELF-LOVE

Media figures least prone to self-restraining rational disciplines have become the idols of modern chauvinism. The western entertainment industry idealizes and romanticizes self-preoccupation. Classic Christian orthodoxy is the remedy against moral license that pretends to be an expression of genuine freedom.

Conscience is the present self comparing itself with what it knows it ought to be. Conscience does not ever go completely away because it is we who are speaking to ourselves, holding up before ourselves our better selves. For self-absorbed narcissists, conscience is merely a bother that distracts from supposed self-fulfillment. Those who are most self-absorbed are more likely to come to the point of wanting desperately to be simply relieved of conscience. But God has planted conscience in every human being and it will not go away.

Those who cling to every habit of mind that the historic church has long rejected have lost their bearings. They are now are being called to account. The healing of bad habits may take as many decades to cure as they have taken to grow. The faithful are learning belatedly how to admonish, discipline, and speak the truth in love. Those who are ready to pray for grace to listen to tested orthodoxy have a much more serene

---

50. First used in *Agenda for Theology* (San Francisco: Harper and Row, 1979); cf. *After Modernity . . . What?* (Grand Rapids, MI: Zondervan, 1990).

51. For examples, see Mercy Amba Oduyoye, *Daughters of Anowa* (Maryknoll, NY: Orbis Books, 1995), a Methodist from Ghana; Catholic Bénézet Bujo of Zaire, *Foundations of an African Ethic: Beyond the Universal Claims of Western Morality,* trans. Brian McNeil (New York: Crossroad Publishing, 2011); and Coptic H.E. Metropolitan Bishoy of Damiette, Kafr El-Sheikh, Barary and the Monastery of Saint Demiana, Egypt, *Deification of Man and the Interpretation of "Partakers of the Divine Nature" (2 Pet 1:4)* (http://www.metroplit-bishoy.org/english/index.htm). Though quite different, all three are founding members of the International Conference of African Theologians called together by the Center for Early African Christianity. Their concord lies in their confession of classic Christian faith.

battle. Penitent faith can stop a bad habit cold turkey, but only by grace permeating freedom.

IGNORING CONTINUITIES IN HISTORY

The modern habit is to ignore continuities in history and stress only changes. That habit misses the joy of seeing how grace sustains faithful communities through hard times. It undermines confidence in the whole idea of the unity of the body of Christ, which is so crucial to classic Christian teaching. That unity embraces all generations of Christian belief, and not modern Christians only.

Faith revels in the steady continuity between the original apostles and life today. It is healthy to celebrate cultural varieties between Christians as long as the unity and continuity of believers with the original witnesses is not forgotten.

A huge literature exists on the conflicting varieties and inconsistencies within Christian history and especially early African Christianity with its angry Arians, overconfident Pelagians, and self-regulating Donatists. But only a very small scholarly literature can be found on how the faith confessed by Christians today is the same faith as that experienced by Mark, Athanasius, and Augustine.

The process of exact remembering and guaranteeing continuity was pioneered in early African Christianity, as seen in its early councils[52] and gradual overcoming of teachings contrary to the unified testimony of the original witnesses to incarnation, atonement, and resurrection.

A massive gap in historical studies has resulted: the neglect of empirical inquiry into those ways in which orthodoxy has remained stable and centered. Today this continuity is poorly understood and under-reported in western higher education. But it was clearly known and understood in African orthodoxy of the third and fourth centuries.

Modern chauvinists do not study the exquisite processes of transmitting a tradition of memory accurately throughout changing centuries and cultures. It is ignored because it does not exist within their range of vision.[53]

This myopia has persisted too long without gentle correction. Modernization since the eighteenth century has an insatiable fascination with change, which has its roots in eighteenth-century Enlightenment. This is accompanied by a sense of boredom about ideas of stability. Modern news media have far less interest in reporting on continuities than on changes. Journalists are socialized to be fixated on what disaster

---

52. See the Councils of Carthage, Synods of 251, 256, 345, and 397; and the Conference of 411.

53. That same diminished vision may keep sincere persons from seeing the economic factors and interests of their own social location. See Peter Berger and Thomas Luckmann, *The Social Construction of Reality: A Treatise in the Sociology of Knowledge* (Garden City, NY: Doubleday, 1966).

is likely to happen next, not on how human cultures have repeatedly learned how to survive heartbreaking challenges.

Much less is acknowledged today of the sturdy consistencies in the Christian tradition than of the ruptures, debates, controversies, and reversals of Christianity. African Orthodoxy has carefully studied both. It has a clear perspective on how the unity of the body of Christ was transmitted through widely varied cultures.

The next question is whether Christian continuity goes back only to Christ and the apostles or reaches back to a larger Hebraic memory of God's promise and covenant.

C. ORTHODOX JEWS AND ORTHODOX CHRISTIANS

Although the idea of orthodoxy matured within Christianity, it was anticipated in Hebraic history. This is why it is illuminating to consider orthodox Judaism in relation with orthodox Christianity.

COMPLEMENTARY READINGS SHARE THE SAME SACRED HEBRAIC TEXT

Many beliefs are commonly held by Jews and Christians: One God, almighty, same Prophets, same Psalms, and the Lord of history who reveals his Name (YHWH, Yahweh, I am who I am) to Israel.

No Christian orthodoxy would exist without the actual history of Israel. Judaism and Christianity both ground themselves in twelve plus centuries of Hebraic memory. In this way they stand together in stark contrast with forms of religion that are based on ideas rather than events. God is known through the events in which he makes himself known.

Classic consensual Christianity has always been illumined by its classic consensual Jewish roots. Talmud was written about the same time as the early patristic writings. The Babylonian Talmud was compiled in the third to fifth centuries. The Jerusalem Talmud was compiled in the fourth and fifth centuries. Like patristic teaching, Talmudic teaching focuses on understanding the ancient sacred texts approved for congregational worship.

Jews have something decisive at stake in the recovery of classic Christianity, and vice versa. Today both experience the same cultural crises and opportunities. Both share the same Old Testament texts. The surprise: Orthodoxy within both Judaism and Christianity is now in a growth stage.

A body of literature exists, both ancient and modern, that seeks to assess the boundary between Judaism and Christianity. In the first four centuries that comparison was an intense issue for African Christians, especially in Alexandria, where Christians lived amid a huge Jewish population. That early interaction between Jews and Christians remains pertinent today. Both traditions have accommodated themselves rashly to modern ideologies.

The relation of Christianity with Judaism was of intense interest to Peter, Stephen, Luke, and Paul in the New Testament. Making cohesive sense out of those New Testament writers in relation to the texts of the Law, Prophets, and Wisdom literature became the special concentration of the early African Christian writers, especially Origen and Augustine.

THE INTERTWINING OF JEWISH AND CHRISTIAN HISTORY

One of the earliest and most far-reaching ecumenical decisions in the struggle of Christian doctrine was against those who sought to be Christian by rejecting Jewish scripture. That rejection led by Marcion began in Pontus and Rome, was resolved in early African Christianity by a teaching consensus that centered in the Catechetical School in Alexandria. Thereafter it was clear that Christianity could never set aside the Torah or Chronicles or Prophets or Psalms or the Hebrew language. African orthodoxy itself has been shaped decisively by its dialogue with the Jews of Egypt.

A Christian who presumed to despise the Jewish scriptures would be thereby disclaiming and abrogating Christianity. All Christians share in the history of the covenant of God with Noah, Abraham, Moses, and the people of Israel, Jews and Christians together are guardians of the same memory of God's almighty presence in the world. This contrasts with all forms of non-biblical religion, since the Jewish canon is a necessary part of the Christian canon.

God's word has always been spoken within particular human crises. Revelation occurs in a unique history, recounting events at specific times and places. This is sometimes called the scandal of particularity, since it remembers God's action and presence especially in distinct and particular events such as the exodus, the captivity in Babylon, and the death of Jesus. The events gave birth to the ideas.

Christian orthodox remembering does not see the Law and Prophets as contrary to Christian reasoning. Rather they are the historic basis for a clear and coherent understanding of the fulfillment of the divine covenants with Israel in the Lord's death and resurrection.

ONE ISRAEL, TWO MEMORIES

To separate faith from its history would be, as Will Herberg said, "like paraphrasing poetry."[54] It is alien to biblical faith to try to explain the meaning of life from

---

54. Herberg, *Faith Enacted in History* (Philadelphia: Westminster Press, 1976), 32.

within the limited terms of natural causes alone, without speaking of the cause of all natural causes. The philosophical attempt to speak of the truth of human existence without reference to any actual risk-laden history is quite different from the Bible.

From Moses and the prophets Christians have learned to resist the elevation of finite values into idols or absolute values. Together Jews and Christians reject any form of worship in which the human story is exhaustively swallowed up in the cyclical rhythms of nature.

The events related in the Bible tell the story of salvation as a particular narrative of actual history, not as a general set of rational arguments about ideas. In biblical religion human freedom plays out in a particular chronicle of bondage and deliverance. African Christianity from its beginnings in Mark, Tertullian, and Clement has viewed salvation as a narrative of an actual history.

GOD'S COVENANTS WITH NOAH, ABRAHAM, AND MOSES REMEMBERED THROUGH THE INCARNATION

God's covenant with Noah was a promise to all humanity not to destroy the earth. As the life of the world was promised to the progeny of Noah, so the Life of the world was in due time revealed in God's Son.

For both Jews and Christians, Abraham is the father of faith who provides the prototype of one who steadfastly trusts the promise of God even when the death of his son Isaac is commanded. For this faith Abraham and his followers are promised a land and descendants who will become a great nation and bear God's blessing to all humanity.

Jews and Christians speak in similar ways of God who gives and orders all nature and history, who is creator of man and woman in God's image and likeness, and who offers a way of divine-human reconciliation when they fall. The differences appear when Christians confess Jesus Christ as Lord who came to forgive sin.

Jews and Christians together understand life in relation to a history of divine-human covenant. Although they may differ on how that expectation is fulfilled, together they view history in relation to its end, to fulfillment that will come in the end time of judgment and redemption. Judaism before Christianity looked to divine grace to bring divine-human reconciliation. This differs sharply from all nonbiblical religions.

A SINGLE HISTORY SHARED

Judaism faces inwardly toward an elect people, a particular holy land and descendants, while Christianity faces outwardly toward the horizon of the world to take God's good news to all humanity. According to Jewish theologian Franz Rosensweig they need each other.

While the elect of Judaism are defined tribally by progenitor and circumcision as the people of Israel, the elect in Christianity are all those who trust in the Word revealed in Jesus. In this way all others who are not children of Abraham ethnically are brought into the covenant of God with Israel by faith in the incarnate Son. Judaism looks toward its Promised Land and Holy City, while Christianity gratefully moves from Jerusalem to the ends of the earth. In their baptism, Christians participate in a new exodus that recapitulates and fulfills the hopes of Israel.

Children enter into the Jewish community by being born into it. They enter into the Christian community by being reborn by faith through baptism. While Jews look toward the promise of a particular land, Christians are more like sojourners in history and strangers in every land and in every society. Although they may be citizens within various social orders and cultures, they do not see their fundamental identity before God as connected with land, place, or ethnicity, but as connected with the faith of Abraham as seen in the light of Christ.

African Christians have never viewed their ethnicity as the source of their salvation. It is a decisive error to limit God's saving action to a literal race. In this way the covenant with Israel has universal significance for all people. Christianity transfigures Judaism by seeking to bring the God of Israel to the whole of humanity, and the world of humanity back to God.

God's revelation does not require a change of ethnic status or circumcision or becoming a part of a particular national identity, seed, or genealogy. Paul wrote: "Now if you belong to Christ, then indeed you are Abraham's descendants, heirs according to the promise" (Gal 3:29 CEB).

The new covenant was first explored thoroughly as a problem of scriptural integrity in African Christianity. The new covenant promised in Jeremiah does not replace the old covenant, but enlarges and fulfills the covenant with the people of Israel, which began with Abraham and in Egypt with the exodus and the giving of the Instruction (Torah) in Sinai.

THE FREEDOM OF GOD

Christian orthodoxy is not embarrassed by the gracious truth that God chose the people of Israel and through them blessed all humanity. Similarly Jewish orthodoxy is not falsified by the premise that God chose a particular people in order to bring God's blessing to all. "You are a people holy to the LORD your God. The LORD your God chose you to be his own treasured people beyond all others on the fertile land" (Deut 7:6 CEB). "All the families of the earth will be blessed because of you" (Gen 12:3 CEB).

The ultimate intention of God's choice of Israel as chosen people was to send the Messiah who would be the Savior of the world. Jesus had to come from the seed of David to embrace all humanity.

The crucial question is whether the Messiah came in Jesus or not. However friendly, Jews and Christians do well to be utterly candid with each other about how they differ on this pivotal point, and how it affects what they believe and teach. Granting that difference and its importance, the difference does not foreclose all further discussion. The one covenant with God may be viewed from two different vantage points: one, the chosen people of God; the other, the people of God in the light of the ministry of Jesus.

SEMINAR 4
ORTHODOX REMEMBERING

A. REMEMBERING THAT WHICH IS MOST WORTHY OF MEMORY

WALKING WITHIN BOUNDARIES

To walk in the orthodox way means to think and live within the boundaries of the ancient Christian consensus of teaching, applying that teaching contextually within ever-new cultural situations. The gifts of mind and conscience guide the application of the truth toward prudent judgment.

The New Testament is an exposition on the Hebrew Bible's prophetic expectations,[55] showing how the life, death, and resurrection of Jesus fulfill those expectations. The first witnesses understood themselves as standing in a tradition of accurate and faithful remembering. They were remembering how their community had been suddenly transformed by the coming of the promised Anointed One.

The exercise of human freedom within orthodox life is protected by boundaries that enhance freedom. No one is coerced into believing, but those who freely believe have consented to live within these boundaries. Within these bounds of free consent, anyone in a subsequent generation who comes to hear the scripture rightly can trust the unique power of the historic consensus. That unique power is the unifying power of the Spirit who accompanies the hearing of the written Word, and who brings it into cohesion in the mind of the believer.

By this means, believers are free to think with the earliest witnesses so as to be assured of receiving reliable testimony to God's coming to humanity. They believe the same truth that was attested by the earliest witnesses. They hold the same core faith in

---

55. That is, the Hebrew Bible in Greek translation (LXX).

God as that of the prophets, patriarchs, psalmists, sages, apostles, saints, confessors, and martyrs. It is one faith variously received within a developing history.

THOUGH CULTURE CHANGES, GOD'S WORD DOES NOT CHANGE

Orthodoxy in all its culturally varied forms follows Paul's strict admonition: "However, even if we ourselves or a heavenly angel should ever preach anything different from [*heteran*, from which we derive our word *heterodoxy*] what we preached to you, they should be under a curse" (Gal 1:8 CEB).

Inventive revisionists are forewarned that their revisions will not gain easy consent in the company of those who have been deeply formed by the apostolic witnesses to the truth of God's Word become flesh.

Classic Christianity is most reliably defined in documented form by the New Testament itself. Even more concisely the gist of scripture is summed up in the primitive baptismal confession, which was entirely derived from scripture as salvation history summarized in its most concise form.

This doctrinal core was recalled in the three most widely received summaries of faith—the Apostles', the Nicene, and the Athanasian Creeds—and their subsequent consensual confessions and interpretations. The faithful in Christ are baptized, according to scripture, in the name of the Father, Son, and Holy Spirit.[56]

HANDING DOWN THE TRUTH FROM ONE GENERATION TO ANOTHER

The root word for tradition is the Latin *traditio* (Greek *paradosis*), meaning the handing down of the Word from generation to generation, just as it was consensually received worldwide, and cross-culturally lived out through two millennia. Tradition means passing along the holy writ received in the Old and New Testaments and respecting its most faithful consensual interpreters.

Nothing would be less orthodox than to assert a tradition that has no basis in scripture, since by definition, tradition consists in passing along scripture. Any teaching that pits tradition against scripture has already lost its orthodox equilibrium, since the Spirit is shepherding the transmission of scripture. Apostolic tradition is itself a memory of scripture interpretation as it has been consensually received over all epochs and locations since the death and resurrection of Jesus.

Readers of the Bible have always understood that the Spirit of God is working within the process of the remembering and hearing of scripture. The Spirit works not merely in the inspiration of scripture, but also inwardly within the hearing process. Thus the faithful are never abandoned to their own private single-culture interpreta-

---

56. Matt 28:19 (CEB)

tions. As they read, they pray that cultural biases be curbed by the Spirit's presence in their reading of the sacred text.

Wherever one text of scripture may appear contradictory to another, the remedy is to reason by analogy from clear passages to those less clear. This is another point in which a principle of interpretation was researched and confirmed first in Africa—notably by Origen, Tichonius, Augustine, and Cyril—and later became received virtually everywhere. Since the faithful hold that all discrete scripture texts are inspired by the same Spirit, every proposed interpretation of any passage must be compared with the other portions of Bible teaching. Classic consensual Christian teaching has looked carefully at both the whole and every part repeatedly over generations so as to seek consensual interpretations of passages that appear to conflict. This does not deny that different interpretations of a passage may be proposed, but affirms that there is a tradition of consensual interpretation by which any given passage has been understood in relation to the whole.

On the basis of the plain sense of scripture, orthodox reading looks for the moral and spiritual message of text, wary of interpretations that ignore the long-standing consensus. If the plain sense is unclear, the reader of scripture prays for grace that the Spirit might reveal its meaning, ruling out anything that might not correspond with the well-defined core memory of historic revelation.

Without the process of handing down the truth from generation to generation there could be no reliable way to ensure that the original truth revealed is remembered accurately.

B. RETURNING TO THE FOUNTAIN

HOW MULTICULTURAL AFRICAN ORTHODOXY IS DIFFERENT FROM MONOCULTURAL AMERICAN FUNDAMENTALISM

Please, I beg you; do not force the assumptions of twentieth-century fundamentalism on the ancient Christian writers. Augustine and Cyril knew nothing of what we now call fundamentalism. It is an uncritical and perverse misnomer to conclude that they who knew nothing of modern fundamentalism were fundamentalists. Early African interpreters of scripture differ entirely from fundamentalism. They were not reacting against modern views like those of Rousseau and Darwin.

Major early African orthodox interpreters of scriptures lived more than fifteen hundred years before the method of modern fundamentalism, which did not emerge until the Niagara Conference 1895, 1500 years after Augustine wrote *On Christian Doctrine*. Therefore, African orthodoxy must not ever be tainted with the controversial Western word "fundamentalism." That is properly called an anachronism—an idea belonging to a period other than that in which it exists.

The rebirth of African orthodoxy is definitely not the rebirth of American fundamentalism. African orthodoxy began in the first century and American fundamentalism did not begin until the late nineteenth. Since then fundamentalism has been defined as strict adherence to five anti-modernist theological doctrines (inspiration and inerrancy of scripture, the virgin birth, substitutionary atonement, resurrection, and the historical reality of miracles). Classic Christian orthodoxy is not restricted to these doctrines, and all five can be viewed as a time-specific reaction against late-nineteenth-century modernist theology.[57] Orthodoxy precedes American fundamentalism by nineteen centuries.

Orthodoxy rejects the cult of newness. From the viewpoint of classic orthodoxy, modern American fundamentalism is a new configuration of good intentions that neglect other aspects of the catholicity of Christian teaching. Fundamentalism viewed itself as a new and simpler compact definition of the essentials of Protestant confession. What was actually new about fundamentalism was its distinctive nineteenth-century historical reactions to Hume, Feuerbach, and Darwin.

Critical orthodoxy today seeks to regain analytical skills of discernment honed through centuries of consensual recollection in liturgy, psalmody, and scripture. Orthodoxy resists captivity within any particular transient worldview.

Orthodoxy is more profoundly multicultural than modern multiculturalism because it embraces the faith of past cultures and not modern cultures alone. The ancient tradition of African orthodoxy provides a tested way of critical reasoning. Classic African teachers of scripture often objected to a lifeless, flat, merely literal view of the scriptural text without listening to its spiritual and moral meanings.

HOW ANCIENT ORTHODOXY IS DIFFERENT FROM NEO-ORTHODOXY

African paleo-orthodoxy is distinguished from Euro-American "neo-orthodoxy" of the last century, which was a once conspicuous school of theology that withered by neglect of ancient Christian teaching. Instead neo-orthodoxy was desperate to accommodate to western culture. Neo-orthodoxy never gained a significant foothold on the continent of Africa. Africans who studied in the West before 1975 were likely to have been impacted by it, but little since then.

The Euro-American neo-orthodoxy of Paul Tillich, Rudolf Bultmann, and Reinhold Niebuhr failed to grasp the central importance of resurrection. The neo-orthodox writers were uneasy with the act of receiving the risen Lord in the Eucharist. Prayer, moral discipline, Christian liturgy, and holy living were not their primary concern. Cultural accommodation, social policy, and philosophical innovation were their primary concerns.

---

57. T. Oden, *Agenda for Theology* (San Francisco: Harper and Row, 1979); George M. Marsden, *Fundamentalism and American Culture* (New York: Oxford University Press, 1980), pp. 4-5.

Some neo-orthodox writers used the term *orthodoxy* to legitimize their cultural accommodations with a diluted view of Jesus as the Savior and a qualified, seemingly embarrassed, view of biblical authority.[58]

In the decades of the 1960s and 1970s neo-orthodoxy and modernity declined hand in hand. Far from a correction of modern temptations, neo-orthodoxy was in many ways a bland reflection of modern western passions and temptations.

It is a misleading habit to connect neo-orthodoxy with ancient Christian orthodoxy. Neo-orthodoxy was not orthodox in any decisive sense except in its attempt to teach the doctrine of original sin as a political reality. I have used the term paleo-orthodox to make it entirely clear that the ancient consensus of faith is starkly distinguishable from neo-orthodoxy. The "paleo" aspect of orthodoxy is its oldest primitive layer, which is significantly African in conception and argument. Global Christian orthodoxy has deeper third-century roots in Africa than anywhere else.

ORTHODOXY DOES NOT LET THE WORLD SET THE AGENDA

The orthodox life seeks to challenge the world's agenda, not succumb to it. It seeks to guard, reasonably vindicate, and wisely advocate the faith once delivered to the faithful. The way is discovered not by borrowing further from the idols of the modern world but by testing them.

Meanwhile the actual fallen world, the ongoing cosmos that runs on regular clock time, is still the subject of God's mercy even if fallen. It is still in the process of being reconciled and its sin overcome. To speak of an "actual fallen world" is to hold up for examination a prodigal history of sin which has not yet come to repentance and faith, and is still being prompted by preparing or prevenient grace, which goes before convicting grace and justifying grace. No one is saved by prevenient grace; only by justifying grace that generates faith active in love.

Classic Christian teaching carefully avoids taking the world in its fallenness more seriously than it takes God's seriousness about redeeming the world. The fallen world is absurdly still searching for the saving event that ironically has already occurred in the incarnation. Classic Christianity has always taken care that it should not be swallowed up by the fleeting power of those who have not yet discovered God's redemptive love.

---

58. This neglect allowed the door to open for those most obsessed with modernity to take command of biblical criticism in the western universities. An exception was Karl Barth, who was far more grounded in ancient ecumenical teaching, but nonetheless remained more indebted to Calvin than Augustine, and more bound to Augustine than to the eastern fathers who had gladly received the scriptural wisdom of the early African exegetes from Athanasius to Cyril the Great.

THE PASSING NATURE OF THE FALLEN WORLD YET TO BE REDEEMED

The fallen world's distracted and distorted imaginations are hardly the final word. The spirit of these times cannot itself dictate the terms of salvation. That spirit is itself under divine judgment. Untested schemes are forever tempted to overestimate the fleeting power of the fallen world.

It has always been and is still misguided to offer vast supposed improvements upon the gospel. The world is and remains under God's grace and direction. His saving mercy is a gift given for all, ready to be received by all who repent and believe.

Christians are continually tempted to be overly awed by the passing vitality of the fallen world. If sins have been forgiven and human freedom empowered by grace, why should sin and fallenness be an absolute and unforgiving preoccupation? Those who are awestruck at the power of evil are tempted to forget the incomparable power of the One who has already acted decisively to save the world from its wretchedness.

The faithful joyfully point toward the majesty of the One from whom all things come and into whom all things return, in whose constant love there is no shadow of change or turning. Sadly, the transforming power of grace becomes carelessly trivialized under the spell of taking the world absolutely seriously while ignoring God's almighty power. When modern cultures seem to be capable of undermining any claim to any truth, it is best to tell the truth simply and plainly. Nothing is more disarming.

The faithful need seasoned teachers who have lived long enough with classic consensus Christian texts and songs and prayers so as to trust them and not be deceived. These teachers are citizens of a global community that is en route to eternal life with God.

THE IDEA OF A "POST-CHRISTIAN WORLD" UNDERSTOOD WITHIN THE ORTHODOX CONSENSUS

Early African Christians would never have accepted the idea of a post-Christian world. The notion that there is a world that has succeeded in permanently outliving God's grace is a desperate fantasy.

Yes there is a world that does not listen to God, but its deafness can never mean that God is not speaking. The world given by God only appears now to exist without God. The total effect of the abuses of human freedom can never be deeper than the ocean of divine grace.

Sin has no power to totally eclipse the work of the Spirit just because the Spirit's promptings are not received. The worst sin imaginable cannot mean that the real world now lacks the forgiving love of the crucified and risen Son.

The world is tempted to proceed as if the Word of God was not revealed. This leads to the illusion that the reported coming of God in time has no abiding relevance to actual humanity. Even when spurned, the transforming power of the Spirit continues to be freely offered. Thank God the fantasy of a post-Christian world lacks empirical evidence and intellectual strength.

C. POLITICAL WINNERS?

IS ORTHODOXY MERELY THE SKEWED MEMORY OF WINNERS?

Is the orthodox way merely a case of political "winners" eliminating "losers" in a world in which power alone determines history? If so, the faithful have a right to know how they have been deluded by a series of cynical power plays.

African orthodoxy has repeatedly examined this important question. It is not a new puzzle, but has a history of serious inquiry in Africa from Tertullian and Clement to Augustine and Cyril the Great. The classic consensual Christian teachers have often set forth reasons why life with God is not explained by an analysis of worldly power alone. Such reasoning has guided orthodox faith repeatedly in gaining confidence in God's presence in actual human history.

Suppose that the only thing the unorthodox voices lacked was clout. Suppose that Montanus and Marcion could have been just as correct as apostolic teaching but just did not have enough muscle, no army, and no police. If so, the history of orthodoxy would become nothing more than the history of a powerful majority, not the history of truth.

Suppose the winners were by definition labeled as orthodox, and the losers by definition as heretics.[59] This is a commonplace modern objection to classic consensual Christianity. Its most familiar form is the Marxist or social location argument. It challenges religious judgments on the premise that they can always be shown to come from some particular social location or vested interest within the economic order. The Marxist explanation of orthodoxy was simple: economic interests prevailed. Ideological winners imposed their views on ideological losers coercively as a matter of power. Though Marxism is in disrepute, dreary echoes of this Marxist explanation of orthodoxy still linger, oddly enough in departments of religious studies in universities originally created by Christians.

---

59. Vincent, *Commonitory*, ch. 6, FC 7. For modern arguments see William H. C. Frend, *Martyrdom and Persecution in the Early Church: A Study of a Conflict from the Maccabees to Donatus* (New York University Press, 1967); Maureen A. Tilley, *The Bible in Christian North Africa: The Donatist World*, (Minneapolis: Fortress Press, 1997); Timothy Barnes, *Constantine and Eusebius*, (Cambridge, MA: Harvard University Press, 1981).

THE MARTYRS SOUGHT NO WORLDLY GAIN

Vincent of Lérins provided the classic answer to this question of winners. It is the evidence of martyrdom. It seeks no worldly gain. It is self-evident that the martyrs had no economic interest in being slain. Their very willingness to give their lives for the truth showed their disregard for all economic gains. Who can buy bread if they have no life?

We are asking what is so wrong with the idea that orthodoxy is an accident of winners. Vincent explained: During the height of Arianism, many orthodox believers had been hunted and persecuted by their more powerful opponents. There is no economic sense in which they can be described as winners. It offends their memory to consider them under the metaphor of worldly winners.

Were the martyrs more afraid of death or of life? Neither. They loved life but loved more the truth for which they died.

LEARNING FROM THE AFRICAN MARTYRS

The actual history of Christian martyrdom among the people of God is galvanizing. The Letter to the Hebrews speaks of those who

> received back their dead by resurrection. Others were tortured and refused to be released so they could gain a better resurrection. But others experienced public shame by being taunted and whipped; they were even put in chains and in prison. They were stoned to death, they were cut in two, and they died by being murdered with swords. They went around wearing the skins of sheep and goats, needy, oppressed, and mistreated. The world didn't deserve them. They wandered around in deserts, mountains, caves, and holes in the ground. (Heb 11:35-38 CEB)

There are abundant examples (gulags, death camps, and salt mines) showing that the political winners were the persecutors of the orthodox.

When times worsened for the earliest African believers under persecution, then God sent in his legions of saints. Some were scholars, most were not. Grace empowers the faithful to die, when necessary, for their faith. They were seldom elite agents of power. By these ironic means, God works to awaken faith among the persecutors. That is a fact of third-century African history just as it is a fact today in Syria, China, and northern Nigeria.

It is absurd to think of the martyrs of the Decian persecution as winners. Nor was Athanasius a winner during most of his hazardous life of banishment. He was exiled five times and pursued all over the Egyptian deserts. Only through the slowly unfolding generations of lay consent would the martyrs become recognized as saints and heroes of the faith.[60] The faithful laity had to discover and confirm the wisdom

---

60. Elizabeth A. Castelli, *Martyrdom and Memory: Early Christian Culture Making* (New York: Columbia University Press, 2004).

of Cyprian and Athanasius before they could become teachers of global Christianity. The price was not cheap.

Similarly in Soviet times, the orthodox faithful were not the powerful but the poor, the dispossessed who were forced to keep their scriptures hidden under their attic floors. The seventy years of Soviet oppression were horrible but in relation to eternity only a slip of time. In 1991 in Moscow just after the collapse of the Soviet Union, I was given a Bible by the Bible Society of Moscow that had survived the seventy years of persecution. It was beaten up and tattered, but it remained the Word of God, and my most poignant remembrance of my days in Russia.

In what conceivable economic or political sense was Antony of the desert a winner? He ate wild grains, berries, and insects. Or consider Mother Theodora? Or blind Didymus? How did Perpetua win any gains in this world? She died horribly for the truth under the hoofs of a maddened cow in a cheering amphitheater. Those who imagine that the consensus-bearers were upper-class elitists know nothing of the biographies of beheaded Cyprian, the tortured Origen, or the murdered Black Moses the Ethiopian.

Winners? Not in worldly terms. Their treasure was in the celestial city.

Origen and Athanasius were among the most learned of the African Fathers, yet they lived most of their lives under conditions that most today would regard as poverty, danger, risk, sickness, and deprivation. Many early African saints and heroes spent more time either in jail, exiled, or being hunted and hounded than they did living safe and comfortable lives.

REMEMBERING THE CONFESSORS

The formation of classic Christian teaching did not happen by popular vote of the civic authorities but came about through general consent of the *believing* laity. They were the ones who remembered the locations of the deaths of the martyrs and who gathered at those places to pray, long before there were any church buildings. These became sacred places that marked a place to pray in recollection of a believer who had died for faith. These places became modest oratories (from *orare*, a place to pray), which often after Diocletian became churches.

The community of faith recognized the decisive importance of witnessing with one's very life. These lives were remembered. Their memory entered into the memory of the church. By a long process of remembering, local voices of consent were repeatedly received into subsequent general consent.

Who brought about consensus? Was it by politics or cleverness? The early church had a clear answer: it was by the guidance of the Holy Spirit.

The "winner-loser" oversimplification drastically misleads. It wrongly applies a competitive sports metaphor to the process of free consent. Fair-minded persons will look deeper before allowing such a skeptical idea to corrupt the memory of classic Christian wisdom.

Modern critics forget how important were women, slaves, and the dispossessed in those circles of ecumenical lay consensus. The Spirit found ways of hearing and making known the voices of the underclass in the broad consenting process leading to the general consent articulated by the ecumenical councils. The Spirit opened ways to awaken general consent, even when worldly powers or hierarchical organizations were determined to resist it.[61] The poor, the widows, the bonded servants, and alienated class citizens of the world composed the decisive jury for ecumenical teaching.

---

61. Athanasius, *Defence of the Nicene Definition*, NPNF 2 IV:149ff; Calvin, *Inst.* 1.6.12–13.

SEMINAR 5
WHY ORTHODOXY PERSISTS

A. NINE REASONS ORTHODOXY SURVIVES

Not long ago it seemed almost certain to western intellectuals that Christian orthodoxy would fail. It seemed to be the least likely contender to survive the overwhelming creativity and power of technology, urbanization, and secularization.

Similarly those who dragged Mark through the streets of Alexandria expected Christianity to disappear. Right away. It didn't.

Those who beheaded Cyprian expected North African Christianity to be wiped out. Apply bloody state power, the authorities thought, and Christianity will go away. It didn't. Instead their blood inspired the community of faith to grow in faith and determination. The more the saints willingly suffered for the faith when necessary, the more the beholders recognized the power of their faith.

The present moment of opportunity is clear: the faithful are learning anew how African orthodoxy today continues to rise out of oppression, blight, war, and the grave, turning death into service and hatred into love.

How did classic Christianity survive all these challenges: idolatry, authoritarian power, plunder, being sold into slavery in the mines, and military conquest? Despite all negative predictions, African orthodoxy has in fact survived, even in Libya, Tunisia, and Algeria, where it once flourished for five hundred years. Why? The real answers are surprising.

Orthodoxy exists:

1. BECAUSE IT IS CROSS-CULTURALLY AGILE

The most surprising feature of global Christian orthodoxy is not its rigidity but its flexibility. Since it was and is centered in life in the eternal Word, orthodoxy remains free to enter willingly into countless hazardous cultural settings on behalf of its all-embracing vision of the truth.

The orthodox way may appear on first glance to be suspicious of other cultures and forever imprisoned in a particular ethnic group. Coptic Orthodoxy looks too Egyptian. Ethiopian Orthodoxy looks too Ethiopian. Catholic orthodoxy looks too Latin. This is because they entered deeply into culture after culture without losing their bearings. They formed cultures without ceasing to be a part of the global confessing people of God. What a poor concept orthodoxy would be if it only occurred in one culture with one language.

The fact that orthodoxy has become very deeply invested in particular cultures is evidence of its flexibility and empathy. This happened in third-century Alexandria and Carthage, fourth-century Ethiopia, and fifth-century Nubia and Libya. African orthodoxy proved itself to be culturally versatile without ceasing to be faithful to the apostolic teaching. Its history shows that it has been uncommonly capable of relating to emergent cultures. The orthodox were eager to reach out deeply to meet, confront, and dialogue with different cultures, to become all things to all peoples on behalf of God's Word.[62]

African orthodoxy has not survived two millennia by being inept in making adroit responses. Rather it is freed by the gospel to make creative and variable cultural responses since it is firmly centered in the unchanging God.

The people of God live by penetrating and embracing each new culture, language, and symbol system as God's special providential gift. The Spirit provides the wisdom to do this in any location.

Cultures and languages change constantly. But global orthodoxy, the same ancient memory of God's presence in the world, is continuing to grow in ever-new cultures and languages. Today it can spread by such a wide range of musical voices as hip-hop, Raï, Swahili, Shaabi, Arabic, and Gregorian chant.

It passes along the most ancient memory by the most suitable means. It both guards the original testimony and communicates it anew within dawning subcultures. To fail either challenge is to default on right remembering. This is not unbending rigidity but high-spirited alertness.

African orthodoxy has been sustained throughout twenty centuries of moving from culture to culture without losing connection to the great cloud of witnesses and without diluting the original witness.

Why has orthodoxy survived?

2. BECAUSE GOD'S PROMISE IS DEMONSTRATED IN ACTUAL EVENTS

God's promise is sure: God will protect the people of God from ultimate and irreversible loss of faith. This promise is not offered in regard to a particular congrega-

---

62. 1 Cor 9:19-22.

tion, denomination, generation, or passing period of history but rather to the whole community of faith viewed from beginning to end.

Will the community of faith survive no matter what? The answer is based on the promise of God that the Spirit will accompany every step of the human future. This gives believers a distinctive confidence in the long-term future, even when the short term appears unpromising.

The one, holy, catholic, apostolic church is promised imperishable continuation, even if particular believers falter. The covenant of God with Israel is simply not threatened by our faithlessness. It is an eternal covenant, not one limited to any particular time or culture. It is sustained by God's own sovereign will.

That will is made known through the real events of real history, as remembered by the people of the covenant. This is standard teaching within classic consensual Christianity. The neglect of this teaching may cause a loss of moral courage. However, the calculation of low odds for survival has never been a foremost concern of the covenant community. As the biblical story of Gideon's army of three hundred shows, low odds make God's power more evident (Judg 7:7). Faith sees beyond human obstacles.

Orthodox faith is not cowed by "these times." Global Christianity speaks confidently of the purpose of God in history because it has seen it work out in history. The community of faith lives by the Word of God and the power of the Spirit. This confidence rests not only on transient historical evidence, but also on the certainty of faith in God's promise. This conviction was brilliantly articulated by Athanasius and Augustine. It now awaits rediscovery by young Africans. Viewed globally, faith is once again ready to reclaim the orthodox teaching of the perpetuity, imperishability, and essential durability of the people of God.

Although the faithful in some times and places may appear virtually extinct, to their surprise they find that there are always "seven thousand who have not bowed their knee to Baal." Although their vitality may become "so obscured and defaced that the Church seems almost quite razed out . . . yet, in the meantime, the Lord has in this world, even in this darkness, his true worshipers."[63] The foundation is standing sure and the Lord knows who are his.[64]

This faith is seen especially in the relentless, persistent tenacity of the communities of believers in the Magreb and along the Nile valley under Arab rule since the seventh century. Their real-life stories of perseverance offer the rest of us a new opportunity to learn once again of the eternal remnant to which we belong. The remnant's continuity is guaranteed not by our cleverness, but by sovereign grace.

This leads to the third reason why orthodoxy persists:

---

63. CC 148; cf. 1 Kgs 19:18; Rev 7:4, 9.
64. 2 Tim 2:19.

3. BECAUSE GOD DOES NOT LEAVE HIMSELF WITHOUT WITNESS

The future of belief is finally left not to chance or human ingenuity but to the patient grace of God. God wills to be known by rational creatures. The divine will does not depend on our receiving it since God is omnipresent whether we receive it or not.

Many branches of the seasonally changing vine may drop off in the varied storms and seasons of passing cultures. Once-vital ideas and institutions may become defunct, but God will preserve the faithful until the end of time. That is a biblical promise. It is a certitude, a sure tenet of faith commonly shared by Protestants, Catholics, Copts, and Charismatics. The ultimate destiny of the believing community of faith is eternally secured, not by human shrewdness but by God's own faithfulness.

Faith alone remains the crucial condition of participating in this secure promise. Where faith is weak, grace continues to awaken and sustain it. The Holy Spirit is determined to prevail over idolatry and disbelief in God's own time. But this assurance is not to be held in such a way as to diminish faithful good works or neglect the responsibilities of human freedom.

This teaching cannot be grasped within the short time frame of only a few generations. Rather it can be best seen within a long-range frame of reference that reaches from the beginning to the end of history.

Though individual believers may face shipwreck and ruin, and even centuries of emerging and deteriorating traditions lose their bearings during periods of confusion and crisis, the people of God who are being guided by the Holy Spirit will be upheld by grace until the end.[65] God will not be left without witness in the world.[66]

God supplies that grace of persistence by which the faithful are sustained in time even while challenged by infirmities, forgetfulness, and persecutions. The worshipping community will be preserved to "broadcast the death of the Lord until he comes" (1 Cor 11:26 CEB). The Holy Spirit does not abandon the ever-forming, ever-renewing community of faith amid these earthly struggles. Meanwhile the community of faith sails on the turbulent seas of history and continues to be vulnerable to all those hazards that accompany historical existence generally.

Against the faithful "the gates of the underworld won't be able to stand" (Matt 16:18 CEB). So Jesus taught.[67] The people of God will never decline into total forgetfulness. The Spirit rekindles the flame and guides them to confirm the promises that always accompany them,[68] even when all the short-term audits do not add up.

---

65. John 16:7, 13.
66. Acts 14:17.
67. Cf. Luke 1:33; 1 Tim 3:15.
68. Luke 12:11-12; John 14:16; 16-13; Matt 23:20.

The community of faith, insofar as guided by the Spirit, never falls entirely away from the central truth of faith or into irretrievable error. It is preserved by grace, not by human craft or numbers or political savvy.[69]

Orthodoxy persists.

4. BECAUSE THE DIVINE WILL TRANSCENDS TEMPORARY DENIALS OF FAITH

As the continent of Africa is surrounded by oceans, so is the African church encompassed by waves of discontent. These challenges are permitted by God in order to test and strengthen faith. Despite temporary, real, and devastating failures, it is unthinkable that God would allow the community of faith finally to become absolutely and continuously unfaithful, or to lose all touch with the righteousness that the Redeemer has once for all bestowed upon the bride of Christ. "You have been given new birth—not from the type of seed that decays but from seed that doesn't. This seed is God's life-giving and enduring word. Thus, *All human life on the earth is like grass . . . but the Lord's word endures forever.* This is the word that was proclaimed to you as good news" (1 Pet 1:23-25 CEB).

The community of faith does not stumble or err so long as it builds upon the rock, Christ, and upon the foundation of the prophets and apostles. Due to the Spirit's guidance, the people of God will not fall away irrecoverably from salvation. The Spirit will not allow all those called and brought to faith to err completely or all at the same time.

We know this is true by looking at the actual history of God's providence. This is not a conclusion of an optimistic view of humanity. It is a teaching grounded in the complete reliability of God's will to accomplish God's purpose.

Jesus promised the faithful of each generation and of all cultures that the Holy Spirit "will teach you everything and will remind you of everything I told you" (John 14:26 CEB). The Holy Spirit has an omniscient memory of the truth, even when we remember imperfectly. Always some seeds of faith sprout from the ashes of the believing remnant. Sometimes such seeds may seem to struggle as endangered species, scattered all too thinly throughout a particular weed-infested culture. Yet wherever the people are hearing the Word and participating in the life of the risen Lord, they are never without effect, for "my word . . . does not return to me empty. Instead, it does what I want, and accomplishes what I intend," says the Lord (Isa 55:11 CEB).

The Spirit ensures the continuity of the Word in history. So the whole church does not at any given time completely err, and it does not err in its foundation, even if it may in temporary and non-essential ways. This is a compelling promise received by the church of all periods and places.

Orthodoxy endures for another surprising reason:

---

69. Matt 7:25.

5. BECAUSE THROUGH HUMAN WEAKNESS THE DIVINE POWER IS MADE MORE EVIDENT

The vulnerable, visible, local assemblies of the faithful are always prone to forgetfulness and fallibility amid the history of distracting temptations. Strategic mistakes, errors of judgment, and lapses of memory are to be expected. The church's imperfection is a stubborn hard fact. Original sin has been said to be the only doctrine that can be empirically proved. Yet the Holy Spirit promises to uphold faith through seasons of forgetfulness.

Unbelievers simply do not have the power to prevent all subsequent generations from hearing the good news of God. When the faithful community frankly recognizes its finite limitations, faith is freed to celebrate God's almighty presence amid those very limitations. The intimidating idea that the church is only one generation away from extinction is short-sighted because it doesn't remember the Spirit's faithfulness through the whole of time.

The community of faith exists within the conditions of the history of sin and will therefore always be prone to corruption and distortion. It will remain vulnerable to those who wish to use it for their own self-interest. Until the last day of history when the incurably wicked will be cut off from the living vine, a mixture of wheat and weeds will remain among God's people. The attempt to flee completely from this scene of human corruption would require fleeing from the distinctive arena of the community of faith in the world.

The consequences of the history of sin will continue to plague the community of faith and limit its temporary growth. Faith continues to battle with the partisan spirit that would divide it, the heterodox spirit that would change it, the permissive spirit that would turn liberty into license, and the legalistic spirit that would turn grace into law.

Despite continuing challenges permitted by a kind providence to strengthen the community of faith, the body lives on. The vine sends forth new shoots. The Spirit enlivens and heals. The Head continues to guide and order the whole body[70] even when its arms are weak.

Those who prefer clean hands to a servant heart may try to hold aloof from the hard challenges of actual life. Not so with Jesus. He ate with sinners and came to visit those most despicable and rejected. Without sin he chose to identify with sinners in his baptism, in his healing ministry, and on the cross.

The living community of believers in Africa continues to struggle with its perennial challengers such as:

- a Gnosticism that would reject physical creation and the resurrection, and treat the body as a prison and the community as an elite group of knowers;

---

70. John 15:1-5; Col 1:18.

- an Arianism that denies that Jesus is the eternal Son of God;
- a Donatism that would exclude communicants who have suffered under lapsed ministries;
- a purist Novatian rigorism that would close its doors to sinners with real moral deficiencies; and
- a Montanism that would individualistically exaggerate its own unique access to the Spirit.

But clean hands do not make a believer, only a contrite heart does so. The people of God living in faith, hope, and love under the life-giving power of the Spirit can never become absolutely, finally, or irreversibly corrupted.[71]

Every challenge presented to apostolic faith still lies awaiting its new occasions. Most of these challenges had to be first fought in Africa. They better prepared global Christianity for meeting these struggles.

Orthodoxy refuses to go away:

6. BECAUSE THE SPIRIT WORKS TO CONVEY CONSENT FROM GENERATION TO GENERATION

The history of the people of God is not one of uninterrupted progress or sustained ecstasy without challenge. It is made of constant course corrections. Athanasius fretted that the Christian faith had often seemed to be on the edge of universal destruction. But every time that it has appeared to be in this condition, God has raised it up anew. Each seeming defeat readies the community for some deeper level of potential understanding. Each apparent victory prepares the community for a deeper level of conflict.

The general consent of the people of God is sustained over very long stretches of time and space. The persistence of that consent provides decisive empirical evidence of the endurance and unity of the community of faith. To be in harmony with this witness is to be aligned with this universal consent.

No one generation can subdue the consent of the faithful. No century of persecution can defeat it, not even twenty centuries, as we see in Coptic Egypt. The Spirit promises to guard from permanent error the apostolic witness. This occurs not mechanically, as if impersonally forced by the Spirit apart from human freedom, but rather by the Spirit witnessing within normal human conditions through conscience, reason, persuasion, and redemptive grace.

The continuing vitality of the community of faith is an amazing story that is recounted in actual human narratives. The worst days of martyrdom were accompanied by the most profound movements of the Spirit. Correctives such as those of Cyprian, Anthony, Athanasius, and Augustine have typically *followed* the deepest seasons of

---

71. Matt 16:18.

dejection. To now, the promise has held, even against great obstacles, whether they be Roman rule or Arab conquest or civil disorder.

Orthodoxy persists despite all hindrances. Why?

7. BECAUSE THE HISTORIC STREAM OF UNIVERSAL CONSENT IS DIVINELY GUARDED

The faithful have found that they can rely on the Spirit over time to bring the truth to light, to remember rightly, and beckon the whole community toward the whole truth. The same fullness of faith is continued in the whole communion of saints around the whole world. If ruined in one country it is alive in another.

It is the Spirit who finally guarantees the unity of the faithful and the valid transmission of the apostolic witnesses. The Spirit continues in a patient way that only divine grace can sustain.

The common reception of the general ecumenical councils provides evidence of the unity and free consent of the global community of faith. This history shows that the Spirit has never ceased working to center the community in scriptural truth.

It is this universal consent that the faithful of all times find always reliable. The longer it persists, the clearer it attests the endurance of the community of faith as a gift of grace.[72]

These are all good reasons faith persists. But there is another:

8. BECAUSE THE FAITHFUL ARE GIVEN PATIENCE

Patience is a gift. It is not earned by grit but given by God as a reflection of the patience of God. "Those who hope in the Lord, will renew their strength; they will fly up on wings like eagles; they will run and not be tired; they will walk and not be weary" (Isa 40:31 CEB).

How can it be that the faithful glory in tribulation? Paul answers: "because we know that trouble produces endurance" (Rom 5:3). How long into the future is orthodox faith durable? James answers: "Therefore, brothers and sisters, you must be patient as you wait for the coming of the Lord. Consider the farmer who waits patiently for the coming of rain in the fall and spring, looking forward to the precious fruit of the earth" (Jas 5:7 CEB).

The victory of general lay consent will finally be vindicated only on the last day. Then wheat and tares will be separated. The unity, holiness, catholicity, and apostolicity of the faithful will then shine forth, though now seen through a glass darkly. This is a conviction of faith assured by the actual history of providence.

---

72. Council of Nicea I, SCD 54, p. 26; Basil, Letter 114, FC 13:241–42; Gregory of Nazianzus, *On the Great Athanasius*, Orat. XXI, NPNF 2 VII:269–80; Cyril, Letter 39, FC 76:147–52.

Temporary lapses in Christian memory will continue. But these do not lead the worshipping community to despair over the truth. Rather these lapses have amazingly revealed the meekness and vulnerability of the remembering faithful. Through this supposed weakness the faithful are disciplined to rely on God's promise, aware of their own finite temptations.

African orthodoxy is hesitant to point to any one time or place in which the consensus was utterly demolished. Having lived patiently through many generations, the faithful rightly doubt any alleged claim to orthodox consensus formed only in a single generation.

Finally, orthodox faith persists:

9. BECAUSE THE ORTHODOX HEART HAS THE ADVANTAGE OF LONG-TERM MEMORY

The long memory of tested Christian truth tends eventually to override the shorter memory of error. The advantage of a very long memory is that it has more levels of applicability and more clarity.

Modern observers are baffled at the tenacity of African orthodoxy. From where does its resilience come? Its persistence seems irrational to many observers who cannot fathom its foundation.

The more durable the consensual memory, the more likely it is to be trustworthy since blessed by the eternal One who is rightly remembered. Any particular assertion of Christian truth must stand under the constant corrective of the growing consent of the faithful over a wide range of time. Its persistence has the advantage of accessing this extremely long memory of many social adaptations without the loss of its identity.

Modern life is often trapped in short-term memory. The long memory of the community of faith is forever overcoming the shortsighted forms of distorted memory of those who live only in a single sub-culture or passing worldview. History abounds with regrettable illustrations of errors temporarily held. Even when corrected, the new correction is often insufficient. In the short term we frequently over-correct.

The Gnostic philosophical elites on the Nile near Nag Hammadi needed the majority corrective of the ordinary community of believers. The regional Donatists of Numidia needed the correction of the worldwide community of remembering. The skeptical Arians needed the corrective of the church's simple confession of the eternal Son of God. And so it goes. In each of these cases the faithful over time sought a reconciling ground to bridge the best aspects of each of these memory failures, complementing them with the rich stores of classic consensual memory.

But these correctives took time. Only a very long historical memory could provide critical balance for the lengthy journey through ever-present and new hazards. It is amazing how many times a fleeting erroneous apparent truth has seemed plausible for a while, only to be corrected by greater historical perspective.

All of the long-term advantages for survival lie on the side of the longer, more nuanced, more refined forms of historical memory. This is the special gift of the orthodox way.

SUMMARY

In sum, these are the nine reasons why African orthodoxy has survived the collapses of modern times:

1. it is cross-culturally agile

2. God's promise is demonstrated in actual events

3. God does not leave himself without witness

4. the divine will transcends temporary failures

5. human weakness shows divine power

6. the Spirit works to enable consent from generation to generation

7. consent is divinely guarded

8. the faithful are given the gift of patience, and

9. orthodox life has the advantage of long-term memory

B. GOING DEEPER: THE KERNEL OF TENACITY

WHY THE FAITHFUL ARE WILLING TO SUFFER FOR TRUTH

To speak of truth without willingness to suffer for the truth is indirectly to debase that truth. No teacher can be taken seriously who refuses to be inconvenienced for the truth she or he teaches. Truth claims are quickly revealed as phony if made by those unwilling to live by them.

The readiness to suffer for the sake of the truth permeates the whole fabric of biblical teaching. It is not an optional part of the curriculum for equipping the faithful.[73] It is what is meant by taking up the cross and following the risen Lord.

---

73. Phil 3:10; Cyprian, *On the Lapsed*, ANF 5:437–447; Kierkegaard, *Attack on "Christendom,"* passim.

It is a fact: The faithful have been willing to suffer for the truth. Not all have, but God raises up witnesses ready to deny themselves and bear the cross, viewing this as an inestimable privilege that their bodies could become the bearers of eternal truth.

The very concept of truth in classic Christianity depends on the willingness to put one's body on the line for the truth. Any alleged truth which it is not worth suffering for is not Christian truth.[74] Otherwise why would so many believers be ready to say yes to one who asks them to share in his life by bearing the cross of innocent suffering? This goes directly against modern narcissism, which says "me first" and "me alone."

Jesus made exceptionally clear to his disciples that "they will arrest you, abuse you, and they will kill you. All nations will hate you on account of my name" (Matt 24:9 CEB).[75] Paul set the pattern for the early church. His teaching was personally validated in the most costly way, by his willingness to suffer "to the point that I'm in prison like a common criminal. But God's word cannot be imprisoned" (2 Tim 2:9 CEB).[76] Jews and Christians have a three-thousand-year history of being willing to take the truth seriously enough to die for it. That remains puzzling to modern narcissism.

WHY THE BLOOD OF THE FAITHFUL CONSTITUTES A UNIQUE FORM OF PERSUASION

Willingness to die for the truth is a special form of evidence that cannot be cheaply countered with theoretical arguments for the truth. When the testimony to the truth is then sealed by blood, as it was with Jesus, Stephen, and Paul, its authority transcends worldly calculus. Its testimony is most powerful when the act of public disavowal of the truth is required by a coercive state authority.

Tertullian recognized the unique role of the martyrs in defense of the apostolic faith.[77] They constitute a stunning form of evidence much more credible and convincing than any conceptual argument. Christianity enters the search for truth with a unique form of authority.

In Africa thousands have been willing to die for Christian truth over many centuries. Today more than ever. Contemporary Egypt, Eritrea, Nigeria, and Southern Sudan all are cases in point. Boko Haram in Nigeria, Al-Shabaab in Somalia, Ansar al-Sharia in Tunisia, and the Muslim Brotherhood in Egypt are explicitly targeting Christians for their religion in ongoing attacks.

---

74. 1 Pet 4:13–5:9; *The Martyrdom of Polycarp*, ANF 1:37–44.

75. See Irenaeus, *Against Heresies* IV.33.9, ANF 1:508.

76. The naturalistic explanation of this resilience falls pitifully short. The willingness to suffer for the truth is reduced either to masochism, sexual distortions, or warped religious ecstasy. Reasons grounded in salvation history are ruled out, hence the phenomena are misunderstood.

77. Tertullian, *Apology*, 50; Vincent, *Commonitory*, ch. 4–5, FC 7:272–275.

Nothing new. Among the first African martyrs were Perpetua and Felicitas, women "whom no force could keep from defending the faith... no threats, no blandishments, neither life nor death, not the palace, not the courtiers, not the emperor, not the empire, not men, not demons."[78] They died for a specific purpose: to prevent the scriptures from being found by idolatrous authorities and desecrated.

In the North African outpost of Tangiers in 298 AD there was a Christian centurion named Marcellus who was required to participate in the birthday celebration of the Emperor Maximian, which entailed sacrifice to Roman gods. He had to make a decision between idolatry and faith. He threw off his belt and weapons and insignia, was brought before a Praetorian prefect, and was killed with a sword. The Christians of Tingis in far Northwest Africa still remember him as a witness for Christ with his own blood.

Origen's father was arrested during the persecution of Septimius Severus; his property was seized and he was beheaded under the Egyptian prefect Lactus. Cyprian died rather than offer a sacrifice to a Roman god, which symbolized disavowal of the one true God Almighty. The church of Alexandria pointed to the death of their patriarch Peter, whose beheading marked the apex of the Diocletian persecution. The choice of Black Moses was to remain in his monastery to die rather than flee under attack.

These witnesses were not forgotten. The modest shrines built in their memory became churches of believers who prized their witness.

All gave their lives for Christian truth. It was not a proposition they died for but a person: the risen Lord.

MARTYRDOM TODAY

Martyrdom remains a relentless feature of North African Christianity. Ethiopian oil workers in Libya were selected to die for no reason other than that they were Christians. When asked, they did not conceal their identity. They were beheaded.

Christian Garissa University students in Kenya were asked by the Somali terror group Al-Shabaab to repeat a Muslim prayer, and if they did not they were slaughtered on the spot.

Martyrdom resists simple-minded this-worldly rationalizations. It cannot be explained merely by the premise of a death wish, political conquest, stiff-lipped courage, or the desire for recognition. Such interpretations do not square with the actual accounts of the confessors. They did not seek death, but faced death when death sought them by requiring them to act against conscience.

THE DIFFICULTY OF EXPLAINING LIFE-AND-DEATH CONFESSION TO CASUAL BYSTANDERS

Providence worked powerfully through these African martyrs and confessors, and "because of their tenacious attachment to the ancient faith" many of its oppres-

---

78. Vincent, *Commonitory*, ch. 5, FC 7:275.

sors were brought to faith. Through these martyrs, God "restored battered churches and brought to life people that were spiritually dead."[79] But those who are desensitized to the value of life have special difficulties understanding the martyrs.

A martyr is a witness. The witness is not to the martyr's death but to his life with God. A martyr is a believer who has borne witness to Christ by shedding life blood.

The risk of martyrdom was a consistent feature of the testimony of the early Christians.[80] African orthodoxy would not exist without that risk. It grew up within an environment of extreme risk, free conscience, and dauntless courage. These were central features of African Christianity before 311 AD, when the Great Persecution ended with the Edict of Milan.

The Greek word *martus* means witness, and those witnesses were willing to suffer gladly for the name (Acts 5:41). The name was Jesus. While a preacher bears testimony by his words, a martyr bears testimony by his death.[81] Christians who suffered death for their witness came to be called martyrs (Rev 2:13; 17:6) in the sense that they attested the truth through their blood.

Stephen was the first Christian martyr (Acts 22:20). The disciples were informed by their Lord that God's messengers would be persecuted (Matt 23:34-35). They were called to take up their cross and follow him (Mark 8:34-38). Discipleship means being ready to suffer for the truth for Christ's sake (Phil 1:29-30; 1 Thess 2:14-15; 1 Pet 3:14).

These witnesses are called today to "the old faith, from modern unreasonableness to ancient sanity, from the blindness of novelty to the ancient light."[82] The special power and authority of the confessors lay in their dauntless stand against accommodation to the world, against prevailing common opinion. They appeal to the ancient faith universally received by prior generations.

TOO MANY GENERATIONS OF AFRICAN FAITHFUL TO IGNORE

If it were only a few African confessors or martyrs for a short time, they might have been overlooked, but there were far too many to ignore. Not only in Roman times; today the horror continues. Their tortures were outrageous. During the Arian persecutions of orthodox believers large numbers were willing to die rather than confess what they knew to be a dilution of the truth. Origen personally knew many of these victims. The martyrdom of his own father became his inspiration. "They preferred to surrender themselves rather than the faith universally held from the beginning."[83] African orthodoxy stands under the discipline of the Prince of Peace.

---

79. Ibid.
80. Acts 5:40-42; 9:15-16.
81. *Martyrdom of Polycarp* 14:2; 16:2.
82. Vincent, *Commonitory*, ch. 5, FC 7:276.
83. Ibid.

The courage, sanctity, and good will of the martyrs and confessors showed forth brightly in the generations, even centuries, that followed them. They did not flinch even amid torture and death. It was an overpowering silent witness, hard to refute. The best analogy in our time is the numberless Christian martyrs whose blood was left on the sands of Egypt, Nubia, Libya, Ethiopia, and Algeria for more than a thousand years. The spiritual authority of these confessors is unrivaled. They reveal the heart of African orthodoxy.

What modern academic or church leader is willing to die for his or her teachings? There may be some modern agnostics who are willing to lay down their lives for their propositions, but few come to mind. There is a reason why: their willingness to sacrifice tends to conflict with their own doubt, if they doubt consistently. Genuine martyrdom is not filled with doubt, according to its confessors.

Orthodoxy cannot be exhaustively explained sociologically as merely a neurotic fixation or a phobic resistance to change or social climbing or habits of sexual compensation. People do not suffer for the truth in order to deal with neurosis or phobia or upward social mobility.

The martyrs were not nostalgic reactionaries enamored with power. In their highest moment of truth they were entirely powerless. On the basis of these naturalistic explanations, there would be no reasonable way to account for the faith of thousands of confessors over the ten major persecutions that happened most harshly in Africa. They were prepared to be jailed, to be tortured, and to die for their life in Christ.[84]

It may seem as if our human efforts are failing, but the Spirit is always working to communicate the Word. The people of faith have not been abandoned by the Spirit who has been forming the one body of Christ worldwide for all of these centuries.

The gospel was first heard in Africa as early as the 60s AD through the Apostle Mark. Mark is now being reheard as an African. His gospel is being again appropriated without dilution, even unto death. God is working amid human despair toward greater ends than we can imagine. His Spirit is quietly awakening a continent, one person at a time.

THE BLUNT DIFFERENCE BETWEEN MARTYRDOM AND JIHADIST SUICIDE

The witness of the defenseless Christian martyrs has been clouded in our time by terrorists who have chosen to kill others brutally while advancing the goal of conquest, with many falsely using religion to cover the acquisition of power. To compare jihad with Christian martyrdom is like comparing coercive conquest with meekness. These are not analogous but opposite cases. Those who best know and love the strengths of Islam view the suicide killers as sick deviations from the deeper faith of Islam.

It is absurd to link the question of Christian martyrdom with suicide killings. Suicide by definition is the intentional taking of one's own life, God's first and fore-

---

84. Cf. Ambrose, *On the Duties of the Clergy*, I.35–42, NPNF 2 X:30–35.

most gift to every soul. It is the final form of self-made tragedy, since it is irreversible self-destruction. What it most dreads is life itself, continuing to live. The radical jihadist form of suicide aims to harm on behalf of a warped vision of conquest. Its stated purpose is to kill or maim.

Martyrdom is entirely different. It does not desire or intend the taking of either one's own life or another's. It desires only to witness to faith even at great cost. The martyr is annihilated in the service of witness to the truth of faith, not for the sake of ending life. Since the martyrs understood their death as the beginning of eternal life, the metaphor of annihilation would have felt absurd to them.

How utterly different is Christian martyrdom from the terror bombings of innocents. The latter deliberately takes away life for a political cause. The former dies for the lives of others without taking another life.

Those who intentionally kill are not worthy to be compared to those who die for the way, the truth, and the life. This false correlation should be firmly answered with gentle and reasoned words.

Some are ready to dismiss the actual history of Christian martyrdom by stereotyping it in the same breath with modern suicide bombing. In the long stretch of villages between Nigeria and Somalia, life has been made cheap out of distorted religious motivations.[85] Likewise, nations have been torn apart. Women and children have paid heavily for the violence of ruthless men.

Sadly there are many more Christian martyrs in our century than in any previous one. Their imprisonments, tortures, and deaths are just as appalling now as those of the ancient persecutions.

WHEN TRUTH IS EMBODIED

God has become personally known in human history. God became human, entered our human sphere in the flesh, was born as we are born, was tempted as we are, died as we die, and rose to vindicate his death. Faith participates in this lived-out truth by personally living it out in daily life.

Salvation is an event in history, not a speculative idea. The truth to which orthodox faith witnesses has become an event in Jesus. Followers are called personally to participate in his life, death, and resurrection.

To tell the truth rightly is to follow the One who is truth. The truth embodied in the incarnate Lord still appears to many to be a "stone of stumbling" and "a rock of offense."[86] But for the faithful it becomes the chief cornerstone.

The truth that is lived is the best evidence of the truth that is spoken. The truth spoken must be embodied to be taken with full seriousness.

---

85. The analogies between Islamic Conquest and Christian Crusade are largely exaggerated and misinformed, but the portion of truth they convey calls for Christian repentance.

86. 1 Pet 2:8 (KJV); Rom 9:32-33; 1 Cor 1:23.

SEMINAR 6

ONE FAITH: CONCORD AS THE GIFT OF THE SPIRIT

A. HOW AFRICAN ORTHODOXY IS STILL NURTURING GLOBAL CHRISTIANITY

Bishop Antonios Markos, Coptic Bishop of African Affairs, a member of the board of the Center for Early African Christianity, was decisively instrumental in founding the unique Organization of African Instituted (Independent) Churches (AIC) in 1978, a group of indigenous African churches not affiliated with any Euro-American mother church. These churches have refused financial support from the West. They prefer to rediscover their own African heritage. The Coptic Church was a founding participant in the AIC since its identity is not borrowed from western sources. No form of African Christianity is more ancient or more indigenous than that of the Egyptian Church that sprang from the mission of Mark the Evangelist in the 50s and 60s AD.

CHRISTIANITY'S PROVEN INDIGENOUS PRESENCE IN AFRICA OVER TWO MILLENNIA

No religion in Africa is more indigenous than African Christianity in its earliest phases. No other religion in Africa has a half-billion adherents today accompanied by two thousand years of experience in Africa, counting from the early conversion of the Ethiopian eunuch (Acts 8:26-40, ca. 34 AD).

No other religion in Africa is more locally diverse in villages and cities than Christianity. African Christians do not need to apologize for their African identity.[87]

---
87. Africanness, sometimes called Africaneity.

Prior to the 400 years of coercive modern western colonialism, they had already enjoyed centuries of indigenous local roots in Africa lasting 1600 years.

The Holy Spirit is at work to encourage unity in the body of Christ. The personal free agents of this unity are faithful Christians in every communion all over the world who share life in Christ. The Holy Spirit is acting concretely and tangibly the world over, but it is hard for us to see the unity when our ears are attuned only to this fragile world and its current cultures. The unity lies in the almighty One who unites: God the Holy Spirit, who can work precisely through signs of contradiction and paradox.

EVIDENCES OF THE RENEWAL OF CLASSIC AFRICAN ECUMENISM

The youngest heirs of modern political ecumenism are gratefully rediscovering their most ancient ecumenical roots. Today African Christians are discovering a deeper form of ecumenism by listening to ancient African orthodoxy to regain their bearings.

Modern political ecumenism has an unsteady history based largely on its modern western roots that have broken contact with the ancient Christian wisdom. African orthodoxy has ancient ecumenical roots that are still deep and vital.

The All Africa Conference of Churches has been moving toward independence from western-based ecumenism. It is no longer viewed as a branch office of the World Council of Churches under obligation to Euro-American management. That is why it refused to call itself a Council. (For a list of member groups, visit http://aacc-ceta.org/en/members/member-churches.html.) Bright young African leaders are discovering that their own African Christian tradition has a deeper unity to offer than modern western political ecumenism. These young Africans are Spirit-led and liberated from secularizing assumptions which have never been very much at home in Africa.

THE HOLY SPIRIT ENGENDERS UNITY

The uniting work of the Holy Spirit is taking form on a breathtaking world scale. It is manifested with special power in Africa. It is finding expression in quiet and inconspicuous ways in local churches, parachurch ministries, and unobtrusive grassroots communities. The Spirit is working in diverse areas ranging from food relief to teaching ministries to concerted evangelization. The Holy Spirit is creating forms of grassroots unity in the church far deeper than a political activism that instinctively turns to flawed western ideas of the human condition.

The promise of the Spirit is to guide the church into all truth. "When the Spirit of Truth comes, he will guide you in all truth" (John 16:13 CEB). The Spirit enables accurate memory of the apostolic testimony. The work of the Spirit in Africa is to remind the faithful of the good news of the kingdom that was so powerfully embraced among the earliest generations of African believers.

The Spirit is at work to transcend and reconstitute western ecumenical bureaucracies. The Spirit's work is not limited to pragmatic cooperation. The Spirit enables the living embodiment of the body of Christ.

Modern political ecumenism has its central bureaucratic location in Geneva in the World Council of Churches. Modern political ecumenism has been irreparably identified with the decaying churches of colonialism in Africa. It is dependent on the West. The rebirth of African orthodoxy is in no way dependent upon the West. It listens intently to Africa's minds in their earliest phases.

WHY "ECUMENICAL" IS NEITHER AN ORGANIZATION NOR A MOVEMENT

The word *ecumenical* derives from the Greek word *oikoumene*, meaning the whole catholic, universal church of all times and places. It is not reducible to an organization. It lives out of the unity created by the Spirit.

There are two views competing for the legitimacy of the word *ecumenical*. The following table gives a brief glimpse of the differences:

ECUMENISM AND ORTHODOXY

MODERN WESTERN POLITICAL ECUMENISM	CLASSIC AFRICAN ORTHODOX CONSENSUS
distrustful of ancient ecumenism	deliberately grounded in ancient ecumenism
accommodates modernity uncritically	critical of failed modern ideas
oriented mainly to modern Euro-American assumptions of the Enlightenment and the Reformation's left wing	oriented mainly to classic Christianity and conciliar teaching, especially of Africa's first six centuries
romantic revolutionary fantasies prevail	an organic view of historical change prevails
assumes human innocence without the fall	keenly aware of the complexity of the intergenerational transmission of human depravity

MODERN WESTERN POLITICAL ECUMENISM	CLASSIC AFRICAN ORTHODOX CONSENSUS
ideologically drawn to the heirs of Rousseau, Marx, and Freud	sees many tragic consequences in Africa from western secularism
impatient and chronically activist	patient, humble, and serene amid historical turbulence
dialogue between bureaucracies	concentrates on social consequences of personal life with God
seeking negotiated institutional unity based on shifting political alliances, utopian planning, and control of charitable activities	unity already found in Christ personal faith working in love
loss of nerve when financially unsupported	confident, resourceful
politics-driven	Spirit-led
begins in 1948 (Amsterdam)	begins in the council of Jerusalem, 46 AD, and the African Councils of the third century
peaks in 1966 (Geneva)	peaks in early ecumenical Councils
now aging and declining	now emerging among youth all over Africa

Those who study the graph carefully will recognize a decisive difference between the two types of ecumenism. This difference has special relevance in Africa, where the classic consensus was significantly formed.

These are descriptions of tendencies rather than absolute differences. They serve to point to distinctions of tone, orientation, and trajectory. But the difference in spirit is stark.

Modern political ecumenism focuses on negotiating organic unity. African orthodoxy seeks to restore classic Christian truth within and despite obstinate divisions such as those between Copts and Charismatics. This uniting work of the Holy Spirit demonstrates that God is at work in grassroots Christianity.

African orthodox teaching is found among Copts, Catholics, Protestants, and Pentecostals who remember and embody classic Christian teaching. All can point back gratefully to their African roots in Athanasius and Augustine. They are not a substitute ecumenical movement but the original and sustained fellowship in fertile continuity with the global communion of saints.

THE WANING OF WESTERN POLITICAL ECUMENISM

Euro-American political ecumenism presumes that the embodiment of Christ depends largely upon deft organizational management, human ingenuity, and western models of revolutionary change.

Political ecumenism imagines that visible unity will be accomplished by getting institutions and denominations together to formally and verbally agree to make common statements, often seeking the lowest common denominator, and resulting in supposedly weighty symbolic political acts that give the appearance of great prophetic courage.

African orthodoxy sees the Holy Spirit as doing something far more unexpected, quiet, and compelling than paper proclamations or building a stronger bureaucracy. Its task is to nurture Christian disciples one by one. African orthodoxy repeatedly survived the collapse of despotisms, controlled economies, and statist arrogance.

The waning political ecumenism is fast disappearing as a force in Africa, as well as in the U.S. and Europe. The activist political church bureaucracies were sponsored by the secularizing West. They tried to export liberal ideology to African villages. They are largely a western liberal Protestant movement not well attuned to grassroots African life, where scriptural teachings, healings, miracles, and mysteries abound.

Coptic and Eastern Orthodox voices have always remained frustrating minority partners under the ascendancy of liberal Protestants. But now that ascendancy is descending. Evangelicals may be viewed by Copts as somewhat deficient in liturgy, yet evangelicals are clear that worship according to apostolic teaching is essential to the health of the church. Meanwhile Copts may be viewed by evangelicals as lacking to some extent in the language of personal salvation by grace through faith, even while they have justifying faith active in love deeply embedded in their liturgy.

Both Copts and evangelicals consent to the apostolic teaching that Jesus is the Son of God and that God the Father gave his only Son to save sinners through the Holy Spirit. That is what we mean here by lowercase, classic consensual orthodoxy.

African Catholics may be viewed by African Pentecostals as lacking in the gifts of the Spirit, while Pentecostals may be viewed by Catholics as lacking a sound teaching of the church and sacraments. These memories of different church practices did not pervade the early African orthodoxy of Athanasius and Augustine. The very nature of global orthodoxy in that period was the permission to join in one voice to praise God the Father and to receive the gift of salvation in the Son through the Spirit. The recovery of this unity is the aim of the rebirth of African orthodoxy.

Emerging African orthodoxy is committed unapologetically to ancient classic ecumenical teaching, especially as formed and sustained by the first African Christians from Mark on through the Council of Ephesus.[88]

African orthodoxy has a high doctrine of scripture, a long-term view of cumulative historical consent, and a classic consensual view of God the Father, God the Son, and God the Holy Spirit. In whatever local or regional community of faith, it adheres to the classic Christian teachings of creation, incarnation, atonement, resurrection, and final judgment. These are fixed boundary stones in the ancient consensus Christianity which we are taught not to move or attempt to refashion. Out of our respect for the truth of the witnesses that bore to us the gospel, we voluntarily draw back from any thought of changing these core beliefs.

In modern political ecumenism these doctrines have become largely submerged under the rhetoric of supposed social and economic transformation. That rhetoric has proven itself to have more mouth than heart, more bombast than holy living.

FIFTY YEARS FROM AMSTERDAM TO HARARE

What began in 1948 with Amsterdam's bold vision ended in the Harare (1998), Porto Alegre (2006), and Busan (2013) World Assemblies of the World Council of Churches (WCC), where conspicuous promises were made to both Eastern Orthodox and global evangelicals that were never fulfilled. After Harare anything at all could be baptized as "ecumenical," whether shamanism, syncretism, clog dancing, group-think experiences, amateur photography, social games, knitting, or mercurial political advocacy. The ecumenical movement that was once firmly grounded in classic Christianity became captive to current fads. This in time turned into demoralization, nonsupport, and a series of accelerating financial crises. These conditions have become the seedbed of the rebirth of African orthodoxy.

Modern political ecumenism is accustomed to viewing all conceivable issues through the eyes of current media trends, liberal political correctness, and utopian advocacy. The faithful have become tired of these trends. All of these obsessions were foisted on the member churches and focused ideologically within western modernity at any cost.

I attended as a youth observer the Second World Assembly of the World Council of Churches at Evanston in 1954, then the Geneva Conference in 1966, and finally the Harare World Assembly in 1998. I have personally beheld the old ecumenism in its earlier, middle, and waning phases. I have seen it move from neonate idealism to overconfident middle-age bureaucratic activism to senile introversion, all in one lifetime. I can personally attest that a radical turn occurred by the mid-sixties toward revolutionary rhetoric, social engineering, and statist politics.

---

88. 431 AD. After the Council of Chalcedon in 451, the unity became much harder to articulate in Africa.

When I participated in world ecumenical conferences in Evanston 1954 and Geneva 1966, I was a dedicated ecumenist. It took me a long time to realize that I was mostly committed to a waning modern political and institutional ecumenism which had an obsession with accommodating uncritically to modern ideologies.

Modern political ecumenism has developed a stubborn aversion toward ancient ecumenism. The Faith and Order Commission which sought without avail to correct the wayward direction was gradually reduced to another echo of political activism. My 1960s ecumenical enthusiasm now seems cheap and phony in relation to the bloody and hard-won testimony of the actual martyrs, saints, and confessors of African orthodoxy.

THE REDISCOVERY OF ANCIENT GLOBAL FAITH

Meanwhile, African orthodoxy is being revived by embracing all global believers who share the consensus of the earliest scriptural interpreters. It is silently reclaiming the courage of the martyrs, the faith of the confessors, the irenic resolve of the early Councils, and the wisdom of the Fathers.

B. DIVERGING VIEWS OF CHRISTIAN UNITY

THE CLAIM TO WHOLENESS, CATHOLICITY, AND WORLDWIDE PRESENCE

The word *ecumenical* (from *oikoumene,* wholeness, universality) implies a claim to wholeness, catholicity, and worldwide presence.[89]

Modern political ecumenism assumes it owns the permanent rights to the term *ecumenical.* But this now is being tested. Copts and Catholics and Pentecostals do not grant to western political ecumenism the claim to be the sole legitimate heir of the office of bringing unity to the body of Christ.

Political ecumenism has been corrupted by a slippery relativism that defies any claim to universal truth. Meanwhile the modernity to which it is seeking to adapt the church is declining in moral power and the power to inspire. The waning forms of modern political ecumenism wholeheartedly accept the ideas of modern consciousness as a permanent feature of every conceivable future. Those ideas have names associated with western Enlightenment philosophical traditions: naturalism, empiricism, idealism, and social engineering. The rebirth of African orthodoxy contests only those points that are inconsistent with classic Christian teaching.

---

89. In describing two ecumenisms, we are speaking of two mutually exclusive visions, competing contrary claims to the truth of the one body of Christ.

Only recently has it become crystal clear how damaging political ecumenism has been to the cause of Christian unity. Political ecumenists who forgot the ancient ecumenical consensus are most divisive when they have offended ancient ecumenical teaching, namely in, permissive sexuality, family disintegration, and the reduction of politics to power. Since the late 1970s the most public test has come in the challenge to the classic teaching of the complementary relation of a man and a woman whose love is blessed by children nurtured in durable caring families.[90]

Ancient orthodoxy is based on apostolic testimony that has sustained genuine worldwide consent through countless generations. Modern ecumenism has deteriorated into equivocal rhetoric and negotiations between bureaucrats. It remains bound by modern culture. Ancient ecumenism owes no such debt.

Modern political ecumenism is in confusion precisely because it has neglected classic ecumenism. False assumptions of modern life cry out for a reexamination of classic consensual Christianity.

THE APOSTOLIC CRITIQUE OF MODERNITY

The faith of the apostles has emerged as a plausible critic of modernity, not the other way around. There is increasing evidence that God is now blessing the renewal of classic Christian ecumenism as it becomes regrounded in the ancient consensual tradition of scriptural study.

The journey has come full circle now, back to Africa where doctrinal consensus-formation first grew strong through the earliest Councils of Carthage (251, 256, 345, 397, and 419 AD) and Alexandria (231, 306, 326, 363 AD).

Now at the beginning of Christianity's third millennium these same ancient African writers are once again available for study by global Christians who understand grace as the basis for repentance, faith, baptism, and new life. This rebirth of classic Christianity is occurring with the wide consent of the most culturally diverse Christian communities all over the world. In China, South Africa, Argentina, and Singapore the same discussion is occurring.

Christians whose traditions have long distanced themselves from each other through separate and often competing church memories, such as Baptist and Catholic, or Pentecostal and Coptic, are now finding their commonality in the ancient classic consensus sustained through centuries. From all these quarters they are finding that the early Christian commentators on scripture most clearly express this classic consensus in a way that can be trusted by all.

Gathered together are magisterial Protestants alongside Eastern Orthodox, Catholics with Evangelicals, and Anglicans with Charismatics. These varied Chris-

---

90. St. Ignatius of Antioch to Polycarp, ANF 1, earlychristianwritings.com; Tertullian, *Ad Uxorum, An Exhortation to Chastity*, 9; Jerome, *Against Jovinianus*, Book 1, 3, 16; Augustine, *On the Good of Marriage*, 8–10; Thomas Aquinas, *Summa Theologica*, Part III, Question 63.

tians find inspiration and common faith within this historic memory because their center is so intrinsically and obviously ecumenical, so catholic in their cultural range, so orthodox in core teachings.

All of these traditions have an equal right to appeal to the earliest Spirit-led history of Christianity. All of the confessing laity of each of these traditions can, without a compromise of intellect or conscience, come together under the guidance of ancient ecumenical teachings common to them all. Protestants have as much right to the councils and the church fathers as do Latin Catholics or Greek Orthodox.

People of vastly different cultures recognize in these witnesses their own unity as the people of God, despite different cultural memories, foods, garments, and habits of piety. Asia Minor and France gave us Irenaeus, but his voice is heard echoing everywhere in global Christianity. The hymns of Ephrem were first sung in Syria, but now are sung everywhere, and nowhere more passionately than Ethiopia. The homilies of Ambrose were first taught in Milan but have entered into Christian common speech, especially through Augustine.

C. THE UNITING WORK OF THE SPIRIT

THE UNITY OF THE BIBLE

Written texts of books of the Bible were transmitted in vastly different cultural settings between 1000 BC and 100 AD, but together they tell a single inclusive story of God's life with humanity. The story is of creation, fall, redemption of sin, and consummation of God's purpose in history.

Ancient African believers blazed the path for others in understanding the unity of scripture in the first three hundred years of Christianity. They looked toward the spiritual sense of scripture without neglecting the plain historic sense of scripture. They grasped the core of apostolic teaching. They prepared the way for worldwide confessional unity in the first four centuries. Though an imperfect unity, it was more consensual than any alternative view. Its core was the first three General Ecumenical Councils.

EVANGELICALS AND ORTHODOX

After centuries of quiet frustration of Eastern Orthodox leaders with evangelicals and vice versa, the ways common to them both are at long last beginning to converge. For too long evangelicals have remained distanced from the Orthodox. Many of the gifts of the Spirit offered in Orthodox teachings of scriptural authority, grace, liturgy, and prayer were ignored or stereotyped by evangelicals. They are more similar than either imagines. Even if evangelicals' congregational polity, free liturgical patterns, voluntarism, and enthusiasm seem odd to the Eastern Orthodox, they confess together the same Father, Son, and Holy Spirit and a high doctrine of scripture.

Often evangelicals have ruled themselves out of orthodoxy because of a distrust of its perceived ethnic fixations, cultural narrowness, and undemocratic hierarchies, but these distances have been narrowed by friendships between Catholics and Copts and evangelicals.

Today the global evangelical communities are being drawn more toward the earliest Christian interpreters of scripture. Evangelical thought has been too long deprived of vital contact with its most ancient sources of classic scriptural wisdom. The world of orthodoxy has become surprisingly intriguing to global evangelicals who previously disdained the work of the Spirit in centuries before Luther.

Christian writers of the past two centuries have seldom thought of the early African writers they quoted as African, seeing them rather as Neo-Platonic or Greek.

Thankfully the hunger to understand the history of the Holy Spirit is now growing in Africa as fast as the Christian population is growing. Protestant pietism inspired the African missions of the nineteenth century. Some of the more dismal consequences of the eighteenth-century Enlightenment did not become evident until the end of the twentieth. Both of these traditions of the colonial period have expressed disinterest in the early classic African forms of scripture interpretation.

Evangelical and Pentecostal African believers have often been caricatured as backward or primitive. But now evangelical, Charismatic, Baptist, and Pentecostal laypersons in Africa are rediscovering the actual history of the Holy Spirit that has been so profoundly remembered in the Coptic communities. As these evangelical and Charismatic traditions mature and deepen, they recognize their need for the scriptural reasoning of classic consensual Christianity, with special attention to its earliest African interpreters.

THE BONDING WORK OF GOD THE SPIRIT

Oneness in Christ is dependent not upon finding a clever way to produce a negotiated settlement but upon recognizing and embodying what is already present in our actual life in Christ through the Spirit's leading and in our prayers and silent hopes.

The Holy Spirit is still mending conflicts that have stood for over a thousand years, like those that have prevailed between western, eastern, and African continental traditions.[91] These disputes have hinged on the mystery of the relation between the divine and the human in Jesus Christ. The unity of the teaching of the apostles was hammered out on the anvil of African martyrdom. It grew to maturity in the decades following that period.

The Holy Spirit had accompanied the martyrs and confessors of all times regardless of their different cultural memories, suffering under appalling conditions of

---

91. The non-Chalcedonian communions are coming into a greater recognition of what they can and do honestly share with the Chalcedonian tradition.

state persecution.[92] Today the Holy Spirit is unifying Christians in different cultures around the classic consensus.

Every scripture text has a history of interpretation. Commentators on the Bible have pursued its meaning in every century. In the earliest Christian centuries this history of interpretation united Christians of varied cultures. Though the consensus was formed through conflict over scriptural interpretation, once resolved these struggles made the unity of the body of Christ more evident. Many of those uniting voices were first heard in Africa in the writings of Cyprian, Clement, Origen, and Augustine. Believers from Asia and the Americas are no longer turning a blind eye upon Africa's gift to world Christianity.

THE TIMELINESS OF THE ORTHODOX MIND

The orthodox mind is both timeless and timely. It is timely in prudential judgments because it sees them in relation to eternity.

The orthodox way of reasoning listens to the most revered voices that best reflect the consenting mind of the people of God of all cultures over the longest stretch of human memory.

The worst habit of those who distrust the consensual scriptural interpreters is their fixation on individualistic innovation. They have not yet learned what the worshipping communities already know: that the consensus does not need to be improved upon but trusted.

The one, holy, catholic, apostolic church celebrated at Nicea in 325 AD existed before Nicea. It is constituted by all who repent and believe, whose lives are shaped by their participation in the living Christ, and who live in this real but imperfect communion. To be the one church, it must be apostolic, mirroring the holiness of God in our lives in the world. It reaches out to all cultures, all classes, and all languages. We behold this one church most fully alive when we see believers ready to put their lives on the line for its truth.

REPRISE FOR PART ONE

Worshipping communities are reframing their priorities as they walk courageously in the sixth millennium of human culture and into the newborn third millennium of Christianity. The earliest millennium of human culture is generally reckoned

---

92. The living body of Christ is growing precisely under conditions of persecution, unjust accusations, imprisonment, and state terrorism. This courage amid peril can only be a work of God the Holy Spirit. No one could have predicted that the Chinese church would grow so fast under such limiting conditions, but the Spirit has enabled this. What has happened to Chinese Christians is subject to objective historical reportage and analysis. It is all too obvious to any worshipping Christian who reads the Bible what the Holy Spirit is doing in China, Sudan, Cuba, and Indonesia. Obstacles are what Christians expect. Through patience in well-doing, the people of God are being united and bonded with people a world away.

as 3000–2000 BC with the transition of culture from hunting and gathering to agriculture and commerce. We are at the beginning of the third millennium after Christ, which is the cusp of the sixth millennium of human culture.

Worshipping communities know that the children of the western sexual revolution have suffered through the high cost of modern living: rootlessness, costly social experimentation, and political delusions. These ailments have hit Africa as hard as any region, as seen in the pandemic of fatherless families.

Orthodoxy persists, despite all contrary predictions, because it is more cross-culturally agile than is modern multiculturalism, and God's sovereign grace provides the basis of its durability. God does not leave himself without witness in the world. Even the weaknesses of the pilgrim community attest the strength of the Spirit. The consent of the communion of saints over generations is divinely guarded and guaranteed.

The faithful are called to patience as they look toward vindication in unfolding history, and finally on the Last Day. Classic Christianity opens doors for wider intellectual freedom than the narrow space that is offered within modern intellectual elites.

PART TWO
SIGNS OF NEW LIFE

What are the leading signs that ancient African Christian teaching is reviving?

In Part Two, I set forth four layers of evidence to show that there is indeed a rekindling of the orthodox spirit in Africa. Here is a bird's-eye-view of where we are headed in this last half of the seminar. These evidences appear in four arenas: the people, their texts, their communities, and their method. Lives are being changed. Time-honored texts are being reclaimed. The Word is coming alive through persons who embody the life of faith. Social effects are being felt in a world searching for multicultural wisdom. Believers are learning to recognize and trust the consensus and recognize ancient boundary stones. Global Christians are rediscovering the classic method of ecumenical discernment.

SEMINAR 7

THE NEW BIRTH OF AFRICAN ORTHODOXY

A. ORDINARY LIVES ARE BEING REVITALIZED ONE BY ONE

The clearest evidence of the rebirth of African orthodoxy is that ordinary lives are being transformed in cities and villages all over Africa. One by one, people are coming to new birth through scripture study, communities of prayer, and classic consensual Christianity.

This first arena of evidence of the rebirth of orthodoxy is autobiographical, expressed in personal narratives of how classic Christian teaching has transformed one particular life. Countless Africans have told their own stories of the power of classic Christianity to transform modern lives.[93] Augustine's *Confessions* and Athanasius's *Life of Anthony* provide the two greatest African narratives of how God's grace was at work in their lives.

Like finding a lost child, we can now look into the eyes of living persons who embody full accountability to God, who seek to live a holy life. They can be found among Protestant, Orthodox, Catholic, and Charismatic laity. They are all "orthodox" in the general sense of joyfully adhering to the teaching of the apostles and their earliest common interpreters.

Whenever these persons witness to their change of life, we are eager to listen. However humble, we know their story will be illuminating. We ask them what happened. How did they rediscover the ancient way of holy living? Even if we hear only one such story, we remember it. It is prized and embraced. It is like discovering a jewel buried beneath deep layers of debris.

---

93. Biographical narratives of orthodox conversions of North Americans have been powerfully honed by Will Willimon, Peter Gilquist, Andrew Walker, Keith Fournier, and George Weigel.

Not long ago the chief places where this life could be expected to be found were largely in the religious orders and lay congregations of Catholic and Coptic Orthodoxy and in deep-going classic Protestant and Charismatic spiritual formation. Now the practice of holy living is encompassing skeptical Protestants, spirited Pentecostals, and African Instituted Churches. It has never been absent from Africa in any century since the first, but only in the twenty-first is it being better recognized for what it is: Africa's gift to world Christianity. That gift harks back to Christianity's beginning.

Among the many personal narratives by Africans turning to classic Christian faith in God, we will note only three here, with more in the bibliography: Professor Lamin Sanneh, Bishop Antonios Markos, and genocide survivor Immaculée Ilibagiza.

First, Lamin Sanneh of Yale University, one of Africa's greatest theologians, has provided the riveting narrative of his personal story, entitled *Summoned from the Margin: Homecoming of an African*, telling of his birth into a Muslim culture, his childhood in the Gambia, his "exile at home," his gradual entry into the highest levels of European higher education, his turning point, his teaching at Harvard and Yale, and his "homecoming" and return to the rock of faith, where he felt "a lively sense of emancipation surrounded by the symbols of the mystery of God in the ungrudging faithful witness of the church."[94]

Second, His Eminence Coptic Bishop Antonios Markos, Bishopric of African Affairs, Johannesburg, has written extensively in three volumes of his medical mission to Ethiopia, Kenya, and all over Africa, including his leadership in the African Instituted Church movement, bringing a wide range of pastors to Egypt to meet with Coptic leaders, and his mission activity from Ghana to Zululand. Like Lamin Sanneh, he is a member of the board of the Center for Early African Christianity and has shepherded the translation of Africa's Gift[95] into regional heart languages of Africa.[96]

Third, Immaculée Ilibagiza, an observant African Catholic from Rwanda, has written her moving story in *Left to Tell: Discovering God amidst the Rwandan Holocaust*, narrating her remarkable escape from the Rwandan genocide and her discovery of faith.[97] Incredibly, she survived the slaughter.

> For 91 days, she and seven other women huddled silently together in the cramped bathroom of a local pastor while hundreds of machete-wielding killers hunted for them. It was during those endless hours of unspeakable terror that Immaculee discovered the power of prayer, eventually shedding her fear of death and forging a profound and lasting relationship with God. She emerged from her bathroom hideout

---

94. Lamin Sanneh, *Summoned from the Margin: Homecoming of an African* (Grand Rapids, MI: Eerdmans, 2012), p. 267.

95. *Africa's Gift* is the short version of *How Africa Shaped the Christian Mind*, condensed for translation into Africa's regional languages, available to Africans from the ICCSPress.

96. H.E. Coptic Bishop Antonios Markos, *Come Across and Help Us*, 3 volumes, (Johannesburg, South Africa: Coptic Orthodox Bishopric of African Affairs, 1988–2003).

97. Carlsbad, CA: Hay House, 2006.

having discovered the meaning of truly unconditional love—a love so strong she was able [to] seek out and forgive her family's killers.[98]

These are among the many powerful narratives of personal transformation that appear in the bibliography. Meanwhile I have my own story to tell.

B. HOW MY ROAD TO ORTHODOXY LED THROUGH AFRICA

A NARRATIVE OF TRANSFORMATION: MY UNEXPECTED JOURNEY

Orthodox teaching resists an undue focus upon personal narrative for a good reason: its subject is God far more than individual experience. Our human stories remain small when measured in relation to God's own story revealed in history from creation to consummation.

Nonetheless, as we see in Augustine's *Confessions* and Athanasius's Letters, personal witness inspires, illuminates, and clarifies faith. In my 2014 autobiography, *A Change of Heart: A Personal and Theological Memoir*,[99] I told the story of how I found my spiritual roots in Africa. Here is a glance of an extended narrative:

> In my forties I went through what seemed to me a lonely, almost solitary pilgrimage that led from modern western leftist political movements to patristic studies and finally to Africa. It seemed a bit lonely for me because I was the only one I knew who was traveling on this road. Few of my friends grasped what was happening to me. This step took me away from obsessive spiritual faddism to stable classic Christian teaching. Whenever I have told this story, even occasionally, I have had people ask me to clarify just what happened.

THE MEANDERING PATH OF A MOVEMENT THEOLOGIAN

During the experimental 1960s I was a "movement theologian," joining one movement after another, whether political, therapeutic, or philosophical. The providence of God was working quietly over many years of wandering in my former (Freudian-Marxist-existentialist) past. Now I celebrate that drifting as having been taken up into a more inclusive understanding of life with God.

My youthful forms of political ecumenism, viewed from the standpoint of the ancient orthodox tradition, now seem lacking in wholeness. Following in the curious steps of my once-Communist, later traditional mentor, Will Herberg, a Conservative

---

98. http://www.hayhouse.com/left-to-tell-7.
99. Thomas C. Oden, *A Change of Heart: A Personal and Theological Memoir*, IVP, 2014.

Jew, I am recognizing a fair amount of self-delusion and demonic deception in ideologies that once appeared to me seductive. Herberg was the first to call my hand. He told me truthfully that I would never become a theologian until I had carefully absorbed the most eminent Christian writers of the earliest Christian traditions, just as he had once committed himself to read the Torah and Midrash.[100]

At the time I thought I was being "inclusive," but did so only within the strict limits of modern ideologies trapped in secular premises. In this captivity I systematically excluded most pre-modern forms of wisdom.

Now I experience a gracious sense of inclusion in a much larger cloud of witnesses. They precede and transcend modern life and will survive its death. The faithful belong to a much more far-reaching communion than is even conceivable within the limits of modern ideologies.

I crawled my way through the beautiful, long-hidden texts of classic Christianity, many from Africa. The deeper perennial questions resurfaced. From this experience I re-emerged out of the secularizing maze to once again delight in the holy mysteries of the faith and the recurrent puzzles of human existence. Rather than interpreting the texts, I found the texts interpreting me.

After years of pretending to be a theologian, after publishing books on theology, and after teaching theology for years, something happened: a reversal, a conversion, an act of repentance and reparation—however it is named—it started with a 180-degree turn. Like a mustard seed growing, it took years to mature.

THE FOCUSED PATH OF AN ORTHODOX THEOLOGIAN: THE ABIDING CONVERSATION

This radical reversal had an abrupt, instantaneous beginning, but it matured mostly through quiet reading in early mornings, and in long conversations with my faithful evangelical, Catholic, and Orthodox PhD students. For me it happened chiefly through tranquil, slow, meticulous reading the ancient fathers of the church. For example: While reading Cyril of Jerusalem on the evidences for the resurrection, I became persuaded that Pannenberg had provided a more accurate account than Bultmann of the event of resurrection. While reading Tertullian on idolatry, I recognized myself in the mirror as one who was worshipping the false gods and absolutized values of modern consciousness.[101] While reading the account of the trial and death of Perpetua and Felicitas I realized how important were faithful women in the story of African faith. Their acts of self-sacrifice were more powerful than any arguments I had been making for social justice.

---

100. See *A Change of Heart*, chapter on the 1970s.
101. Ibid., chapters 5 and 6.

Every question that I had thought was new and unprecedented I found had been already much investigated in third-century African writings, and they had left a profound imprint on later European and eastern writers.

Earlier as a "movement theologian" seeking to legitimize Christianity by accommodation to modern thought, I had put inordinate trust in psychological methods: behavioral engineering, client-centered therapy, and psychoanalysis.[102] As I absorbed the writings of the ancient Christian teachers, I was gradually coming to view interpersonal transactions in the light of God's becoming fully human in the incarnation.

Earlier I was blown by every wind of doctrine and preoccupied with social and psychological fads amid the spirit of hyper-toleration. That came to a dead end when I came to grasp the consensual reasoning that occurs so effortlessly within classic African Christianity.

I became fascinated with the social dynamics of orthodoxy, the process of transmitting apostolic tradition, and the received canons of classic consensual teaching. I was on the threshold of the intergenerational wisdom of the ancient community of faith, which I found was still persisting as a living, caring community

AN ENLARGED FREEDOM OF DIALOGUE AND PRAYER

Unmerited, I now stand within the blessed presence of the communion of saints of all generations. There I experience greater, not less, cross-cultural freedom of inquiry. Subjects previously blocked from investigation are now open: creation and providence, divine foreknowledge, revelation in history, demonic temptation, and the lives of saints.[103] These partners in dialogue have become my daily bread. They can be read by anyone with a basic education.

The orthodox mind finds itself at home in every conceivable historical and intellectual environment by offering anew the unchanging Word in each new cultural setting.

African writers especially (Cyprian, Augustine, Athanasius, and Cyril the Great) have freed me from the narrow modern dogmatisms in which I had become entangled. I delight in their gracious flexibility. They personify and embody a Spirit-led life of grace. The names of these major African consensual interpreters of scripture are no secret. Among them are Clement, Origen, Didymus, Cyprian, and Optatus. These mentors weaned me away from the narrowness of modern perceptions.

This orthodox community melds and unites all that I now do. I have glimpsed the centered teaching of these classic witnesses. I am grateful to have been liberated to orthodoxy.

It is not a fabrication or projection that I once was a militant pacifist, a psychotherapeutic follower, an early Simone de Beauvoir/Betty Friedan feminist campaigner, an avant garde existentialist, and a zealous advocate of convenience abortion. I have served

---

102. Ibid., chapters 4 and 5.
103. Ibid., chapter 5

my time in all those liberation armies. That period of my life left an extensive record of activity and writing.[104] I had to squeeze myself out of that hyper-modern cocoon.

WHERE I COME FROM

I once distrusted even the faintest hint of orthodoxy. I was in love with heresy, the more unruly, the more seductive. *Now* I have come to trust the very consensus I once belittled. I now relish studying the diverse rainbow of orthodox voices from varied cultures spanning all continents for over two thousand years.

I once demeaned Catholic and Orthodox views of scripture. Now I embrace the language and life of orthodoxy. I esteem nothing higher than holy writ as ecumenically received and consensually explained. My daily work as a teacher of graduate students came to focus on our meeting with classic minds who have freely consented in varied cultures and times to the Christian narrative of the history of salvation. This was a highly focused textual dialogue. The seeds planted by the apostles always bear fruit in due season.

This is not about color since the good news is addressed to all persons of all hues. By celebrating African orthodoxy as a North American male, I do not mean that I have perfectly understood such a great continent but I have understood it well enough to be humbled by it.

The homecoming of which I speak in this book is to ancient consensual Christian wisdom. I myself have experienced this coming back home, especially to the wisdom of ancient African teachers. Seldom have I been told that my skin prevents me from knowing the depth of alienation of another skin. The power of empathy can be greater than the power of hate.

No boredom can linger long where the awe of God abounds. Everywhere there is wonder: the creation itself, time, providence in history, the penetration of grace and freedom, sin in believers, and radical judgment at the end of history. The lamp of scripture illuminates all and makes all things new.

This I learned from African voices speaking before 400 AD: that this creation is being redeemed; that all things work together for the good; that God's mercy covers all human misdeeds; that the seed of the Word is everywhere being planted precisely within the fertilized soil of passing cultures. My personal story is about how I learned to sit at the feet of Africa's best minds, and how they transformed my life and what I do.[105]

THE CORRUPTED HUNGER FOR ORIGINALITY

Ancient African intellectual achievements have forced me to retreat from all pretenses to originality. Modern life always pretends to be original because it thinks

---
104. Ibid., chapter 4.
105. See *How Africa Shaped the Christian Mind*, chapter 1, IVP, 2007.

the newest is best and the oldest is worst. Yet modern life's surface originality is jaded when compared to the great tradition of witnesses. What is not worn out is the Light of the world that shines radiantly upon our iniquities.

Africa has given world Christianity a priceless, ever-renewing gift. The gift is wisdom as vast at the continent itself. I have learned to listen intently to those who best demonstrate general consent to God's coming in the flesh. This gift is offered to all of the community of saints from all times and cultures.

It was not until I met ancient orthodoxy, especially in its earliest African form, that I entered the doorway of what was for me a genuine community of holy living. After that I came into rich conversation with orthodox believers far different from my ultra-liberal self. This has been a great legacy I received without merit.

Since then I have often felt like a translator between remote dialects, conflicting historical vocabularies, moral languages, and cultural memories, or sometimes like a lonely bridge-builder between distant islands of separated religious traditions.

THE PLEDGE TO UNORIGINALITY

It was while reading the texts of the early African writers that it first dawned upon me how universal consent to apostolic teaching was achieved, how boundaries were marked that remain today, how worldwide decisions were made, and how the Spirit nurtured unity of consent by way of agreement on the essential elements of faith.

About this same time I found my way back to Augustine's handbook[106] of wisdom and the method of recollecting faith first received by the apostles and passed on to Tertullian and Athanasius and later to Vincent of Lérins. Only with Vincent did I see explained the ecumenical way of truth that I already found embodied in the early African councils. Everything I have written since then is based on a commitment to offer nothing original. Presumed originality is the plague of theology. That is not a joke but a solemn pledge. I am trying to curb any pretense at improving upon the apostles and their earliest exponents.

---

106. *Enchiridion on Faith, Hope and Love.*

SEMINAR 8
RECLAIMING THE SACRED TEXTS

African orthodoxy is returning to its foundations because its most ancient texts are being rediscovered. They are being dug out of mummy masks, ancient junk piles, ceramic epigraphy, and secreted libraries in the sands. They are not just being read but being believed. These texts are now ripe for application to social processes, family governance, prayer, and ordinary life. People are learning to listen to scripture through the community of believers.

In this section I will seek to clarify:

1. How time-honored reflections on scripture are being reclaimed and restudied,

2. How communities of believers are celebrating their African heritage,

3. How the Word is coming alive through persons who embody the life of faith, and

4. How social effects are being felt in a world searching for multicultural wisdom.

A. LISTENING TO SCRIPTURE THROUGH THE COMMUNITY OF BELIEVERS

African orthodoxy connects with and contributes to the search for equitable justice by strengthening and deepening multicultural empathy and social consensus. No modern multiculturalism is as deep or fertile as historic Christian multiculturalism. It exceeds the strength of both secular multiculturalism, which is hamstrung by political correctness, and Islamic multiculturalism, which is bound to a single language for its holy writ.

SEMINAR 8

COUNTERING MODERN EXCESSES IN BIBLICAL STUDIES

Under modern western influences, biblical studies have sought to interpret sacred texts out of narrow modern experiential premises. African biblical scholars trained in the West have for decades sailed the troubled waters of these frequently changing winds of academic criticism. They better than most know the hazards.

Avant-garde scripture studies easily turn into ideological outrage pretending to rest on empirical evidence. When African youth and pastors have attempted to digest the results of western historical studies of scripture, the outcomes have been disappointing. God has not blessed this undertaking.

The task in African biblical studies is not merely to understand the Bible historically, but to understand history biblically. Western methods of literary and historical criticism were not equipped fully to reveal that history itself in precisely the arena in which God is becoming known. Real history is far more complex than can be dealt with solely by the narrow methods of present-day historical criticism, however important those studies may be in western universities. Spirit-led Bible studies need deeper grounding than can be acquired solely by modern historical-critical studies.

Brilliant young African students who have sought higher education in western universities have sometimes returned with a philosophical bias toward discounting everything supernatural and exalting everything western. When back on the ground in Africa they soon recognize the limits of faddish western criticism.

The last several generations have lived through dozens of chapters of literary, textual, and historical criticism. Most of these have been reduplicated in Africa. But Africa has its own great scripture scholars who verse by verse dig deeper into the spiritual reading of scripture: notably Origen, Augustine, and Cyril the Great.

The ancient African Christian writers were primarily addressing laypersons in a worship setting. They offered scriptural meditations weekly or in some cases daily for the community at prayer. They shunned speculation and loved plain speaking. Communities of prayer and ministries of compassion are now returning to the wisdom of ancient Africa to deepen their spiritual formation and social wisdom.

The wisdom of classic African scripture teachers remains unfamiliar to many highly trained clergy. Highly literate biblical scholars who were trained in the ever-narrowing methods of western scientific criticism have hardly heard of Origen except to dismiss him as an allegorist. That stereotype forgets his avid passion for language, context, and the plain sense of scripture.

Evidence of the modern neglect of classic African interpretation is seen in the appalling lack of reference to classic African scripture scholars. Many of the once authoritative classic African commentators on scripture remain untranslated into international languages. The need in Africa is to translate early African sources into current African regional languages. Even classic Buddhist and Confucian commentaries in modern China have not suffered the fate of such neglect. Many students are left wondering why the university or seminary is unprepared to teach the history of orthodox exegesis. All too few biblical and historical professors are prepared to show them the way in the history of ancient African biblical interpretation.

These facts reveal the problem, but what is being done about it?

RECLAIMING THE SACRED TEXTS

The faithful are looking toward expanding historical study, not diminishing it, by extending its range to orthodox scholars. They are bringing scripture studies ever closer to the evidences of God's self-disclosure in the actual events of human history.

God's own coming in history in human form is open to historical investigation. Faith is free to investigate whether the incarnation is true history, whether the resurrection actually occurred, and whether the providential work of the Holy Spirit is indeed a factor in actual historical outcomes. These questions tend to be more open in Africa while remaining closed in the west.

The Holy Spirit has promised to help the faithful reader of scripture remember rightly (John 16:13). The Spirit will not allow a defective testimony to be transmitted permanently or irreversibly to the community of faith.[107] As we see in Luke's Gospel,[108] historical accuracy is a central value in reporting the good news. Questions of historical evidence can be subjected to the stringent tests of accurate historical reporting. But if these tests rule out God and revelation prior to the investigation, that is not openhanded inquiry.

TOWARD OPEN INQUIRY

The remembering community of faith in Africa has for centuries savored the inspired words of the prophets, psalms, and apostles. Hearing these voices anew is like relishing the sounds of a beautiful musical masterpiece echoing through the fragile words of human memory. This has occurred at a time of weakness in the intellectual rigor of western universities, preoccupied as they are with the policing of language, financial crises, and failing ideological dreams.

It is hard to believe that the Holy Spirit would leave such an important matter as the transmission of the truth of God's coming to the jaded imagination of those whose values are shaped exclusively by the narrow methods of a transient cultural landscape.

Contemporary observers remain free to evaluate any proposed viewpoint by its correspondence with the consensually received testimony of the original witnesses.

---

107. See Thomas C. Oden, *Classic Christianity: A Systematic Theology* (New York: HarperOne, 2009), Book III, on the perpetuity of the church.

108. Luke 1 and Acts 1.

God is blessing the fruits of those who are taking seriously the historic Christian consensus. That testimony has a multi-century record of trustworthy transmission through varied cultures without losing its unity and power.

B. THE CHURCH'S BOOK

THE PLACE FOR HEARING SCRIPTURE

The worshipping community is the best place to hear scripture read. The natural home of the sacred text is in the worshipping community, not necessarily the academy. It is addressed to a community and borne by a community.

The academy needs to become more tolerant. The reading of scripture is not merely an act of adapting the Word to modern worldviews; it is rather an act of praise, humility, worship, and glory in the mystery of God.

When an interpreter presumes to be in charge of holy writ so as to become the measurer of scripture's correctness, it is fitting to ask whether the historic consensus of classic interpreters should be considered and, if not, why. Those who seek to be gatekeepers to the Bible need to listen to the historic consensus even if they disagree with it. Many believers in the worshipping communities, having tried out the modern methods, say: "Give us back our scriptures. They belong to the community of faith that has transmitted them into your hands."

When the creative imagination of the interpreter is exalted above the plain sense of the Word, then the community of faith appeals to the consensus of scriptural understanding held by the most widely respected interpreters from over two thousand years of history. Those schooled in African orthodox scripture study can easily spot the limitations of many modern biblical commentaries: over-speculation, philosophical bias, controversial slanting, and aggressive control of the text by a predisposed interpreter. These habits spring from a persistent compulsion to impose modern western worldviews so as to express dominance over classic interpreters.

This prejudice tends to view the biblical text exclusively through whatever modern lens is used to correct and readjust the sacred text. Almost any modern lens will legitimize; almost any pre-modern lens will delegitimize. Within orthodoxy, however, respect for the hundred generations[109] of consensual interpreters has great weight based on demonstrable consensus.

Consensual reasoning out of scripture, such as that found in Augustine and Cyril the Great, comes as a gradual work of sanctifying grace, not merely of clever scholarly research. It is a mature work of the Spirit. It seeks to articulate what can only be spoken after much prayer, study, and historical listening. Even then the humble listener for the Spirit in the Word can only exclaim, as did the father of the convulsive child

---

109. Viewing a generation as twenty years, now almost one hundred generations since the apostles.

in scripture: "I have faith; help my lack of faith!" (Mark 9:24 CEB), and say with the tax collector: "God, show mercy to me, a sinner" (Luke 18:13 CEB).

THE INTERWOVEN FABRIC OF SCRIPTURE

The classic African teachers developed a highly refined pattern of scriptural cross-referencing: each scripture text is illumined by other texts and by the whole of the history of revelation. Every text therefore has other correlated texts interwoven with it to confirm and extend its meaning. Each verse is rightly understood in relation to the message and credibility of scripture as a whole. Thus the whole of scripture illumines each part.

Ancient commentators weaved many scriptures together rather than considering one apart from the whole substance of scriptural revelation. This deliberate interweaving of references has been unfairly caricatured in modern studies as the alignment of texts to support an argument without taking into account their context.[110] What the modern caricature may fail to see is the interconnection between different texts on related themes, which was the special genius of early African exegesis.[111] The comparison of text with text is essential to orthodox scripture teaching. No scripture text stands alone as if apart from the whole story of God with humanity.

The early baptismal confession, which was behind closed doors discreetly passed on to and ordinarily memorized by all believers, often under conditions of persecution, has always been consensually viewed as a reliable and concise guide to the heart of scripture. Out of that simple confession came all subsequent systematic theology.

GUARDING THE SCRIPTURE

Under conditions of persecution, the hunted community had to rely on memory rather than written texts. When the Roman authorities required believers to give up their scriptures, these believers died rather than yield the precious manuscripts to the enforcers of idolatry. The brevity of Mark's Gospel may have sprung from a need for a short form of Peter's preaching that could be committed to memory. Coptic accounts of Mark recall him as a member of Peter's extended family.[112]

During the three centuries of African persecutions, the privilege to cite scriptural texts was properly thought to belong to the worshipping community who preserved them from confiscation by the authorities. When the idolatrous Roman civic

---

110. Sometimes called proof-texting.

111. Cyprian and Didymus the Blind are notable examples, both of whom memorized large portions of scripture.

112. See Oden, *The African Memory of Mark* (Downers Grove, IL: IVP, 2011).

authorities wanted to possess scripture, believers hid them and resisted public exposure, as in the case of the twelve North African Christian men and women of Scilli who were executed for their beliefs on July 17, 180 AD. That day marked the beginning of Christian persecution in North Africa. It all had to do with protecting the scriptures from seizure. The scripture manuscripts were the most valuable property the church possessed. They could not be turned over to idolaters. The modern situation is similar.

The orthodox tradition in Africa invites rigorous study of particular texts of scripture that seek to grasp the flow of events within which the revelation of God has become known, spoken, written, and transmitted. These writers welcomed serious investigation into the language and contexts in which God has chosen to reveal divine mercy and grace. In doing so they resisted the intentional distortion of the meaning of the sacred texts.

WITHOUT APOLOGY

It is the habit of orthodoxy to make reference to texts of holy writ without apology. Yet it has become a modern habit to assume that each scriptural reference must be doubted or accompanied by lengthy justifications. The reading of scripture practiced by the early African exegetes was especially committed to seeing each text in relation to its larger context within the whole course of scripture.

The reading of the bible grounded in the consensual tradition prevents the reader from reducing the text to a detached historical exercise of investigating the disconnected words of holy writ. Peter at Pentecost did not divert his sermon into historical inquiry into the root word for "repent."

Study of the context surrounding the divine address remains a valuable exercise, but not when the context becomes an end in itself. The eyewitness of the apostles is crucial to the historicity of the Christian narrative, for where else can you find the eyewitnesses to the incarnate risen Lord except through the eyes of those who saw him?

RESPECTING BOTH THE PLAIN SENSE AND SPIRITUAL SENSE OF SCRIPTURE

The wisest early African teachers of scripture (Cyprian, Clement, Origen, and Didymus) respected both the plain sense and the spiritual sense of scripture, as well as its moral application and its significance for eternal life. When words are excessively symbolized, the plain sense may be missed. When words are not allowed to have metaphorical significance, the spiritual meaning may be overlooked.

When its moral sense is not applied in the lives of hearers of the word, it bears no fruit. When the text is not studied in relation to its significance for eternal life, the end-time sense is overlooked.

Just as the person has body, soul, and spirit in union, so does the interpretation of scripture have not only a plain, literal, and historical meaning, but also a moral meaning for holy living, as well as a spiritual meaning for communion with God, and a final meaning for life after death.[113]

The Holy Spirit had veiled the outward expression of some texts whose meanings were meant to be fully revealed in God's own time.[114]

It is fitting to let the Spirit speak through the text. Where uncertainties appear in the text, seek guidance from the leading classic consensual interpreters. Humbly the faithful community prefers to let God speak freely; not imposing their own vested interests on the interpretation of the Word of God.

The purpose of the study of the sacred text among the orthodox is to humbly listen to the best minds of the church seeking the wholeness of the truth that the revealed scriptures convey. In fairness, the modern reader has no legitimate right to impose overconfident modern assumptions upon the text that overrides the plain sense of the sacred page.

The freedom in orthodoxy to let the text speak for itself provides ample room for varied spiritual interpretations, provided they arise out of the text itself and do not ignore what the historic consensus confirms.

THE RELATION OF EARLY ORAL TRADITIONS TO WRITTEN TEXTS

Jesus taught his disciples not by writing but primarily by his life. His only known writing was in sand.[115]

His words that interpreted his life were carefully remembered, and in due time written down in order to be preserved accurately. Thus an oral tradition may precede the written tradition, yet once written and widely received in worshipping communities, the written Word takes precedence over alternative claims of an earlier oral tradition. Preaching from canonical texts continues the oral interpretation of the written Word.

An oral tradition of preaching clearly existed before the written texts that became the New Testament. The teaching of the apostles was spoken before it was penned. Hearing the word preceded reading the word. The word spread first by oral preaching, which later became fixed in writing and was ultimately received as reliable everywhere for use in public worship.

---

113. Irenaeus, *Against Heresies*, III, ANF I; Origen, *De Principiis*, IV, ANF III; *Against Celsus*, V.60, VI.7, ANF III; Tertullian, *Against Praxeas*, 18–21, ANF III.

114. Paul wrote: "But their minds were closed. Right up to the present day the same veil remains when the old covenant is read. The veil is not removed because it is taken away by Christ." (2 Cor 3:14 CEB).

115. John 8:3-8.

Paul valued highly and commended both the received written tradition and the tradition of oral interpretation based upon it. In the New Testament's earliest written documents, Paul called the Thessalonians to "stand firm and hold on to the traditions [*paradoseis*] we taught you, whether we taught you in person or through our letter,"[116] meaning whether orally heard or in writing. We can imagine various possible forms of proclamation that existed in the new Christian communities before that time, but we do not have many of them in written form, except for the texts that were preserved in the written tradition. Hence they do not carry the same weight of reliability and durability as the canon of holy writ whose authenticity was carefully examined.[117]

Scripture became written so that the events it attested might be more accurately preserved and transmitted. The written text was recognized as more stable than an oral tradition. Oral speech will always be subject to more varied and volatile interpretations than a written text. The text did not distort the memory but stabilized it in writing. The written Word was assumed to be consistent with apostolic preaching.

The same Spirit who inspired the prophets and apostles was also at work to inspire the reading of the text and its reliable transmission. The whole process of inspiring the Word, proclaiming it orally and in the written word centuries later has always been viewed as a work of the Spirit. Its transmission stood under the protection of the Holy Spirit. The Spirit works to reveal the word and to teach all things necessary. "The Companion, the Holy Spirit, whom the Father will send in my name, will teach you everything and will remind you of everything I told you" (John 14:26 CEB). "When the Spirit of Truth comes, he will guide you in all truth" (John 16:13 CEB).

What books belong in the public readings within the church is not for later critics to determine because it was decided by the end of the fourth century and has been trusted by generations of believers with abundant fruits of the Spirit. To change the canon would be to disrespect generations of believers whose lives give evidence of the reliability of the canon.

Holy writ is the primary source, ground, and criterion of all Christian teaching, as in Jewish teaching. The faithful of all generations have always known that. Even the heterodox despisers of the consensus appealed to scripture for their arguments. To enter the arena of Christian worship is to enter the arena of scriptural truth.

THE VULNERABILITY OF ORAL TRADITION

It is hard to discern what other oral traditions may have been remembered in the earliest centuries, and we do well not to speculate wildly. The written word is sufficient. Among examples of early holy tradition are baptism in the name of the Father, Son, and Spirit, common prayer on the first day of the week, the sign of the cross, and bending knees in prayer to rise anew as an analogy of death and resurrection. In

---

116. 2 Thess 2:15 CEB, italics added.

117. Obviously the examination occurred in the fourth century and could not have assumed current criteria.

these cases little residue of written apostolic tradition remains, but that absence did not diminish their value.

Saint Basil, whose work *On the Spirit* was highly valued in early African Christianity, argued that the practices just noted were received and conserved consensually as unwritten traditions from the apostles, and remained graciously shrouded in silence "out of the reach of curious meddling and inquisitive investigation. Well had they learned the lesson that the awful dignity of the mysteries is best preserved by silence. What the [catechumens] are not even allowed to look at was hardly likely to be publicly paraded about in written documents."[118] In this same tradition of awe, especially under conditions of persecution, the consensus received the same written documents that had been circulating from earliest memory. Basil thought that the apostles had passed on certain recollections orally from the beginning, but none that would undermine the written tradition.[119]

Moses did not open all parts of the tent of meeting to everyone. Unbelievers did not enter at all. The Levites alone served in worship, offering sacrifices. Only one priest could enter the most holy place, and then only once each year. By analogy, not everything was reported in scripture, but only that which is necessary and sufficient for salvation.

Oral tradition, however valuable, is always more vulnerable to falling prey to abuse, uncertainty, and division. Thus the focus of orthodox Christian teaching remains fixed upon the Spirit's presence in the written word and upon the early written documents setting forth the meaning of that word to the worshipping communities worldwide.

C. FOLLOWING THE WORD IN ORDER TO HEAR IT

Jesus said to a woman in the crowd who blessed him: "Happy rather are those who hear God's word and put it into practice" (Luke 11:28 CEB).

---

118. Basil, *On the Spirit*, XXVII.66, NPNF 2 8:42.

119. Basil applied this analogy: "If, as in a court of law, we were at a loss of documentary [written] evidence, but were able to bring before you a large number of [oral] witnesses, would you not give your vote for our acquittal?" On this basis Basil cherished the phrase "with the Spirit" in the doxology as a legacy of the fathers, and here he specifically cited Irenaeus, Clement, Origen, Dionysius of Rome, Gregory Thaumaturgus, Firmilian, Eusebius, and Africanus. Basil did not want to be falsely perceived as "an innovator or creator of such new terms." These precious oral traditions, he argued, go back to those who were "pillars of the church and conspicuous for all knowledge and spiritual power." Thus he argued that memories and practices evidently familiar to those generations immediately following the apostles and "continued by long usage" should remain highly valued in Christian teaching. These words were passed down by champions of the word to "whole nations, cities, customs going back beyond the memory of man" (Basil, *On the Spirit*, III.29, NPNF 2 8:45-47; cf. Augustine, *Letters*, FC 12:252-3).

PRACTICING LIFE IN THE WORD IN ORDER TO LIVE OUT ITS MEANING

James wrote: "You must be doers of the word and not only hearers who mislead themselves" (James 1:22 CEB). The Word of God teaches us how to live so that we will hear, "Well done! You are a good and faithful servant. You've been faithful over a little. I'll put you in charge of much. Come, celebrate with me" (Matt 25:23 CEB). The Word must be applied behaviorally to be rightly understood. To treat the text as a hypothetical word or suggestion of God is to not take scripture seriously as the Word of God.

In classical scripture study it was assumed that readers could not even begin to approach an elementary discernment of the meaning of the text if they refused to take seriously its revelation so as to seek to live accordingly.

They assumed one must practice its truth in order to hear its meaning. Holy writ was rightly not even to be possessed by those who were as yet unready to put it into practice. The right to hear the sacred text is based on the reader's willingness to take the assumptions of the text seriously.

THE JOY OF WALKING IN THE NARROW WAY

Eugene Peterson paraphrases Jesus in Matthew 11:28-30: "Are you tired? Worn out? Burned out on religion? Come to me. Get away with me and you'll recover your life. I'll show you how to take a real rest. Walk with me and work with me—watch how I do it. Learn the unforced rhythms of grace. I won't lay anything heavy or ill-fitting on you. Keep company with me and you'll learn to live freely and lightly" (THE MESSAGE).

As Jesus bore the cross for the joy set before him, so do his disciples. "Let's throw off any extra baggage, get rid of the sin that trips us up, and fix our eyes on Jesus, faith's pioneer and perfecter. He endured the cross, ignoring the shame, for the sake of the joy that was laid out in front of him, and sat down at the right side of God's throne" (Heb 12:1-2 CEB).

It is usually from a history of suffering that God makes us ready to hear his calling to us to love the neighbor. From personal struggle we come to know how God is calling us to respond to the struggle of others.

African Christian history shows that it is only through a history of adversity and readiness to die for the faith that the depth of God's love is revealed. "Those who don't pick up their crosses and follow me aren't worthy of me" (Matt 10:38 CEB). "All who want to come after me must say no to themselves, take up their cross, and follow me" (Mark 8:34 CEB).

THE UNFOLDING OF VOCATION

Even though I did not know it clearly in my rootless days, I now realize that my vocation has been from the beginning to teach classic Christian orthodoxy. It is from this experience of wandering that I came to see Africa as the key place where the intellectual formation of Christian teaching most deeply occurred and where the faithful were willing to suffer for the truth. I would not have learned the full breadth of my vocation without having gone through the circuitous path that led me to the great minds of early African Christianity.

My vocation has grown directly from my own hunger for roots, my seeking them without avail in the liberal ethos, and my thirst for historic grounding beyond my former world of intellectual faddism. It was not until I died to idolatry that I shared in the resurrection. My chief idol was modernity, the lure of the ideologies that modern consciousness had made absolute. The resurrection of my dead life was the apostolic witness as recalled by its earliest interpreters.

Earlier my search essentially consisted of a moral search for virtue, goodness, and social justice. Only later did it become an awareness of God's search for me. I changed by moving closer to that which is unchanging, toward the still point of the turning world. I had to taste the dregs of movement theology and faddism before I could come to that centered equilibrium.

D. TOWARD A WIDER CROSS-CULTURAL CONSENSUS

A GENTLE CAVEAT FOR THOSE WHO EXPECT ANCIENT WRITERS TO ADAPT TO ONE-SIDED MODERN ASSUMPTIONS

If one starts with the narrow assumption that modern thought is superior to all ancient wisdom, then the classic exegetes will always appear as dated, quaint, and laughable. They will either seem comic, mean-spirited, or oppressive if judged only in terms set by modern moral judgments. The deeper question for critical analysis is the adequacy of modern moral judgments.

It is foolish for any modern writer to assume that any ancient writer should have had access to ideas that had not yet been written. Moses never read Frantz Fanon, although he may have been an archetype in Fanon's mind for national liberation movements.

Christians of many diverse forms of ethnicity, politics, and culture are learning to listen for witnesses to the truth that are less culturally narrow, attested by a broader range of historic experience than is provided by modern ideas alone. The story is about the meaning of the whole of history, not just now.

ORTHODOXY AS MAXIMUM MULTICULTURAL EXPERIENCE

African orthodoxy is by definition cross-cultural. It finds a home and becomes profoundly indigenous to Africans in the Egyptian culture, the Ethiopian culture, the

Berber culture, the cultures of Nubia, Namibia, and Libya—all these in the first six centuries, and hundreds more languages and cultures after that.

An evidence of the rebirth of orthodoxy is its continuing interest in transforming culture. Wherever Christians are found, they are living lives that impact culture formation. From its beginnings African orthodoxy, which emerged in Alexandria, Cyrene, and Carthage, invested itself in grassroots cultural transformation. Orthodox life has a practical capacity to energize great love for a particular culture while remaining in healthy connection with the worldwide community of faith.

Classical Christian orthodoxy exists far more as a global and multicultural phenomenon than do strictly modern secular visions of happiness and justice, since its cultural variations embrace twenty centuries while modern models have only one or two centuries of experience. Orthodoxy proves that it has resources and energies for social transformation unavailable to its secular counterparts.

Growing evidence confirms the higher social outcomes of faith-based charitable acts and services as compared with government and secular services. The western citadels of modernity are belatedly recognizing the social value of traditional Christian moral reasoning. The sociological evidence is pouring in on what makes for sustainable societies: family, education, and moral responsibility. Those rooted in tested moral teaching are more effective in implementing positive behavioral change than are supposedly value-free agents or bureaucratic planners. This evidence rises from scientific social analysis and studies of the relation of religion and culture and from cross-cultural studies, public policy, and strategies for social effectiveness.[120]

WHERE POLITICAL CORRECTNESS MEETS A WIDER MULTICULTURAL ORTHODOXY

Intrinsic to African orthodoxy is its profound multicultural history. The major centers in which African orthodoxy was worked out, from Luxor to Hippo, were as multicultural as any in the world. From those centers classic Christian teaching spread throughout the Nile and Medjerda Valleys and south toward the heart of the African continent as rapidly as seafaring and land exploration allowed.

By the fifth century, classic Christian teaching had spread to dozens of cultures and languages beyond those of Egypt and Proconsular Mauritania. This is a tribute to the intrinsic original multicultural character of African orthodoxy. A map of episcopal and arch-diocesan centers in fifth-century Africa makes that plain.[121]

---

120. Thomas Sowell, *A Conflict of Visions: Ideological Origins of Political Struggles* (New York: William Morrow, 1987).

121. See Angelo Di Berardino, *Historical Atlas of Ancient Christianity* (St. Davids, PA: ICCS Press, 2014).

The modern fairness revolution seeks fair opportunities for every living person regardless of sex, race, class, education, culture lags, or bodily condition. It has both secular and religious forms. The fairness revolution seeks legal and attitudinal remedies for unfair treatment of persons.

The history of the human rights movement makes clear the deep historic connections that led from vital Christian faith to efforts at human dignity, respect for others, and fairness. Classic Christian moral teaching motivated many aspects of the fairness revolution. Although the secular forms of the search for human rights seek to embrace all human cultures, the ideological range of vision is often decidedly recent, western, and secularist, omitting ancient, classic, Catholic, and African models, which embrace so many more generations and cultures. Christian moral judgments do not revolve exclusively around the recently achieved moral views, but are far more cross-cultural than those grounded in modern assumptions only.

The modern multicultural experience base is thin in comparison with that of consensual Christian multiculturalism, which has in fact embraced many thousands of cultures and subcultures over two millennia. The secular fairness revolution wants to include all cultures in the modern democratic scene, but with a rigid qualifier: only modern cultures. Meanwhile it sustains an intractable prejudice against any culture perceived as pre-modern. Any view that might appear to be old-fashioned, traditional, or conservative is treated harshly, as if it had no place in the legitimate thought world. This is the unfair underbelly of the fairness revolution.

The fairness advocates of recent times tend to reduce the vision of human change largely to political tenets and legal constraints, especially as viewed by stereotyped victimization claimants. Often missing are prudential judgments and weightier matters of the heart. This turns into comic exaggeration when the knowledge class appears to love sperm whales, white sharks, and razorback suckers more than actual people and organic human social processes.

Orthodoxy cannot be forced into being interpreted exclusively through the four modern moral prisms (class, gender, ethnicity, and identity). Orthodoxy is about God's forgiveness for all who receive grace, not niggling and finger-pointing.

African orthodoxy is not intimidated by modernity, and does not permit modern western assumptions to stand as absolute judge of apostolic truth. The task of Christianity is to introduce the language police to the languages of a global community of discourse that has weathered many centuries of presumed modernities.

THE CALL FOR A MORE RADICAL DIVERSITY THAN IS POSSIBLE WITHIN NARROW MODERN ASSUMPTIONS

The classic concept of broad universal consent (wholeness, catholicity, universality) spans many generations, even millennia, while the modern idea of diversity spans but a single century or less. At times the modern vision of diversity spans only a tiny slice of one generation, or even one subset of one generation, as if that elite ethos alone is superior to all others. It has no time or empathy to listen to other generations. It insists upon a massive loss of wisdom. The ideal of absolute tolerance has been advocated by those least tolerant of historical experience.

The modern idea of inclusion is less inclusive than the classic Christian understanding of inclusion, which arises from the more radical inclusiveness of God's mercy toward all. God's mercy, as creator of all, redeemer of all, and consummator of all history is humanity's most inclusive concept. God's work in creation is given to all, even if many refuse the gift. God's action on the cross reaches for all, even if some reject it.

The modern passion for absolute tolerance is often less tolerant than the ancient moral value of long-suffering forgiveness grounded in divine forgiveness. Modern media-driven tolerance depends on a relativism that gives up on the search for cross-cultural historic truth before it begins.

Classic Christian forbearance is based upon the joyful reception of the truth revealed in actual history. It is constrained by humility, repentance, and cross-bearing. Modern hyper-tolerance seeks the lowest common denominator, the desire not to be offended, whereas classic Christian forbearance seeks the highest common denominator, human participation in God's incarnate life and sharing in God's temporal and eternal gifts. Out of this comes a higher level of energy for social reconstruction less deceived by illusions.

Absolute egalitarianism consists in the absolutizing of the idea of equality. Any finite good which is elevated to become presumably the absolute source of good is by definition idolatry. This process of elevation began as a great eighteenth-century aspiration that took two and a half centuries to go sour in the twenty-first-century limits on freedom of speech.

The modern portrayal of absolute equality survives on the thinness of passing human sympathies with select in-groups. The classic Christian understanding of compassion radiates the full depth of God's own compassion for all humanity, as shown in God's willingness to become flesh and die for the sins of all humanity.

Classic Christianity is not a product of democratic idealism but the most long-lasting and profound tangible model of it.[122] In the classic understandings of catholicity, wholeness, and universality we find the deepest roots of modern democracy.

That can be confirmed by comparing all the societies lacking Christianity with all those steeped in it. None is perfect, but there is a difference between Kabul and Detroit, even though they may at times look a lot alike.

Classic Christian teaching calls for a more radical diversity than is possible within narrow modern assumptions. It is more profound than its worst examples, such as the Crusades and the Inquisition, which are often used to dismiss vast historic achievements.

---

122. Contemporary democratic teaching stands in need of being regrounded on the premise of the principle of long-term general consent over millennia. For an exposition of this point, see *Classic Christianity*, sections of Book I on creation, providence, freedom, and sin.

HOW ORTHODOXY ELICITS CONSTRUCTIVE SOCIAL CHANGE

Classic Christianity is the historic source of much social compassion that has added immense compassionate energy to social betterment. Optimal food relief for the poor and voluntary medical missions are not necessarily elicited by those who seek the phantom of absolute equality. No community in early Africa was more excluded than Christians, but they overcame the exclusion by entering into the most inclusive worldwide community embracing all cultures, castes, and ethnic identities.

The self-deceptions of the modern fairness revolution are not irreparable. They can be changed by critical reasoning, repentance, and faith.

Christian social vision does not stop with governmental efforts but seeks to enlist faith active in love that walks the second mile. From the small scale of the widow's mite to the international relief agencies, it does not stop with legal remedies but seeks to redeem the heart. This is in part why faith-based social services show better outcomes and greater imagination than do supposedly value-free secular government programs that may solve short-term problems with longer-term dependencies. The most aggressive social justice advocates often do not recognize classic Christian teaching as a vital source of renewal, motivation, empowerment, energy, prudence, and justice.

Classic Christianity has two millennia of experience across many cultures storing wisdom not easily accessible to secular models of giving. They often tend to focus on coercive actions, legislation, and judicial activism, and approaches that have a history of failed social experiments. Often these experiments have been rejected by the very constituencies they were supposed to protect.

The European Enlightenment's record of secular social experimentation is strewn with failures, especially in its unexpected secondary consequences. For example:

1. Rousseau's nativist experiment with his own four sets of children who landed in Foundling homes became a prototype for fatherless families today.[123]

2. Marx's desire to coercively plan other people's lives led finally to the Siberian gulags.

3. The attempt of Khmer Rouge party leader Pol Pot to nationalize and centralize the peasant farming society of Cambodia led to the totally unanticipated consequences of the Cambodian genocide.

---

123. In Rousseau's letter to Mme. Maréchal de Luxembourg, he wrote: "Five children were born of [our] liaison, and were placed in the Foundling's Hospital, and with so little thought of the possibility of their identification that I did not even keep a record of their dates of birth [or of their gender]." William Kessan, "Rousseau's Children," *Daedalus* 107 (1978): 155.

4. The superhuman Nietzschean dreams evolved into the Nazi holocaust.

5. The Maoist Revolution in China became a disastrous expression of misguided modern social planning schemes.

None of these were conceived apart from the coercive utopianism of the suspicious heirs of the eighteenth-century Enlightenment. When these vaunted western ideologies were exported to Africa through colonialism, they ended with the fatherless boys of Soweto, the fury of Rwanda, and the boy militias of the Congo.

THE PERSISTENCE OF THE CORRUPTION OF THE WILL IN THE HISTORY OF FREEDOM

Utopian schemes for absolute equality flounder precisely because of their own failure to recognize the vulnerability of freedom to stumbling. Lacking historical experience, they ignore well-defined temptations. They systematically forget standard forms of social wisdom readily available in classic Christianity. The illusory ideal of immediate equality is tempting but evasive.

For the orthodox mind this recalls the biblical teaching of the persistence of temptation, sin, and evil that passes to the third and fourth generation.[124] The social consequences of bad choices multiply exponentially from grandparents to grandchildren.

Paul wrote: "Just as through one human being sin came into the world, and death came through sin, so death has come to everyone, since everyone has sinned" (Rom 5:12 CEB). And John: "If we claim, 'We don't have any sin,' we deceive ourselves, and the truth is not in us" (1 John 1:8 CEB).

Biblical teaching provides the fairness revolution with a more realistic grasp of the entrenched nature of human self-assertiveness. Unplanned consequences carry with them a predisposition to new forms of distortion. This is the story of human freedom from the beginning of history. The freedom God gives humanity is always subject to being twisted. The grace of repentance is offered anew in each misjudgment.

Orthodoxy provides tested historic wisdom rarely accessed by modern biases. The orthodox tradition offers to the fairness revolution profound new insights and energies for social change, for principled courage, and for persistence in well-doing. These energies come from gratitude for God's gifts in creation and redemption, not from human imagination alone.

The rebirth of African orthodoxy has practical relevance for the deeper grounding of Africa's quest for social justice. Classic Christian moral reasoning shows a better way toward social fairness without falling into self-justifying egalitarian or utopian illusions.

---

124. Traditionally called original sin, since in scripture it has persisted since the first humans.

THE ORTHODOX WAY OFFERS WIDER INTELLECTUAL FREEDOM

Orthodoxy offers a broader arena of inquiry than that available within rigid modern prejudices. It offers intellectual options beyond modern experimental failures. It offers vast varieties of intellectual alternatives that have boundaries and that call for humility every day.

The feast of learning is offered in this enduring community of faithful memory. To enter into the arena of the true love of learning, the believer is offered tested premises to try out personally: divine providence, the Father's love made known through the Son by the power of the Spirit, and the expectation of final judgment. These freeing assumptions manifest themselves in actual living communities of worship that embody the orthodox way. There one sits at a large table to enjoy an eternal feast.

The steady habit of the orthodox mind is the willingness to listen attentively to history, to human experience in the past, and to bring its reasoning into the present. Faith comes to the table ready for the feast prepared. This way of reasoning cannot be reduced to modern sociological insights, philosophical arguments, or scientific data. Orthodox wisdom opens up vistas closed by secularizing modernity.

The honored tradition of orthodox reflection permits the faithful to reason afresh amid their actual ongoing history of the worshipping community. It reasons out of a history of God's self-disclosure. Contrary to modern expectations a high priority is granted to thinking freely out of a huge, robust, experience-oriented base of faithful confessors of all epochs and cultures.

Current guardians of historic faith respect earlier layers of consensus. This community of faith over many generations has assumed that the formation of consensual teaching was led by the Spirit amid the hazards of history.

It is not the habit of orthodoxy to pit Christianity against critical thinking. It is the habit of orthodoxy to incorporate many correlated methods of critical thinking and bring them into fresh understandings of God in history.

ANSWERING STEREOTYPED CHARGES OF MISOGYNY AND ANTI-SEMITISM

Misogyny means hatred of women, or more generally contempt for or ingrained prejudice against women. Anti-Semitism means hostility to or prejudice against Jews. The orthodox interpreters of scripture have sometimes been criticized for misogyny and anti-Semitism. This becomes such a stumbling block to some modern readers that it prevents them altogether from even listening to any ancient wisdom.

The reasoning of the classic African writers was not framed in regard to the hatred of a race or class or gender. They as much as we today celebrate the role of women in the history of salvation, as we see in their reflections upon the narratives of Hannah, Esther, the sisters Mary and Martha, and above all Mary the mother of the Incarnate Lord. While pointing out the self-righteous temptations of late Judaic legalism, the classic African interpreters celebrated the significant place of the Jews as the elect people of God in the history of the divine-human covenant that is fulfilled in Jesus Christ.

The orthodox views that appear to modern readers to be misogynist or anti-Semitic in most cases have a typological reference that did not imply race or gender. Rather they were constantly looking to scripture for types of character formation or events that would be instantly recognizable to those who read scripture. Their method of discerning these types was by means of analogies within biblical reasoning. It views the difference between Jew and Gentile or man and woman not merely as a matter of genetics, race, or gender but under the promise of messianic assumptions.

Biblical typology is the study of how clusters of events in scripture can be understood in relation to a type or typical figure, so that Noah becomes a type of the covenant of promise, Jacob becomes a type of the chosen people, and Esther becomes a type of one who uses only persuasion to save her people.

Compare the writings of Rosemary Radford Ruether and David C. Ford[125] on these controversial anti-Semitic and sexist issues. Ruether steadily applies exclusively modern standards of justice to judge the sins and inadequacies of the ancient writers. Ford seeks to understand the ancient Christian writers empathically from within their own historical assumptions, limitations, scriptural interpretations, and deeper intentions. While both treatments are illuminating, Ford's treatment comes closer to a fair-minded assessment of scriptural intent. Early Christian writers would not recognize themselves in modern charges of racial anti-Semitism and inferior gender status. Even in their harshest criticism against Judaizing threats to the gospel, the writers of the New Testament did not consider Jews as racially or genetically inferior people, as modern anti-Semites are prone to do. Paul exalted "the woman [as] man's glory" (1 Cor 11:7).

---

125. Rosemary Radford Ruether, *Gregory of Nazianzus: Rhetor and Philosopher* (Oxford: Clarendon Press, 1969); Rosemary Radford Ruether, ed., *Religion and Sexism: Images of Woman in the Jewish and Christian Traditions* (New York: Simon and Schuster, 1974); David C. Ford, *Men and Women in the Early Church: The Full Views of St. John Chrysostom* (South Canaan, PA: St. Tikhon's Orthodox Theological Seminary, 1995). Cf. related works by John Meyendorff, Stephen B. Clark, and Paul K. Jewett.

SEMINAR 9
CONSENSUS RECOGNITION

A. LEARNING TO TRUST

BLENDING THE VOICES OF A HUNDRED GENERATIONS

The sustaining of a two-thousand-year consensus seems completely implausible when viewed as a sociology project. From where would the energy to span so many centuries of testimony come? The ancient church knew the answer: God the Spirit is providentially guiding but not coercing the future unfolding of the church. The consensus is not an achievement of human cleverness; it is the gift of the Spirit.

How has orthodox experience extended the range of human wisdom while still remaining true to the ancient apostolic consensus?

The Son prayed that the Spirit would come to make us one as he and the Father are one (John 17:11). Much about the work of the Spirit is entirely beyond finite understanding or reasonable prediction. But we do know from experience that the Spirit finds unexpected ways to proclaim the same Word of truth to different cultures. This steady witness continues today. This wisdom is offered anew to be rediscovered in each emerging generation.

Faithfulness must be lived out in time and space, not just in ideas. The Spirit uses renewed human minds to apply tested remedies. Christian testimony deepens by being applied.

The innermost wellsprings of energy underlying consensus formation and maintenance are gifts of grace awakening human reason, conscience, and practical ingenuity. These communities learned how to apply Christian wisdom to emerging cultures of all sorts. The Spirit does not resist natural reasoning but deepens it.

SEMINAR 9

THE HOLY SPIRIT SPEAKS ALL LANGUAGES

The first lesson the church learned in its founding on the day of Pentecost was that the Holy Spirit speaks all languages. The church that is sent to the ends of the earth must learn to speak all the languages of the earth, insofar as possible, and dwell in the earth's spaces. This differs from Islam, where only Arabic is the sacred language.[126]

The life of faith active in love was poured forth from Pentecost not just for Jerusalem but for alienated Samaria, then went forward, first to the Ethiopian eunuch, who was baptized before Cornelius and Paul as a gift to Africa, and from there on to the ends of the earth (Acts 2–8). The implications of this Pentecostal event emerged as its truth was tested out in new situations.

African orthodoxy laid the groundwork for world consent in the third century. Then a remarkably unified consensual understanding of faith sustained through time gained worldwide consent by the fourth century, as seen in the Ecumenical Councils of Nicea and Constantinople.

Even on the day of Pentecost the language of the apostolic teaching was expanding from its primitive Aramaic to the fifteen languages and ethnic identities mentioned in Acts: the Parthians, Medes, Elamites, Mesopotamians, Judeans, Cappadocians, and those from Pontus, Asia, Phrygia, Pamphylia, Egypt, Libya (Cyrene), Rome, Crete, and Arabia. All that happened on the first day of the church, according to Acts 2:9-10.[127]

From these locations and languages the gospel entered into ever-widening streams, conveyed initially by the great international languages of the Greco-Roman world: Greek, Latin, and emerging Syriac. Soon to follow were Coptic, Ge'ez, Tigrinya, Berber, and Arabic.[128] All were spoken on the African continent in the fifth century. In due time there would be hundreds more regional languages in Africa through which people would hear the good news. Each language was addressed by the same Word through the same Spirit. Nothing necessary to salvation was forfeited by translation into these languages.

The general consent of the worldwide laity to Christian truth has never implied that everything could be crammed uniformly into one single language pattern or cultural perspective. The implications of the gospel were expanded, not diminished, by engaging its message in other colloquial languages and regional cultures.

---

126. Lamin Sanneh, *Translating the Message: The Missionary Impact on Culture*, 2nd ed., American Society of Missiology Series (Maryknoll, NY: Orbis Books, 2009).

127. There were at Pentecost "Parthians, Medes, and Elamites; as well as residents of Mesopotamia, Judea, and Cappadocia, Pontus and Asia, Phrygia and Pamphylia, Egypt and the regions of Libya bordering Cyrene; and visitors from Rome (both Jews and converts to Judaism)" (Acts 2:9-10 CEB).

128. Not until about 350 AD was the Arabic script developed by the Aramaic-speaking Nabataeans of Jordan; see http://www.scaruffi.com/politics/arabic.html.

THE LATE ARRIVAL OF WESTERN COLONIAL LANGUAGES IN AFRICA

Africans are aware that the later languages of colonial Africa—Portuguese, Spanish, English, German, French, and Italian—were very late arrivals in the Christian history of Africa when compared to Coptic, Berber, and Ge'ez. Christianity in Africa had ten centuries of indigenous continuity before the Portuguese arrived in Sierra Leone in 1460. Only after Charlemagne did most of the modern romance languages emerge. There is little to no consensual Christian teaching or writing that existed in these romance languages prior to the ninth century. The time frame for these modern western languages amounts to less than one-third of the entire span of centuries in which consensual apostolic teaching was active in Africa.

Africans who imagine that Christianity is essentially a European phenomenon do well to remember that African orthodoxy was intact and indigenized centuries before those colonial languages gave birth to literary traditions. Christians were speaking and praying in Ge'ez a thousand years before the Portuguese missionaries arrived in sub-Saharan Africa.

Today the heirs of eighteenth-century evangelical revivalism and the twentieth-century Pentecostal expansion of those revivals have the same right as do the Orthodox and Catholics to appeal to the same consensual patristic and matristic voices and conciliar teachings.

CROSS-CULTURAL LISTENING FOR CONSENSUS

The worshipping community has never assumed that absolute unanimity is required for general ecumenical consent. Otherwise no question could ever be settled. A small cadre of grumblers could block any ecumenical teaching and unity in Christ. Consent may be perfect among the faithful in the celestial city, but on earth it remains imperfect and always subject to reexamination among the conditions in transit.

All who sincerely wish to benefit by the ancient ecumenical consensus must learn to listen for it with good judgment and fairness. This is less a skill than a gift, but the gift must be received in order to actualize the intent of the gift. That reception requires a heart that trusts in the forgiveness of the Son and the unifying work of the Holy Spirit. Then it becomes attuned to the silent heart of the believing community in all times and places. The good news has not changed through ever-changing languages.

To engage in this kind of consensual reflection demands a receptive mind and a desire to hear the symphony of voices of the best minds of classic Christianity. Those voices that best sing in ecumenical harmony must be listened to attentively and comparatively, with an ear for the whole range of cross-cultural Christian testimony.

Any singer of familiar hymns can readily access the historic consensus. Consensus recognition is not a judgment by an elite literary class but the harmony of the whole people of God, the laity, who consent together to the good news. It is not so hard to recognize. Some voices do not belong in the choir. They quake with uncertain dissonance that makes the faithful cringe. Others seek to sing in harmony with the apostolic witnesses.

When one hears a voice that blends with the saints of all times, its authenticity is easy for the gathered faithful to recognize. They say: "Amen" (so be it).[129] On the other hand, when one hears a voice that may pretend to sing on key, but only imagines itself to be in harmony while remaining at odds with historic consent, the perceptive faithful easily recognize the dissonance.

Where classic consensual Christian reasoning differs from some particular expression of it, the whole is preferred to the part. There is one place where any layperson can learn this way of listening: the language of the liturgy and the songs of the hymnody. Most Christian believers get it.

ENTERING THE SANCTUARY

First it is necessary to drink deeply from the spring of worship, praise, and moral reasoning of the Bible itself and of the cross-cultural generations of faithful teaching. Nothing is more pathetic than an innovator who has failed to listen carefully to the immense varieties of orthodoxy, yet claims to be a leader of the people of God.

If one tries to impersonate the historic consensus without entering deeply into the worshipping community, without singing the hymns of the church, without being immersed in the written Word, without walking daily in the way, without life in Christ, that voice will quickly betray itself with evidences of dissonance. Such discord can never elicit a broad level of lay trust over an extended period of time.

It would be folly to ignore the experience-based authority of those who have years of practiced attentiveness to classic Christian teaching. To hear a corrective, one goes back and listens carefully to the varieties of expression of the one apostolic mission in its beautiful multilingual variations from the east and west, African and Asian, without the slightest loss of unity in the body of Christ.

The imperative is to listen! Within this huge language universe of classic consensual Christianity, allow time for many shades of allowed interpretation. Orthodoxy does not seek only one exclusive interpretation. Special joy can be found in its variety. Yet the variety never loses its link with the first eyewitnesses.

Charity seeks to discover that level at which all share closely in the unity of the one people of God. This unity can only be perceived by watching it go through varied symbol systems and changing cultural memories without misplacing its equilibrium. The orthodox way seeks to make peace between scripture interpreters of different languages, periods, ethnicities, and moral assumptions, yet who share the same faith in the same Lord and the same bread and wine of the same confessing community. Orthodoxy is only forced by persistent error to draw boundaries.

---

129. Rev 7:12.

It is unrealistic to expect anyone to attain a high quality of classic Christian discernment without sustained exposure to the worshipping community with its ancient texts. Those who do not journey within this remembering community are not prepared to measure it. Those who have already decided that there can be no consensus are not in a position to say it cannot be found in the Eucharist.

BEARING WITH MISUNDERSTANDING

Learning to listen to many different cultures and languages is the habit of seasoned orthodoxy. Lacking that habit, it would have turned out to be unbending and rigid. The apostolic requirement was to teach the same good news in all these languages.

Orthodoxy seeks to identify a proximate consensus of the most widely received ancient Christian texts and sources, even while acknowledging that there will be dissenting voices at every turn. When differing interpretations of scripture conflict, the Deuteronomy rule applies. It was repeatedly appealed to by the ancient writers: "Ask your father, he will tell you about it; ask your elders, they will give you the details" (Deut 32:7 CEB). The simple command is: "Don't remove an ancient boundary marker that your ancestors established" (Prov 22:28 CEB). Interpreters who are already captive to a single monolithic modern worldview are far more limited in critical judgment. Those who allow the ancient ecumenical consensus to guide their praying and believing find the orthodox way to be full of gladness and the beauty that reflects the awe of God.

These boundary stones were firmly established in Sinai and Jerusalem and in the early Christian councils as early as the Council of Jerusalem about 46 AD. They endured intact in the continuing memory of the ancient consensual teachers. Those who "rashly seek for novelties and expositions of another faith" are always eventually going to be found wanting by general lay consent.[130]

In listening for the unity that the Holy Spirit is creating, orthodox reasoning must prepare ironically to bear the burden of being caricatured and pushed into whatever particular pigeonhole a puzzled observer finds convenient. This is a yoke to be borne joyfully, with comic sensibilities where possible.

Those who have not been exposed to the prayers, songs, liturgies, and sacred texts of ancient Christian teaching may not grasp its intellectual challenge. Not until one personally tests alternative voices again and again in comparison to the ancient consensus can one become rationally persuaded of the living fact of orthodoxy's historic coherence.

Recognition becomes easier the longer it is practiced. This discernment grows gradually with earnest prayer and scriptural study within a living community in common worship. The unity of Christ's body is becoming more palpably manifest by being held accountable to historic consensus.

---

130. Lateran Council, 649, SCD 274, 105.

B. DISCERNING THE POWER OF THE CONSENSUS

WHY THE CHURCH'S LEADERS ARE CALLED TO SAFEGUARD CONSENSUS RECOGNITION

The worshipping community is both witness and guardian of scriptural truth. The apostolic teaching has been given cohesive form and conveyed through its most consensual and earliest interpreters through a due process of examining scripture. From this deliberation, orthodox views have become embedded in the liturgy, in Christian education, and in pastoral care.

Due process assumes that many voices have already been factored into general consent to apostolic teaching. Only over many generations and cultures do they reflect durable expressions of universal consent. This consent occurred very early on the African continent with clarity and sustainability, even on such difficult questions as the eternal Son of God and the triune teaching, always emerging through the discourse of varied exegetes seeking worldwide consensus. The ancient consensus of the faithful is taken as reliable unless there are compelling reasons to quarrel with it.

Lay consent over centuries has firmly defined and confirmed the consensus. It has proven itself to be cross-culturally durable. The canon of Holy Writ, the rule of faith, the baptismal formula, and the ecumenical councils were all authenticated many times over by general lay consent and thus hold time-honored and reliable authority. They do not have to be rewritten by every gathering of Christians in every village.

Believers are always free to apply reason and conscience in asking the toughest questions of presumed authorities. But as these voices repeatedly radiate the spirit that comes from the center of the worshipping community, gradually the faithful are willing to trust the tested leadership. Genuine ecumenical authority must undergo repeated testing over a period of several centuries in order to retain that level of trust. Breaking the unity of faith is a serious offence when we come before the Lord who enables that unity.

SHIELDING THE TEXTUAL TREASURY OF FAITH

Few would have guessed only a few decades ago that the youngest children of the African churches would now be turning to the oldest African sources.

Paul instructed Timothy to guard what had been committed to him.[131] Timely Christian teaching consists in "what you have received, not what you have thought up; a matter not of ingenuity, but of doctrine; not of private acquisition, but of

---

131.   1 Tim 6:20.

public Tradition; a matter brought to you, not put forth by you, in which you must be not the author but the guardian, not the founder but the sharer, not the leader, but the follower."[132] The community of believers seeks not to invent a new gospel but to proclaim the ancient gospel ever anew, so that "by your expounding it, [the gospel] may that now be understood more clearly which formerly was believed even in its obscurity."[133] When interpreters pretend to improve upon apostolic testimony, it usually comes from tampering with the evidence. The evidence lies in historical observation, conscience, reason, and the presence of the living Lord.

This does not imply that there can be no advances in our ever-inadequate attempts to articulate orthodox teaching. The interpretation of faith progressively unfolds not because it is changing but because our relation with it is maturing. The idea of "progress" in orthodox understanding does not refer simply to change, since a change can be deterioration. True knowledge advances in understanding that which has been already once for all given fully and adequately in the apostolic confession of faith.[134] As God does not change in substance over time, so does the Word of God not change, although it may be reflected differently in changing cultures. Being of the very nature of God, the Holy Spirit "works in others a change to grace, but is not changed Himself." For "How is He capable of change Who is always good?"[135] "Every good gift and every perfect gift is from above, and cometh down from the Father of lights, with whom is no variableness, neither shadow of turning" (Jas 1:17 KJV).

It is rash to think that philosophical imagination or historical inquiry will finally bring the gospel to more perfect clarity than that grasped by the Lord himself, his apostles, and centuries of steady confirmation. Nothing that modern life offers is able to match that continuity of experience. No new proposal can make out of date the apostolic testimony.

Orthodox remembering challenges the idea that the core of Christian teaching changes in substance from culture to culture. That is a common error of modern hubris. The confession of faith does not itself significantly alter from one meaning to an entirely different meaning that contradicts that which the apostles first proclaimed: God became flesh once for all to die for our sins and be raised to new life. We may participate in life in Christ in different ways unique to persons. But it is not the eternal Son who has changed, but our own lives.

Brighter light may be shed by the good news upon present and future generations. Clearer conceptions of its cross-cultural truth may arise. But the light that will come will shine not from human genius but from God, who is the Way, the Truth, and the Light.

---

132. Vincent of Lérins, *Commonitory*, XXII.27.

133. Vincent, *Commonitory*, XXII.27, FEF 3:264–65 (2173)

134. Vincent, *Commonitory*, XXIII.28, FEF 3:265 (2174).

135. Ambrose, *Of the Holy Spirit*, V.65, NPNF 2 X:102; cf. John of Damascus, OF I.9, NPNF 2 IX:12; Thomas Aquinas, SCG, I.13, pp. 86–9.

The written treasure that the Lord has given the church is its scripture. The church may have a passing treasury of temporal goods, but compared to the scriptures the rest is of little value.

THE DEBASEMENT OF UNIVERSITY STUDIES IN RELIGION

The academic study of religion abounds in exaggerated modern worldview prejudices. Its methods allow the modern critic to become doorkeeper of the text. No one can get to the text except as they pay this doorkeeper. The doorkeeper prevents traditional readings of any text that challenges the modern ideological consensus. The doorkeeper allows the sacred text as revealed Word to be buried under the immense sludge of extensive historical analysis.

The Euro-American academic study of religion professes to treat classic African Christianity objectively and fairly. Meanwhile it is unaware of its Eurocentric prejudices toward Africa. Hence it has deprived itself of the African memory of Mark, the aesthetic disciplines of Sketis, the conciliar method of the Councils of Carthage and Alexandria, and the countercultural tenacity of the African saints and martyrs.

Scripture warns against turning over God's word to alien caretakers, reminding us that bad actors always appear as angels of light. "Since, therefore, they cannot make any change in the [scriptural] facts recorded, they bring novel principles and theories of man's devising to bear upon them."[136] Having found the pre-modern text itself irritating and unacceptable, the modern western critics scramble to imagine some novel way of interpreting it.

The special burden of African orthodox scholarship is to answer these illusions truthfully. The African orthodox way is to trust the Holy Spirit to transmit the witness accurately. Studies in the university must be complemented by studies in the worshipping community, where there is more freedom to investigate their historical memory.

DUE HUMILITY IS REQUIRED IN SPEAKING OF ORTHODOXY

The features of modern hubris that are most evident to the orthodox mind are its narrowness, overconfidence, and self-righteousness. The gospel calls for simplicity, meekness, and self-critical restraint.

The preparation to hear the accents of the ancient African Christian mind begins with humility. This requires listening to it speak in its own language and intonations, with empathy toward pre-modern voices. It must be allowed to have its own history, saints, hymnody, and liturgy.

---

136. Hilary of Poitiers, *Trinity*, II:2, NPNF 2 IX:53, translation amended.

This does not happen without empathizing with a distant culture. When we become immersed in the many generations of orthodox life, we better grasp the limits on our own culture.

Orthodox life produced many different expressions in history. Some are more akin to modern values than others. Meanwhile we all remain fallen human beings. Familiarity with only one or two ethnic expressions of orthodox life may lead us to be intolerant with others. It is better to listen to orthodox accents of many different ages and times before judging.

Too quickly we imagine that the frail, tiny modern part we happen to know about orthodoxy gives us a whole picture of orthodox life. Meanwhile classic Christian reasoning is still pointing not to some part but to the wholeness of teaching of the one holy catholic apostolic church.

A type of critical mind is required that is made critical by the history of orthodoxy itself. Critical study and meekness are not opposites but complementary.

By intensive study of the varieties of orthodoxy we learn its deeper habits that transcend its particular cultural expressions. Even when study becomes a lifelong task of discernment, it always falls short, since it is always incomplete. This incompleteness brings us to our knees in grateful humility.

THE POWER OF ORTHODOXY TO RENEW CULTURE

The deep renewal of global Christianity will occur exactly at the point when the rootlessness of modernity drives us to hunger for the guidance of ancient and tested consensual Christian teaching. This simple decision is being blessed by the Holy Spirit.

The ancient African faith can rehabilitate flawed aspects of modern cultures. We know this because it has happened before. Where?

- in the renewal of holy living that began with Anthony of the desert;
- in the ways the African Councils under Cyprian brought peace;
- in the renewal of biblical interpretation that was initiated by Origen;
- in the Augustinian vision of universal history;
- in the defense of the global unity of the church that was embodied by Optatus.

Believers today can be encouraged by previous historical periods in which this renewal has in fact occurred. These seeds are ripe to be harvested.

This begins to happen when we experience the freedom to listen anew to the earliest voices of African Christianity. They speak clearly on law, marriage, the economic order, and human relationships. Each of those categories would require a series of different seminars. The African written tradition has astute wisdom on all these subjects. This wisdom is now being discovered by young African scholars and leaders. African youth are finding unexpected insight from their own earliest African interpreters of human history, psychology, song, poetry, and social process. The African church is filled with the Spirit even when Western Christianity is dispirited.

The faithful people of God, who once appeared so isolated, so vulnerable, are once again gaining confidence in laying hold of the history of their esteemed forefathers and mothers. The bride of Christ herself, the community of faith, who once seemed so abandoned, is again rediscovering her unique relation to the bridegroom, the risen Lord.

Evidences of health and new growth abound among the orthodox, catholic, and Spirit-led people of God. Even amid cultural accommodations and leadership failures, these worshipping communities are re-grounding themselves in the sacred texts of early African Christianity.

C. LEARNING TO SAY NO

After many decades of western moral permissiveness, the African generations dazed by them are now turning toward rigorous moral reflection grounded in African experience that predates both the Arab conquest and European colonialism. The rebirth of African orthodoxy is providing clear and tested moral boundaries that modern relativism and narcissism have little courage to define.

THE RECOVERY OF CHARITABLE ADMONITION

After years of permissive ethics, there is emerging a felt need to rediscover the moral boundaries lost in an era of decadence. There is an avid interest in boundary definition in global Christian teaching. In embracing the gospel of forgiveness, it is important to learn to say no to self-indulgence, despair, malice, and idolatry. A firm No must be said on behalf of the larger Yes of God's grace that sustains societies during periods of gross recklessness. This certainty points beyond our impatience to the patience of God. God has time to allow for changed hearts and lives. The ultimate good news comes from God himself in his incarnate life and atoning death.

The gentle task of Christian teaching is to make peace among the faithful and their cultures, but in doing so the boundaries of faith must be carefully recognized with joy and without regret. To mark these boundaries requires a retrieval of once-available critical skills now being relearned. These boundaries must be marked with humility and firmness. Relativism has run its course.

SPEAKING TRUTH IN LOVE

A strong affirmation requires a clear denial of that which is its opposite. When two views are mutually exclusive, no one can honestly affirm them both. This is why classic Christianity cannot be rightly affirmed without clarifying the behaviors those affirmations necessarily repudiate.

Orthodoxy required the discipline of identifying the boundaries which distinguish the holy life from a life of dissipation that will never be blessed by God. It is foolish to say Jesus Christ is Lord and act as if the ruling cultural majority is absolute. A burnt-out addictive life cannot be life with God, though it may be a prelude to life with God.

Classic Christian teaching requires careful analysis of ancient rejected arguments and perennially false teachings, how they recur, and why they do not make men and women happy. After many decades of secularization, the faithful are relearning how to draw these boundaries. Orthodox teaching gently shows how false teaching cannot be allowed to masquerade as true. Meanwhile peacemaking efforts must show how diverse expressions of apostolic teaching can celebrate the one faith in the one revealed God.

IN SEASON AND OUT OF SEASON

Every battle line against unhealthy reasoning requires robust and persuasive argument. But argument itself must be grounded firmly in a generous conciliatory spirit that understands where the center lies.

Both cultivating and pruning are required to tend the vineyard of the faithful. It is necessary to hoe the garden to help healthy vines take root. To pull out weeds by the roots is a necessary function of a gardener. The garden of which we speak is not the civil political order but the nurture of the healthy Christian community grounded in apostolic teaching. Without a charitable center, the boundary-making task becomes belligerent and prone to smugness. Orthodox life celebrates what lies peacefully inside the borders of faith.

The modern western love affair with relativism and permissiveness has made it easier to seek an uncritical peace rather than defend the truth against attack. There are times when defense of the innocent is required. Ancient African orthodoxy is equipped to assist modern African Christians in their desire for a proper balance.

Conciliatory efforts fall short if they have grounding only in what contemporary believers have in common, ignoring what Christians of many eras and cultures hold in common. The children of permissiveness are ill-prepared for reasoned argument and charitable disagreement with those who hold fast to classic Christian faith.

LEARNING A GENTLE NO ON BEHALF OF A LOFTIER YES

The yes is God's forgiveness. The no is self-denial. It is only when the faithful have the courage to say no that saying yes has moral force. Only when Anthony was willing to say no to his wealth was the monastic movement born. Not until Athanasius unambiguously challenged Arius did the church's faith in the incarnation become clearly defined. The yes to the truth of God does not happen without a tough no to what is falsely opposing.

Young African Christians are relearning how to mark boundaries established through centuries of multicultural experience. Athanasius was told by intended mediators to "back off" and "ease up" and be more sympathetic with the Arians, to view them in relation to their linguistic challenges or psychological histories, and not forget their good intentions. On such a pivotal issue as whether the Son is truly eternal God, Athanasius was wise enough to say, "No way. Never again." He was not the first African Christian mind to mark boundaries but undoubtedly the most forceful and clear.

THE DUTY OF CHARITABLE ADMONITION

We most owe the duty of gentle admonition to those we most love. To those to whom we are closest we owe the greatest duty to bring their missteps to their attention in a loving spirit. This is especially so for those with whom we hold jointly pledged and covenanted responsibilities: spouses, brothers, sisters, children, or partners in promised solemn trust.

To admonish with meekness is a gift of the Spirit. To fail to do so is negligence. Wherever religious leadership has weakened into a cycle of permissive compromise, the faithful laity must answer them clearly and confidently, well-instructed by the ancient Christian consensus, always with empathy and charity.

Where the hearts of solemnly pledged leaders have turned away to idolatry and deception, we first owe them the duty of patience and charity, but in due time we owe them the tougher act of honest conversation and finally confessional truth.

Grace enables persons to speak the truth with love. Modern excesses will be corrected only by courageous tenderness. This requires candor, but the candor must be grounded in the awareness of the mercy of God. Seared conscience and bad faith are the end results of leaving blatant disavowals of faith unchallenged.

When idols are preferred to the One God, the faithful must be clear in saying no. The worshipping community cannot, under the umbrella of toleration, sanction the false teaching that Christ's death has no decisive meaning for humanity. The confession of God Almighty demands a repudiation of those teachings that claim that God cannot be distinguished from creation, that God is ignorant of the future, or that God is finally as limited as we humans are.

D. HONING A CRITICAL ORTHODOXY

CHRISTIAN UNITY IS GROUNDED IN CHRISTIAN TRUTH

Christian unity springs from Christian truth. Unity eludes those who diminish or avoid telling the truth. Healthy orthodoxy calls for the clear rejection of half-truth parading as if the whole truth. This difference requires a discerning critical spirit. It can flourish only through constant alertness precisely at those points where faith is being falsely distorted or threatened. To pretend to be faithful is "like a deadly drug with honeyed wine."[137]

When unbelief sings the same hymns as belief and wears the guise of orthodoxy, the sorting task becomes more difficult. There is a teaching task to be done for those who have not learned the most simple and generally received consensual teachings: God the Father sends God the Son through God the Spirit, who becomes flesh and dies for humanity's sins and is resurrected from the dead, whose Spirit dwells in his people. In every phrase of that summary, African faithfulness is already strong.

Jesus taught that both healthy and polluted fish are in the same pond, the church.[138] They will be sorted out finally, but within finite history they must be distinguished as far as possible. Ordained ministers are specifically called and set apart to protect the community from toxic teachings, yet sometimes they themselves add to the confusion.

The idea has become popular that no boundaries are required either in moral discipline or religious community—an illusion sponsored by good intentions. Healthy freedom sets limits. The idea that freedom opposes limits is a consequential confusion. True freedom lives gratefully within the limits set by finitude and grace.

A community with no boundaries elicits trouble from its neighbors. It is the border that marks the boundary of an ordered space. So it is with a garden, and so with the boundaries of moral tolerance. To eliminate the boundary of the garden is to confuse the idea of a garden.

ON PRETENDING TO DO WITHOUT A CENTER

The conflict with unbelief is a struggle to specify the rightful boundaries of the worshipping community. God's good news is addressed to all who are willing to hear. Those who enter the door of baptism are by that act called to learn what their baptism means.

Those who claim to have no boundaries have not examined the ordering of physical space or individual choice. When all boundary-making is ruled out of bounds, an absurdity lurks. It is the logical inconsistency of making a rigid rule against rules. No reasonable mind could pretend to accept such a ruling. Logically one must recognize the need for some boundary definition lest the truth be lost.

The word *heresy* means that which has been thoughtfully ruled out of bounds by a long history of consent. The task of identifying boundaries is what has traditionally been called the discussion of heresy. We may not like what it is called, but we cannot avoid what it signifies. It means "out of bounds." A soccer match with no boundaries is not a game. At times a Christian mentor must serve as a referee who increases the joy of

---

137. Ignatius, *To the Trallians*, 6, AF 94.
138. Roger Olson, *Counterfeit Christianity: The Persistence of Errors in the Church* (Nashville: Abingdon, 2015), with DVDs.

the game by tending the boundaries and protecting the innocent by calling outs. Those who do not play by the rules or make them up as they go are not playing the game.

Some think it an unsurpassed accomplishment of freedom that all talk of faith's boundaries has been banished in polite discourse. This gives the appearance of perfection in an always flawed community. In modern polite company, it has become unspeakable to speak of heresy. So a polite rule is invented: do not mention the boundaries of freedom. That would be impolite and might offend. This habit has grown into a plague of acquiescence. Jesus would turn over temple tables to prevent such compliance (Matt 21:12; John 2:15).

Wise instruction begins with humility and seeks to bring believers into a harmony with that glory that reflects the unity of the body of Christ. Those who remain adamantly unwilling to examine their flaws have not learned what it means to come with changed hearts and lives to the Lord's Table. If they show up there without repentance, they condemn themselves, as Paul writes: "Those who eat and drink without correctly understanding the body are eating and drinking their own judgment" (1 Cor 11:29 CEB).

Christian heterodoxy becomes nondiscussable in the spin rooms of modern elites. The word *heresy* itself could only be spoken in soft voice, screened through a thousand qualifiers. It is only within the fantasy world of absolute toleration that the very concept of heresy has become unmentionable. This is one of the controlling myths of standard modern worldviews. But what if we do not live in a modern world anymore? What if it is already disappearing? Many have learned that we now live in a period following the demise of the modern ideologies.

Those not captive to flawed modern assumptions are freed to mark boundary stones within the moral order. They are not intimidated by the absurdity that to mark any boundaries at all would be a danger to freedom. The freedom that once existed in public discourse, and then became lost, is now being recovered.

Some would prefer that the apostolic tradition be forever malleable, with no definable shape at all. But this is accomplished only by constantly twisting the sacred texts into forced interpretations that end in bizarre speculations.

Meanwhile the apostolic testimony remains eternally pertinent. In its firmness, it retains an inwardly centered flexibility capable of correcting human folly when and wherever needful.

E. RECOGNIZING ANCIENT BOUNDARY STONES

DEALING WITH ALLERGIC REACTIONS TO BOUNDARIES

The community of faith under the guidance of the Spirit has learned that strife and pride are tamed and purified, not increased, by stating clearly and accurately where rational boundaries lie. Setting boundaries is an act of rational justice. To respect a boundary set by the rules of a game is to honor the game and trust that fair referees will blow whistles when needed.

Some cannot entertain the thought of any boundary definition without immediately rehearsing the most flagrant examples of witch hunts, inquisitions, sexual repressions, involuntary servitude, and the list goes on. Rather than obsess on the civil abuses of *the last five centuries,* the community of believers today is returning to the best wisdom of *the first five centuries* of flourishing consent to apostolic truth. The classic Christian consensus shows gratitude that God has marked clear boundaries between belief and unbelief.

The recurring temptation is to once again embrace the ancient heresies long ago rejected, especially when they reappear under the guise of newness and supposed creativity. African orthodoxy was born under conditions of state persecution when believers were powerless, but that did not silence the faithful. They were willing to speak through their blood if necessary to set more fitting boundaries upon human injustice.

MODERNITY'S "FINAL SOLUTION" TO HERESY

Modernity's fantasized "final solution" to heresy is to imagine that no boundaries exist. This is an act of pure imagination.

There is virtually no dialogue about the idea of heresy, even in places where it might rightfully be a matter of legitimate investigation, like the role of tradition in human bonding, or the social function of continuity, or the history of boundary making. The word *heresy* and all its derivatives are banned. Only silence will do. It must be frozen completely out, with zero tolerance.

What an accomplishment! Religious instruction, after its long record of inventing the university, building libraries and faculties, and struggling against the imbalances of past distortions of the truth, now has come upon this chilling "final solution": suppression of classic Christian teaching and loss of moral borders. This fantasy is proposed as an historical fact, and then imagined to be irreversible.

This we have achieved in the land of eternal permissiveness. The myth of absolute toleration can appear only in a society where a previous generation has had to fight for the rule of law. Absolute toleration ends in either anarchy or tyranny. That intolerance is ironically a reigning ideology in the modern West. That ideology should no longer be a model for African Christian education.

THE OBSESSIVE DREAM OF THE FLAWLESS COMMUNITY

The rhetorical centerpiece of the ideology of absolute tolerance is "inclusiveness." Yet in the name of inclusion, all who are seriously orthodox, catholic, or evangelical are preemptively excluded, wherever the modern myth reigns.

In those places theology is reduced from the study of God to the study of competing perceptions about God. In these quarters it is permissible to speak of language about God, but only within confined bounds, and only if it means something other than a reference to One who is omnipotent and omniscient and final Judge and Incarnate Lord in history. These dear folk are hunted down by the toleration police because they may tend to make uncomfortable someone who is trying to relax in the modern bubble.

Talk of moral boundaries is unofficially banned in some of these spaces—unless you might be thinking of offenses against inclusivism, such as terms that offend against political correctness, like Father or Son, or final judgment or sacrifice. Such terms are excluded.[139]

Of course the Bible is assumed to be still studied more or less within the university, but not with the assumption that it is the living Word accompanied by the inward work of the Holy Spirit in the inward citadel of the heart. Meanwhile it can be read with almost any other premise.

Under the prevailing rules of absolute relativism, all notions of original sin are radically contextualized in terms of psychological, sociological, or economic determinates. Those who think this is an exaggeration may not have recently been to a course in sensitivity training.

These western norms of higher education are already being challenged in Africa. The Christian tradition spawned these universities at a time when it was basically orthodox, but by now they have become plagued with ideological advocacy. Reform can occur, but not without courage and wit.

F. REGAINING EQUILIBRIUM

CONCERNING THAT WHICH IS "OTHER THAN" CLASSIC CHRISTIANITY

The Greek root *hairesis* derives from the metaphor of arbitrary choice. The root meaning of heresy is capricious self-willing. Heterodoxy is to will "other than" (*heteran*) or contrary to the settled historical reasoning confirmed by the intergenerational community of believers. All forms of settled truth are regarded with suspicion.

Hairesis presumes that it is improving upon the apostolic testimony. It defiantly chooses a path presumed better than that of the apostles. In Africa it was promoted by dualistic Gnostics, Arians, adoptionists, and Pelagians, many of whom sincerely

---

139. In popular thesaurus word searches, certain words familiar to Jews and Christians such as *millennialism, circumcision, soteriology, pneumatology, seduction,* and *paganism* cannot be found, as if they did not exist.

believed that they had discovered a better way than that of the apostles as remembered in the consensus of faith. The mistake is "that of the expositor, not of the text."[140]

RECOVERING EQUANIMITY

If heresy is a persistent vertigo exhibiting loss of balance in walking according to the wholeness of faith, sound teaching seeks a good balance in walking in the way of faith. Believers are regaining their composure, temporarily lost amid the excesses of recent decades.

The tendency toward waywardness chooses willfully to depart from the internal cohesion and stable balance of classic Christian teaching. It asserts severed, segmented fragments of religious truth in disconnection or disproportion, so as to lack the wholeness, composure, and confidence of the New Testament faith. Distrust springs out of a *loss of equilibrium* in appropriating the balanced truth of the classic tradition. It carves and slices the wholeness of faith into parts and chooses its own private preferences. These fragments then may so disconnect that they lose all affinity with the wholeness of ancient Christian teaching. In isolation they become unrecognizable.

Bad teaching thrives where some legitimate dimension of faith is elevated out of proportion. It loses balance and proposes the partial view as a new principle of interpretation for correcting the whole pattern of Christian teaching. This results in the denial of the unity and proportionality found in classic Christianity.

THE EMBROIDERY METAPHOR

Think of the power, beauty, and subtlety of ancient Coptic embroidery, where intricate chains of connection make up a single whole design. "The Coptic weavers and embroider[er]s used chain stitch, cross stitch, whipped running stitch, satin stitch, stem stitch and split stitch, pattern designing from the first century AD onwards."[141] These linen tapestries can still be seen in the Coptic Museum in Cairo.

Suppose some self-assured skeptic wanted to improve the design of the embroidery. Suppose the critic focuses on one square inch and says: this is the brilliant aspect of this tapestry, the stitching on the lower right corner. Then out come the scissors. That misses precisely the wholeness of the image which makes it able to convey the pattern of the holy life.

In making its private selection of preferred glimpses of Christianity, the innovator misses the wholeness, internal texture, and socially received reasonableness of the historic consensus of faith.

---

140. Hilary of Poitiers, *Trinity*, II.2, NPNF 2 IX:53.
141. http://www.artwis.com/articles/coptic-embroidery-and-needlework/.

THE TESTED LONGEVITY OF AFRICAN ORTHODOXY SINCE MARK'S GOSPEL

The length of a generation in earlier periods of history, when humans mated younger and life expectancy was shorter, averaged about twenty years. Two thousand years after Mark wrote down the Gospel, quite possibly in Alexandria, there have been over a hundred generations of African Christians. The composure and balance of African orthodox memory has been tested by all the generations since the apostles. Its core is found in the Christology and triunity evident in the Gospel of Mark where God the Father offers his Son through the power of the Spirit.

The accumulating balance of consent to Mark's Gospel has increased with each generation. Its reliability has been confirmed as valid testimony by each successive generation of Africans. Mark's Gospel portrays Jesus as truly human, truly God. From the first verse he writes: "The beginning of the good news about Jesus Christ, God's Son" (Mark 1:1 CEB).[142] Many have been willing to die to guard that testimony and attest its truth. The conditions of modern life have not changed his testimony.

The wisdom of early African Christianity emerged very soon in rigorous language study on the meanings of Hebrew and Greek words. African writers were especially detailed in their scrupulous comparison of prophetic and apostolic testimonies. This method was first explored in depth in Africa by Origen and Didymus the Blind, and later dispersed throughout the Christian world.

THE UNINTENDED PROVIDENTIAL CONTRIBUTION OF HETERODOXY TO ORTHODOXY

Heresy has never been regarded as entirely beyond the bounds of providence. Nothing is. Classic Christian teaching looks for the providential design lying hidden within the divine permission that paradoxically allows the faithful to struggle with false teaching and grow from that testing.

Providence permits bad teaching to emerge out of fallen freedom in order to strengthen good teaching through the community's grasp of the wholeness of faith. The unintended positive contribution of heretics to the formation of orthodox consensual teaching is that they challenge faith to think through smaller partial views and answer them with larger whole views.

The faithful of two millennia have marveled at God's providential working even through the objections of the heresies. A stronger faith has emerged by being challenged. The Council Fathers concluded that the faith is "defended with the best results when a false opinion is condemned even by those who have followed it."[143]

---

142. These are the kinds of phrases that form critics wish to remove from the earliest canon.
143. Ecumenical Council of Chalcedon, NPNF 2 XIV:258

There is good reason today, as in past centuries, to reexamine the ancient heresies carefully in order to understand clearly how they are fragmented elements of truth. Within classic African orthodoxy, the reasons for false teaching have been as rigorously studied as the reasons for true teaching. The two inquiries belong together, always intertwined.

Here is a point where providence and comic perception intersect. Since comedy depends upon unexpected contradiction, every good surprise outcome of a dubious act has a comic quality.

Human will is always tempted to fall. When new false teachings appear, usually they turn out to be the old ones reinvented. Young African believers have the great privilege of being able to appeal to Africa's earliest historical memory of these struggles in applying them today.

DISTINGUISHING SCHISM, APOSTASY, AND HERESY

Wherever heresy leads to a breach of unity in the community of believers, it is called schism. This may signify either strife within the community or actual separation from it. Faith ceaselessly works for the reunion of the divided body of Christ on the basis of the revealed Word as ecumenically received. In the rebirth of African orthodoxy the hope is to avoid schismatic temptations and pray for the unity of the body of Christ through the power of the Spirit.

Apostasy, which is different from schism, refers to a falling away from an earlier confession of faith. It points to some substantial failure to remember the gospel as it was delivered. It is a failure to recognize the truth embodied in one's baptism. Apostasy is most disturbing when asserted by ordained ministers who voluntarily have been commissioned and have solemnly covenanted to defend the faith, yet neglect or rail against apostolic teaching.

At times the stable lay leadership of the worshipping community has a better sense of orthodox equilibrium than those who have been chosen to lead. The clergy do well to trust the instincts of the faithful laity.

Anyone can join the gathered faithful in singing the songs of the church, praying its prayers, and sharing in its charitable acts. Those best grounded in these hymns and prayers and acts of mercy are often quickest to spot it when the leadership is tempted to unbridled novelties or dull forgetfulness, or to schismatic impulses.

The laity are puzzled by heresy. It is not the song they were taught to sing. They can see that some proposals run counter to the faith they received in their baptism. This is the irony: The clergy sometimes betray their promises to the laity, the very ones most vulnerable to being hurt, when they do not guard the integrity of classic Christian teaching. The Epistle to the Hebrews anticipated this falling away, and its remedy: We need "someone to teach [us] an introduction to the basics about God's message" (Heb 5:12).

THE TIMELY REVULSION AGAINST WESTERN PERMISSIVENESS

There was a time when prudery, Victorian sexual rigidity, and priggish scruples needed to be rejected in order to break through to a deep affirmation of God's gifts to females and males of the joy of sex and the bonding it creates and encourages. That rejection occurred. Now is not such a time. Rather the pendulum has swung fiercely to the opposite side, where covenant fidelity in sexual bonding cries out to be reasserted.

Those who look only to here-and-now satisfaction never get it. Lasting only a moment, its consequences may persist for generations. They could avoid such anguish by listening to classic Christian wisdom. After decades of sexual experimentation, there is today a revulsion against permissiveness. Most have seen enough of it. We have seen its devastation on families, marriages, and children. It is a commonsense recognition of the outcomes of tasteless indecency, coarse vulgarity, and unconstrained indulgence that pretends to be trendy. The great tradition of African music has suffered from this imported coarseness.

The rediscovery of legitimate boundaries to faith is becoming a central feature of the rebirth of Christian moral life. Christianity in Africa is increasingly gaining the courage to ask where more humane boundaries are to be found in the old religion.

It always takes more time to correct than make a serious blunder. At times the church must come to hard repentance over an accumulated chastisement for decades of unexamined recklessness. Religion cannot befriend moral pollution without costs.

Those who do not know any history are most likely to repeat it. Each repetition is more costly. Meanwhile they continue to imagine that their problems are unprecedented. They complain that they are the first in history who have ever had to face basic challenges.

G. RECENTERING FAITH

WHY THE CHURCH'S LEADERS ARE CALLED TO GUARD CONSENSUS RECOGNITION

In the New Testament the superintending shepherds of the body—the *episcopoi* (bishops or overseers)—are those to whom the defense of the faith is especially and solemnly committed.[144] They represent the unity of both the historic and present community of faith. As they bear responsibility for guardianship of the faith, they defend it against error, and guide the whole people of God toward undiluted apostolic teaching as understood consistently from its earliest witnesses.

---

144. Free church traditions also have superintenents, not called bishops, but overseeing the church.

When leaders teach contrary to faith or fail to guard the faith, the offense becomes damaging to the whole body. The flock looks to the shepherd for its defense, and when it is absent they are understandably bewildered. It is intensely disappointing and disgraceful when those assumed to stand in the tradition of the apostles fall into blatantly contrary teaching.

Just being an ordained leader does not guarantee that one has the gift of nurturing the church in the unity that is offered in Christ. There is a strong presumption that any church leader will be honestly accountable to classic Christian teaching. Little if anything will be set right until the larger body of believers insists that its highest leaders avidly guard Christian teaching.

When deceptive voices seem most persuasive and even temporarily triumphant, the Spirit does not cease to work among them to correct and regain the peace of the community of faith. The Spirit is not rushed, for God's justice has plenty of time. Conflicts which once seemed to display irreconcilable differences may be resolved when divisive passions diminish.

THE REFORM OF FALLEN CLERGY

How far should those who mock historic affirmations of ancient African Christianity be left uncontested? Patience and tolerance are great virtues that have been long nurtured in the worshipping community.

God's patience with sinful humanity is long and merciful, but those who go astray are not forever left uncorrected, as we see in the history of Israel. God gets fed up with sin. Only by God's great mercy does it continue at all, allowing a time for repentance.

Well-intentioned candidates for ministry often come to theological education strongly motivated to study the self-disclosure of God according to scripture. I have seen them come and go. This is my world. To their surprise these young men and women often find themselves instead sitting at the feet of those who inwardly detest classic Christianity. The fair-minded know that this must and will end. But by what means? By re-grounding of theological education in the good news that has called forth the worshipping community.

It is the clergy into whose hands the laity have solemnly entrusted themselves and their faith. When persons in the clergy have fallen farther away from faith than the laity, then laypersons rise to the occasion of reminding where the center lies.

The worshipping communities have a legitimate interest in ensuring the clergy's apostolic guardianship role. They are discovering that they cannot afford to bless clergy who are seduced by error and fantasy. Those to whom ministry has been entrusted have voluntarily given up their right to teach conjectures that defy settled Christian doctrine. False teachers can no longer be presumed to have unlimited license to teach anything they please in the church. The church has its own conscience shaped by walking with Christ.

The faithful are not gullible. They have a decisive interest in the quality of the leadership they are asked to trust as apostolic, holy, catholic teaching. Today good stewards of the church resources are taking an increased interest in the causes and activities they support.

RECENTERING FAITH

Ancient Christianity has a unique center: the One God who creates, redeems, and brings history a fitting consummation. The persistent divisions in Christianity have cast doubt upon the idea that the church is one in Christ. Christian teaching has a center but it has been obscured. Now it is rediscovering its center.

Western churches have exported to Africa a divided Christianity. Lacking the deep historical memory and theological bearings of early African Christianity, the western exports have become a wild playground for political and sexual liberations and utopian social experiments. Young African believers are looking deeper into their own African roots on African soil for correctives. They are finding that some of the most astute interpreters of scripture arose in the earliest African Christian centuries. These communities spawned the leadership of great minds like Athanasius and Augustine. Those who have experienced a lack of unity in the one body of Christ are now turning to ancient African teaching in the search for unity of humanity in the incarnate Son of God, the new Adam. "In the same way that everyone dies in Adam, so also everyone will be given life in Christ." (1 Cor 15:22 CEB).

RECLAIMING LAPSED INSTITUTIONS

The institutions of which we speak are not only local churches, but also schools, regional conduits of leadership, and mission agencies. A common classic vision shared by catholic, orthodox, reformed, and charismatic believers is gradually repossessing those divided church institutions that have fallen into forgetfulness. Orthodox voices are exercising increasing influence within congregations previously written off as incurably willing to accommodate to culture.

They do not dance to the tune of the relativists or identify with perishing worldviews. African youth who do not view themselves as being in any way connected, even sentimentally, to North American old-line traditions are the leaders in this transformation.

What a great work God the Spirit is doing among the faithful within these congregations. They are finding that confessors of apostolic faith can form a plausible accord which effectively resists the temptations to waywardness. They can unite with trustable and doable efforts to reclaim the wandering communities of faith to theological integrity and acts of mercy. They can set a new trajectory that will not slide toward either heterodoxy or moral imprudence.

The renewing and confessing believers in Africa are beginning to find their voice. These existing churches are like a sleeping giant still capable of once again inhabiting their earlier memory of orthodox belief. Much would be lost by the collapse of these institutions. Orthodox believers are not just walking away from them, but working to reform them.

The orthodox mind views these present dilemmas in a very long historical perspective, not merely in relation to a specific political problem or legislative action. They look not simply to a decade or generation but to twenty centuries of an established consensus of faith. They know the power of the Holy Spirit. They have reason to believe they can reclaim their sleeping institutions. They have good reason to call other believers to pray for their efforts to center the church.

ON FURTHER DIVIDING THE CHURCH

The one body of Christ is sternly warned by scripture against schism. They dare not further divide the church which has suffered enough already under the divisiveness of ideological advocates who presume to speak for the future of Christianity.

No one hears the gospel without some community to convey it. None are flawless. To quit contending for the faith in these flawed communities is to hold cheap the baptismal vow. Purists and perfectionists are tempted to slide into a despairing act of abandonment of communities and institutions to which their forefathers and mothers have long given blood, sweat, prayers, and tears, and through which the apostolic teaching has been transmitted. These institutions can be reclaimed to their deeper apostolic roots.

To quit prematurely is often to leave behind mounting problems the quitter is unwilling to help solve. The churches need loyal and steady critics more than purists, loners, or deserters.

The faithful in these institutions have remained voiceless long enough. They stand in need of articulate biblical reasoning and wise prudent action to counter unwise teaching. Lack of lucid argument reinforces the stereotype that classic Christianity is incoherent and ignorant. If we abandon the church we have, we may find that we have no place to stand in stating the case plausibly. The thin air of pure ideas is not as reformable as actual historical institutions that yearn to be centered.

Though we respect and empathize with those who have found the reform of their congregations virtually impossible, there is good reason to believe that we stand in a moment of opportunity to reengage and bring fresh energies to the wandering church.

The Holy Spirit is working to renew the church with all of its flaws. Confessing Christians are being invited to become an active part of this renewing work of the Spirit. Those who walk away are like parents leaving a family in distress just at a time when a fresh new start is possible. The Holy Spirit has called us to pray for the church that brought us to faith and to remain as agents of witness and reconciliation within them.

TAKING SERIOUSLY INSTITUTIONAL FORGETFULNESS

When property is stolen, its owners usually have just cause to inventory precisely what has been lost. A legal due process then follows for making an accurate claim for its recovery.

Faithful laypersons are now attempting fairly to assess such a claim. The social justice issues among liberals have lost much of the classic memory. These believers are respectfully asking that their historic properties be returned—not only the ideas that the church has shepherded for generations but also the tangible endowments for Christian educational purposes, libraries, and missional institutions.

Laypersons have watched some of their finest religious institutions erode and disappear. Little will be recovered until lay leaders gain the courage to speak the truth in love. Especially in need of correction are the huge endowments gifted by the faithful but used for faithless ends. Where courage is lacking to do this correction, the problems will grow more entrenched.

Most laypersons have trusted their leadership and institutions. It is only when they have been repeatedly disappointed by those in whom they have trusted that their frustration arises. Often it is their own ordained and credentialed leadership that has most disappointed them. No one should be surprised when the injured ask the injurers to return what has been taken and abused. If they depend for financial support upon orthodox believers, they must be accountable to orthodox believers.

H. CUTTING THROUGH THE RHETORIC

WHY INSTITUTIONS WEDDED TO MODERNITY BECOME WIDOWS AFTER THE DEATH OF MODERNITY

Religious institutions wedded to modernity have become widows with the dying of modernity. Worshipping communities are now extracting themselves from the desperate desire of a generation of leaders who wanted to be *totally liberated from classic Christianity*. The institutions designed to guard orthodox teaching—ordination, episcopacy, and preparation for ministry—have been co-opted under the ploy of innovation.

Sadly, the religious community that fastens itself parasitically on the latest movement in current culture does not easily survive the collapse of that movement. When its host is dead, the parasite loses its nourishment.

Just at the moment when modern exaggerations are collapsing, those who think of themselves as most up-to-date are being abruptly outdated. They are the last to recognize the rebirth of orthodoxy.

THE DESPERATE MODERN DESIRE TO BE FULLY LIBERATED FROM CLASSIC CHRISTIANITY

The liberators who stand on the shoulders of many previous generations typically refuse to recognize that they depend upon classic Christianity even in their rejection of it. Some consider most ancient Christian moral traditions oppressive. They fancy themselves as free from traditional constraints of all sorts, all past oppressions, and all old ideas. They think of themselves as socially compassionate, morally non-judgmental, theologically flexible, sexually tolerant, politically visionary, and above all economically innocent. Now they must cope with a wholly unexpected situation: the decline of modernity itself.

The orthodox pray for the return of these wanderers, who have virtually no immune system against heresy, no criteria for weighing or even testing out the legitimacy of counterfeit religious currency. The faithful laity, who have long delayed gentle admonition, must now enter the conflicted arena of rebuilding, healing, and re-grounding religious discipline as they enter the freedom of life in God.

POST-MODERN PALEO-ORTHODOXY

The spirit of orthodoxy is embodied in the student who has been through the rigors of education, through the storms of political engagement, through the fixations of popular therapies, and through a dozen sexual messianisms, and some into the hazards of drug experimentation. Through all this they have at last become weary of the garish motions of frenetic change.

Finally they have come on Christ's living presence in the world in an actual community of practicing Christians. They now have set out to understand what has happened to them in the light of the classical texts of scripture as understood by its earliest interpreters. This is the agenda for theology in the twenty-first century.[145] They are preparing the post-colonial Christian community for its third millennium by returning again to the careful study and respectful following of the central tradition of classical Christianity.

This is truly the postmodern agenda, but ironically the polar opposite from what western intellectuals have been calling postmodern. I introduced the term "post-modern paleo-orthodoxy" in the 1970s to describe my best PhD students who were yearning for an articulate orthodoxy. It was only later, after the mid-1980s, that Foucault, Derrida, Fish, and Rorty began to use the term *postmodern* with a

---

145. Thomas C. Oden, *Agenda for Theology* (San Francisco: Harper and Row, 1979).

weaker, thinner, hyped definition of modern thought. Postmodern became modern on steroids. It belatedly caught the imagination of ultramodern liberal academics in literary and critical theory. Only then did the popular press catch sight of the ironic idea of postmodern. The journalists fell hook, line, and sinker for a bloated definition of *postmodernity* as *ultramodernity*. Since then the media elites have controlled this definition, and it has intruded itself upon university religious studies.

Reborn African orthodoxy rejects deceptive language ploys. Classic African Christianity has a strong hand to play in this situation, since it is armed with a deep historical memory. Hence it is sturdier than those who try to live without that memory. It is a pathetic ploy to treat modernity as permanent when it is bleeding in its vital parts.

The actual rebirth of African orthodoxy points modestly away from pretended newness toward what is most ancient with no pretenses of gaining points with decaying modern intellectual trends. The humble rebirth of the orthodoxy we are describing is instead happening in the worshipping communities without press management, and without seeking the praise of the knowledge elites.

Journalists have not grasped this irony. It has not been investigated. Secular postmodernity is like a moth circling ever closer to the flame of instant fad death.

SEMINAR 10
REDISCOVERING CLASSIC ECUMENICAL METHOD

The single defining primary text of ancient orthodox consensual method was written by Vincent of Lérins around 432 AD. He himself was a pilgrim, a traveler, and a very mobile observer, and it is likely that he either visited the Egyptian communities of holy men and women or heard reports of them through travelers like Egeria, Jerome, Martin of Tours, and John Cassian.

Vincent's recollection was an Act of Remembering, or *Commonitory*, that is still pertinent to classic Christian remembering today.[146] It is fitting for African leaders to reexamine this way of recollecting which had its deepest roots in the cities and wide spaces of Africa before 400 AD. Vincent's brilliant analysis remains the most astute explanation of the method of consensus formation of the first millennium.

A. AN AID TO REMEMBERING

Christians are quietly relearning how to think consensually in classic terms. But how is this consensus discovered? This requires telling a story.

THE CLASSIC METHOD OF RELIABLE REMEMBERING

Shortly after the Council of Ephesus in 431 an obscure but well-informed Christian monk withdrew from a very active life of travel into a monastery off the southern coast of France. We know him only as Vincent. In the monastery he began to summarize what he had learned about the classic consensus method for discerning the

---

146. For a more complete analysis of the Vincentian Method, see Thomas C. Oden, *Classic Christianity*, Epilogue.

truth. He picked a beautiful, quiet spot, offshore from the city of Cannes, on a tiny island known as Lérins. If Cannes symbolizes the bold, hyper-modern film industry, Lérins symbolizes the quiet reflection on the earliest ways of identifying the ancient consensus on the hardest questions of theology.

The monastery founded by Honoratus at Lérins in 410 AD became the first center of monastic spirituality and inquiry in the Mediterranean linking two continents, Europe and Africa. It focused on spiritual counsel, ascetic exercise on the holy life, and the global Christian conversation. On this quiet island, more than anywhere else, the vital energies of early Egyptian monasticism (roughly 320–430 AD) were transmitted to Europe by key figures such as Honoratus, Rufinus, Egeria, and especially Palladius, who lived nine years in Africa, visiting the monastic communities of the upper and lower Nile and writing about it. They were all reporting back to the European and Palestinian teachers about those amazing ascetics in the Egyptian desert who were serious about pursuing the holy life.

Vincent the traveler was among those who came to this little island for spiritual rejuvenation. The ascetic models at Lérins were the earliest African spiritual athletes: Anthony, Athanasius, Macarius, and the Desert Fathers and Mothers.

It is likely that Vincent himself had some form of firsthand information of the intense debate leading up to the decisions made at the Third Ecumenical Council at Ephesus (431 AD), where the complex biblical and liturgical issues of Nestorian teaching were debated. They were about how to make proper distinctions between Christ's human and divine natures and whether Mary should be called *Theotokos* (God-bearer). It is a likely but unproven hypothesis that Vincent himself may have attended the Council, and it is entirely plausible that he knew key figures who attended. His act of remembrance shows evidence of being a report on the ecumenical method that preceded Ephesus.

VINCENT OF LÉRINS'S WAY OF CONSENSUAL RECOLLECTION

The ancient ways of gathering consensus on contested scriptural passages were under intense investigation. These same ancient texts, methods, and decisions of global consensus are still being actively revisited in our time. Much of this investigation occurred first in Africa, with figures like Origen, Athanasius, Didymus the Blind, and Augustine leading the way.

Today young African women and men are pursuing a profound reexamination of how the ancient consensus itself was formed in the early Christian centuries, how African teachers shaped it, and of how the same methods remain viable today.

The contemporary revival of the Vincentian rule is closely interwoven with the rebirth of global orthodoxy. Vincent shows how scripture repeatedly reawakens the tradition-bearing community and how the Spirit guards right remembering of scripture.[147] It is a window into the process of classic Christian identity formation as understood by the ancient church.

Africa is the place where the orthodox consensus was first made secure for global Christianity through the efforts of Cyprian in the west and Athanasius in the east. Lérins is the place where the way to consensus was first clarified. The orthodox consensus had been known and practiced before Lérins, but it awaited Vincent for its clearest formulation. The method of Lérins could not have been defined without the previous labors of Origen, Athanasius, and Anthony of Africa. Vincent provided a clear description of how orthodoxy was born and sustained.

WHEN, WHERE, AND WHY THE COMMONITORY WAS WRITTEN

Vincent's short book might be entitled a *Recollection of a Wanderer*,[148] containing a way of remembering so as to avoid nonconsensual errors. Vincent himself is the wanderer, the peregrine, the soaring bird that circles high above the vast land and surveys it. He identifies himself only as a traveler, a pilgrim, an outsider, a foreigner. Aside from this enigmatic signature, we know little of him except what can be inferred from his text.[149]

He reveals straightaway why he is writing this study: Christians need to learn how the classic Christian consensus was first discerned, so that it can serve as an *aid to recollection* today. It is addressed to anyone who wants to think with the whole community of believers under the authority of scripture about the apostolic testimony so as to fend off odd and idiosyncratic views of scripture.

Vincent is not writing about doctrine per se, but rather about the process by which right doctrine is conceived. His study is more like a sociologist gathering information on how consensus has been gained. Vincent is not remembered for any particular doctrine he defined or defended, but rather solely for the method of discerning its reliability.

Vincent has in his possession a torrent of information issuing from the Third Ecumenical Council, whose decisions were reaffirmed by African Christians both Coptic and Latin. He condenses the process into a compact systematic statement of classic consensual method. He shows strong evidence of having been engaged in an extensive conversation with church leaders of Antioch, Alexandria, and Rome.

Picture him in his monastic cell or a scriptorium with notes and manuscripts strewn around: He seeks to discern the central intent of the mind of the believing

---

147. This final chapter sets forth the flip side of our argument for doctrinal boundaries in Seminar 9. We now focus on irenics rather than polemics.

148. *Commonitorium*, under the pseudonym *Peregrinus*, or "traveler, itinerant observer."

149. Vincent's feast day is May 24, the same day as Wesley's Aldersgate experience in 1738, when his heart was "strangely warmed" by the reading of Luther on Romans. Wesley would later write on "The Catholic Spirit."

church. He listens carefully to the varieties of cultural voices within worldwide Christianity.

He describes himself as having been "long involved in various unstable and saddening whirlpools of secular strife."[150] What was this secular context? The Hun tribes were threatening the peace of the church and the empire all across the northern perimeter of the Mediterranean, steadily encroaching toward the New Rome.

The worldwide Christian community stretching from Spain to India struggled for proximate unity amid enormous historical diversity. Vincent evidently knew, all too painfully, the strife of that world. He sought the widest database possible. He would have encountered it in Ephesus.

All his initial attention focuses on this simple question: If believers quote scripture with different meanings, who is to decide? How do believers who understand scripture in differing ways come to the truth of Christianity in a way that can be validated by global Christianity so as to transcend mere cultural and linguistic variables and private opinions?

In the quiet of Lérins, France's monastic island closest to the African vortex, Vincent had a chance to stand at a distance from these whirlpools, taking ample time in a serene place to recall accurately the complex process of ecumenical consent. Having been out there on the seas of historical struggle, he is grateful now to be safely in this silent harbor to reflect on his journeys. He seeks to account meticulously for the deliberative process by which the heart of what has been generally received as unchanging apostolic faith has been defined, especially under conflicted conditions.

As he stands before God, he writes of his distinct calling to remember accurately. He hopes to prevent time from snatching away the specific contours of his memory immediately following the Council of Ephesus.

At Lérins nothing distracts him. He can daily practice that which is sung in the liturgy. He can be still and know God. There he can draw together these varied threads from this vast experiential database. As he takes pen in hand, he is especially concerned about the integrity of his task as an historian and truthful remembering in the presence of God. It is as if this remembering process takes place in a divine theater with God as the primary if not sole auditor.

Underneath this remembering there is a crucial premise: the Holy Spirit has promised to help believers remember accurately. The Holy Spirit is the Advocate, "whom the Father will send in my name, [and who] will teach you everything and will remind you of everything I told you" (John 14:26). Vincent is living in a community of prayer and faithful remembrance. This was not an exercise of private opinion or ecstatic vision. Rather there is a reliable process that can be objectively and dispassionately observed, reported, and described.

---

150. Vincent, *Commonitory*, ch. 1, FC 7:268.

THE CONTEMPORARY REVIVAL OF THE VINCENTIAN METHOD

My purpose is to set forth a concise account of Vincent's calm description of that process of conciliar deliberation, definition, and decision. I present this not merely as a history that means nothing to me. Rather his conclusions touch the heart of what I also believe. It describes what I have come to regard as most eminently trustworthy in scriptural testimony, for I also live within this worshipping community, as one baptized within it and willing to die for its truth.

For Vincent the worst possible outcome is that he might remember poorly. He imagined his work falling into the hands of godly persons who have a more intimate knowledge than he. He was worried about not receiving their vindication.

He was not attempting to address the general intellectual culture or the civil order but those who already best know the faith. Hence this is less an apologetic exercise intended to convince unbelievers than a recollection of and for believers already convinced.

Vincent had no thought or aspiration to teach the faithful what they already know. Rather he was simply trying to state accurately just how they came to know it so firmly as to warrant their complete trust. His own opinions, inclinations, and impulses do not appear within this frame. He does not set forth his own subjective feelings about the process; rather he sets forth the historic church's recollection of how it has gained consensus on the apostolic testimony to God's matchless revelation. Hence we know almost nothing of his biography. We barely know his name. Yet we walk away from his recollection with a very clear picture of the process he is describing.

HOW VINCENT DISCOVERED THE RULE BY OBSERVATION

Vincent reveals that he had long been engaged in what we today would call an empirical inquiry, a careful sampling process, something like a poll or interview research. He had been deliberately inquiring of many believers, especially those well-grounded in holy living, about this simple question: *How does the global Christian community come to distinguish the truth of Christian faith from falsehood amid conflicted opinions?*

Since he had being traveling widely among diverse cultures, meeting with confessors, bishops, theologians, ascetics, and articulate laypersons, he asked the faithful everywhere he went: Is there a reliable way to sort out wheat from chaff when believers differ? Suppose I wanted to look for a reliable rule that would distinguish fraudulent expressions of faith from true faith. How would I find it?

He was astonished at his survey. Virtually every believer had the same core answer. Its short form had two parts: (a) scripture and (b) the central tradition that guards scripture. But to say only that would oversimplify.

This short answer led him to inquire further with believers: If we have scripture, why do we even need a continuing teaching tradition? Isn't the scriptural canon itself complete? Isn't it sufficient for salvation? What more needs to be said? Why then do we need councils and contemporary Christian teachers if we have scripture?

Answer: All agreed that the apostolic writings were the rule of faith for Christians of all subsequent times. That had been well established before his time. Every patriarchate jurisdiction (Antioch, Alexandria, and Rome) possessed a list of writings that were permitted to be read in church, the scriptural canon,[151] the register of writings recognized east and west and south as fit for public worship. Earlier Athanasius in his Thirty-Ninth Festal Epistle, 367 AD, had clarified the scriptural canon in a way that became a widely received pattern for consensus formation.

But not everyone fully concurs on what canonical scripture as a whole conclusively teaches. Key areas of disagreement remain on the particular interpretations of many sacred texts concerning the mystery of the incarnation and on plausible ambiguities within those texts, as well as on ways of comparing those texts. If Valerius reads it one way, Arius another, Eunomius, Sabellius, and Pelagius in other ways, how can one know who comes closer to the truth of the text?

The trend of the interpretation of the prophetic and apostolic texts must be understood in accordance with some general rule, plausible across varied cultures of the church universal as to what constitutes the mind of the believing church.

But what is that rule? Again the answer rang clear from all whom he asked. This has become known as the Vincentian rule: *In the worldwide community of believers every care should be taken to hold fast to what has been believed everywhere, always, and by all.* (Its Latin form reads: *quod ubique, quod semper, quod ab omnibus creditum est*).[152] This short answer came from the hearts of virtually everyone Vincent interviewed. So this is not a rule that Vincent invented, but one that he acknowledges was widely understood long before his inquiry, that he sought only to articulate accurately.

EVERYWHERE, ALWAYS, AND BY ALL

Classic Christian teaching holds fast to what has been believed and consented to around the world by Christians of all times and places. If you know that, you can rest assured that you are following orthodox faith. Three Latin words—*ubique* (everywhere), *semper* (always), *omnibus* (by the free consent of all) sum up the ancient ecumenical method of scriptural discernment. The direction and momentum of interpretation is guided by a process of fair-minded historical inquiry aided by the

---

151. By the fifth century largely undisputed.
152. Vincent, *Commonitory*, ch. 2.

Holy Spirit into what has been believed in all cultures where faith has been lived out and believed since the beginning of the apostolic witness, and believed by general lay consent in the whole church over the whole world in all generations.

These three criteria are summarized in three terms: *universality, antiquity, and conciliar consent*:

1. It must be the same faith that the church confesses the world over (universality).

2. It must be the same faith confessed by the apostles (antiquity).

3. It must survive testing by cross-cultural generations of general lay consent (conciliar consent).

If it passes these three tests, it indeed expresses the mind of the believing church. So it is to be believed as trustworthy. Whatever fails these tests may still be open to ecumenical debate, but cannot be confidently termed Christianity, whether in Africa, Asia, or Europe, the three known continents of that time.

When any assertion claims to be Christian, the faithful can examine its reliability with these three questions: (1) Does this opinion echo out of a particular locale, or is it shared generally by the whole community of believers around the world? Thus the first criterion is universality. (2) Is this claim something new or the old intergenerationally received faith? This criterion is apostolic antiquity. And (3) Has this teaching been confirmed by a worldwide ecumenical council, or by the broad consensus of the ancient Christian writers? Do we have a documentary tradition of the consenting laity generally affirming those conciliar decisions?

Truth-telling within Christianity takes place within three arenas: *a space frame, a time frame, and a fairly ordered consenting process*. It has a cross-cultural sociology and geography—*everywhere*! It moves through all times following the ancient apostolic witnesses—*always*! It is constantly being tested out by a fair-minded, comparative, deliberative process under contrary challenge—by all the faithful!—not clergy alone but the whole laity—*conciliar consent!*

CLASSIC CHRISTIANITY HOLDS FAST TO WHAT HAS BEEN BELIEVED

Presented graphically the rule looks like this:

Everywhere	Always	By All
Cross-Cultural Space	Intergenerational Time	Fair Deliberative Process
Universality	Antiquity	General Consent

The received faith has won agreement at all three levels: spatial range, temporal continuity, and fair deliberative consent. If so, it can be assured to be reliable Christian truth.

It is fair to ask whether this consent requires absolute unanimity. It is seldom if ever possible within any historical process to obtain an absolute one hundred percent agreement, nor is it required. Every important question has been contested. Only those scriptural interpretations that have been disputed are here under examination. Vincent sought not an absolute or unanimous perfectionism that never occurs in history but a reverberation of harmony among the great cloud of witnesses. Christian consensus is less a vote than a vibe.

Can believers, using these three criteria, summarize briefly and surely what Christians believe? The answer to this must emerge clearly from general lay consent, having been confirmed over many generations. This we already have received textually from the earliest times, for example, in the concise earliest baptismal rule of faith learned upon entry into the believing community, and in the earliest creeds, such as the Apostles' Creed. It sufficiently expresses the same ancient ecumenical faith into which all Christians are baptized.

At its zenith the great city of Rome came as close as anywhere to symbolize universality in Christian antiquity. The Apostles' Creed is known as the Old Roman Symbol. Its triune structure substantively corresponds to the same faith as that of the Nicene-Constantinopolitan Creed, and the Quicunque Vult (sometimes called the "Athanasian" Creed). These are the "three creeds" that have enjoyed the widest ecumenical consent over the longest period of time, east and west.

To answer in greater detail why Christians believe what they believe requires a larger database of historical information going beyond this baptismal summary to how the Holy Spirit has led the community of believers into general consent to God the Father, God the Son, and God the Holy Spirit—One God.

While all Christians have access to this familiar summary of baptismal faith, and closely analogous forms of it, not every lay believer has the time or interest to investigate its history systematically as an historian might. Each believer is assured of the trustability of the core memory of the meaning of baptism.

B. FOUR HISTORIC PROTOTYPES OF CRISES OF CONFIDENCE IN GENERAL CONSENT

Vincent examines case studies of four crucial historical crises, showing how issues have actually been resolved with these clear criteria.

Already by 431 AD, the worshipping community had undergone a series of major crises in the process of testing the reliability of tradition transmission. Vincent explores each of these four as decisive model cases—each beginning with "what if?" Each reveals the providential path by which, in actual history, the faithful have gained confidence in the consenting process. These four profound challenges were sufficient to bring the truth of Christianity into greater clarity—case by case. Each represents a threatened breakdown in the consenting process. Once solved, each resolution is commended as reliable teaching to the future worshipping community.

These four cases test these four challenges:

1. What if a part rejects the whole? (applying the "everywhere" standard)

2. What if a "new gospel" is preferred to the old, apostolic faith? (applying the "always" standard)

3. What if ancient witnesses themselves might be wrong? (applying the *ab omnibus* standard, which ensures conciliar consent by due process) Finally,

4. What if no conciliar precedent is defined on a particular point that requires further interpretation of conciliar consent?

Taken together these exhaust most challenges.

These four are carefully analyzed by Vincent.

FIRST, WHAT IF A PART REJECTS THE WHOLE?

The first is a disruptive scenario: What if it is found that some few members of the community of faith break away from the global communion of the previously received faith over many generations? This crisis emerges when an idiosyncratic, particular regional minority voice rejects the inter-cultural, worldwide orthodox consensus that emerged under the guidance of the Spirit in the first three centuries.

If scattered, isolated contemporary members abandon the historic faith, the ecumenical remedy is clear and straightforward: the faithful appeal to the "rationality of the body universal" instead of the temporary idiosyncrasies of the dissent.[153] The soundness of the body universal ought rightly to hold against the variability of a few.

Christian teaching under that challenge prefers the universal to the particular. It prefers the classic to the eccentric, the whole to the part. Orthodox faith looks to the multicultural, intergenerational community of believers for validation rather than to a few individual experts or to alleged private revelations or to bizarre ecstatic reasoning. Built into classic Christian thinking is a consensual principle that anticipates later democratic forms that would point the civil order toward proximate political consensus.

There can be no worldwide consent if the confirmation is not global. Regional consent is not ecumenical consent. Insofar as possible, orthodox teaching must be shown to be received and owned worldwide by the worshipping community. Once defined, the consensus does not need to be forever retested, unless its testing becomes necessary.

---

153. Vincent, *Commonitory*, FC 7:272, cf. NPNF 2 IX:152.

Suppose, while claiming to stand in the apostolic tradition, a couple of dissenting voices put together a small caucus or regional group that claims to represent better "apostolic teaching" than that previously held in the generations of Christian communities everywhere. Suppose they claim that they have a particular interpretation of key scriptural teachings which supersedes even that which had once been universally accepted. Then the orthodox way is fairly to compare the proposed view with what general Christian consensual teaching has most broadly concluded. This is an objective testable criterion. It requires comparison of the proposed local view against judgments shared by the whole historical community of experience.

If the interpretation of scripture itself is contested, or one text pitted against another, these views may be tested by the whole body of classic intergenerational consent. The orthodox way thus provides a counter-individualistic criterion: the universal historic community memory stands more reliably than the partial, regional, ecstatic, or individualistic memory.

Does this imply that no local or regional or individualistic scholarship can ever be orthodox? No. It means that local views that rail against the consensual memory must be tested by that broader memory.

This is the first criterion of general consent. It applies a geographical, *spatial* metaphor to the question of truth: Is it believed *everywhere*?

SECOND, WHAT IF A "NEW GOSPEL" IS PREFERRED TO THE OLD, APOSTOLIC FAITH?

The second criterion is different. It has to do with *time*: Has it *always* been believed after the original eyewitnesses? This challenge is all too familiar to the faithful: What if a new and contrary teaching pretends to supersede the received gospel, the canon of apostolic testimony?

Or consider a worst-case scenario: What if even the majority of the worldwide Christian community in a given period has temporarily broken away from the historic apostolic faith? Now we are getting closer to the contemporary dilemma of divided Christianity. What if some contemporary members, perhaps even in huge numbers, abandon the historically received recollection and assert the contemporary opinion as if it were historic faith? Orthodoxy confidently answers: "Then, one will endeavor to adhere to the voice of antiquity, which is evidently beyond the danger of being seduced by the deceit of some novelty."[154]

This second level of crisis emerges when a new branch of the vine falls temporarily into some deterioration. In that event, the believing community is not limited only to the first level of appeal (to believers everywhere, *ubique*). It also has the second level of appeal: to *antiquity* (*semper*), the ancient apostolic faith which precedes and regulates the newer proposal. The orthodox mind therefore argues not only from

---

154. Vincent, *Commonitory*, FC 7:271.

cross-cultural experience (universality), but from intergenerational experience (faith shared over time from antiquity), a very different criterion from the first.

This criterion applies even when vast numbers of believers wrongly consent to temporary error. Against any emergent voices, even those claiming to be a majority, orthodoxy still can appeal to the most ancient writers, because antiquity is beyond being contaminated by contemporary distortions.

Athanasius made this appeal to pre-Nicene formulations in response to the Arians. Augustine made a similar appeal to Paul against the Pelagians and Donatists. Luther similarly appealed to Paul (along with Augustine) against late medieval scholastic misreadings of justification. Even if today's fad theologians might have been enamored for a time with the "death of god" or the cult of the "new age," that does not change one iota the continuity of orthodox teaching. Apostolicity trumps contemporaneity. The original eyewitnesses to revelation override legions of opinions of those who have not been eyewitnesses to revelation, no matter how well-intended.

Does this imply that no new scholarship can be orthodox? No. It means only that any new scholarship claiming fidelity to the apostolic tradition must be tested by the texts of the written word, and the earliest consensual historic memory of the meaning of the written word. Ecumenical consent depends on scriptural interpretation. Since the earliest Christian witnesses are those most qualified to bear the good news, the highest level of authority in contested matters lies with the scripture, consensually received.

In Christian teaching the constituency is never reducible to a contemporary constituency since by definition the contemporary cannot exclude the intergenerational consent. Contemporary ideas are compared with those held by the whole historic community of believers who have given voluntary consent to life with God according to apostolic teaching.

Hence when a novel or false idea of Christianity arises, the faithful are always free to ask how it corresponds with the larger historic constituency of believers of all epochs and cultural settings. If everyone agrees, the decision is self-evident. But "everyone" here is not defined only by modern voices but also is inclusive of all ancient voices of believers who stand in accord with ancient apostolic teaching.

If a view of Christian truth is without precedent, it is bound to be misconceived, because the Holy Spirit would not have failed to guide the church in all previous centuries and cultures. The contemporary community falls under the criterion of apostolic antiquity,[155] which asks whether a view has a record of being affirmed from apostolic antiquity to the present.

---

155. Was this proto-democratic method invented by Vincent or can it be found throughout the apostolic tradition? Might it be that Vincent himself just hatched this method out of his own imagination? If Vincent's method could itself be shown to be new, then it would intrinsically contradict its own criterion of apostolic antiquity. It would indeed seem incongruous to try to fight heretical innovation with a fashionable, new, innovative method. If the claims of apostolic antiquity are not rightly understood, Vincent recognized that his own arguments could be used precisely against ecumenical consent. So he set forth historical evidence showing

This is a perennial dilemma of political consent: Should a legislator weigh constituency numbers (votes) or listen to his own sense of right and wrong (through conscience)?

When these disagree, which way must one go? These two sides of modern democratic theory were anticipated by Vincent in the interface between the first rule (everyone) and second rule (of all times, *semper*, always). The wisdom of ecumenical method lies in the tension and equilibrium between these criteria. When constituency consent corresponds with the rule of antiquity (the voice of historic Christianity) then the consensus is trustable. The analogue to scripture in a constitutional system is the Constitution itself.

THIRD, WHAT IF ANCIENT WITNESSES THEMSELVES MIGHT BE WRONG?

Now we come to a harder case, the third scenario: What if the ancient intergenerational faith, and even the criterion of antiquity itself, comes into question? Suppose its claims are argued to be unreliable or outmoded. How can apostolic antiquity remain a reliable criterion if apostolic antiquity itself is chargeable with being unjust or wrong? What if a new teaching claims to supersede entirely the alleged truthfulness of the old faith?

If the consensus of apostolic antiquity is itself challenged, or if an error is detected in the otherwise trusted ancient consensual writers, then it is time to refer it to a conciliar process, a local or regional council, or ultimately an ecumenical council, to settle the matter fairly, to discern and affirm the unity of the faithful in all times and places. The conciliar process looks diligently for what is consistent with apostolic teaching as generally received cross-culturally and across all Christian generations. If you can find this third level, you have identified classic Christian teaching. If an Arian teaching should arise today that says "Jesus was almost but not quite the eternal God," it is an easy matter to compare it with established conciliar consent.

Suppose someone comes along and says with a straight face: "The sacred text itself errs. Look how unjustly it colludes with crusades and slavery and gender oppression." Suppose the prophets and apostles not only disagreed among themselves but also erred substantially on crucial points, whether morally or reasonably or with faulty memory. What if it is claimed that the transmitted text itself is spurious or untrustworthy? In that case orthodoxy appeals to an entirely different principle that completes and amplifies both universality and apostolic antiquity. This third criterion is a textually tested combination of the first two criteria (*universality* and *antiquity*) in an appeal to *conciliar consent*, which must affirm the decisions that already respect

---

that this method is itself not new or original to him, but rather has been the established custom and practice from the outset of Christian witness, as indicated by the counsel of Jerusalem reported in Acts, and in the tradition from Paul to Nicea to Ephesus.

universality and antiquity. But remember that the concept of conciliar consent makes no sense at all without the premise that the Holy Spirit is guiding that consent.

To review these first three crises: (1) If some isolated contemporary members abandon the historic universally received, worldwide faith, the church prefers the *universal* instead of the *particular*. (2) Even if the whole community of believers for a time seems to go astray in a new culture with a new idea unfamiliar to the apostles, the church can always appeal to *antiquity* above *innovation*. (3) *If the reliability of apostolic testimony itself is questioned, the one body of Christ can appeal to ecumenical conciliar precedent* by looking fairly at long-held conciliar decisions, where almost everything necessary to salvation has been already debated. Vincent's threefold rule encompasses universality, antiquity, and general intergenerational lay consent.

Any believer may freely question the authenticity of a supposed inauthentic Christian tradition. That is done by submitting the historical evidence and looking toward the confirmation of general ecumenical consent. If that consent is not forthcoming or is unclear, however, then the first three criteria need to be supplemented by a rare final fourth option, which we now consider.

FOURTH, WHAT IF NO CONCILIAR PRECEDENT IS DEFINED?

Now we come to a fourth scenario, a variation of the third, and which might be viewed as plan B of the third rule: *What if a contested case arises in which arguably no council has ever acted upon a particular question?* If there is no historic and universal conciliar act to which to appeal, how would you decide, short of seeking to call an ecumenical council? What if an alleged truth purports to be apostolic but has never been adjudicated as such by fair conciliar process?

This brings us to the more complicated fourth scenario described by Vincent. In most cases an issue can be settled on the basis of the first three criteria. The fourth offers a more discriminating level of emergency appeal. If after pursuing the three previous criteria uncertainty remains, then you interrogate the prevailing opinions of *the most reliable consensual teachers of the ancient Christian tradition* who have lived in various periods and at different places, but have nevertheless remained in communion with the broadest consensus of the one worldwide historic community of faith. This is the criterion of the classic consensual interpretation of scripture. It is an extension of the third criterion of general consent, focused not on conciliar action but on commentary on key scriptural texts under dispute.

In this case we are still seeking what we have sought all along: consensuality—the Spirit-led voice of the one, holy, catholic, apostolic community of believers. You interrogate not just contemporaries, but also the writings of those classic teachers who best span the bridge between the apostles and all later generations over a long chronological time frame, and the widest possible geographical frame, those most generally received, east, west, north, and south, in the furthest range of time and space by the *communio sanctorum*.

But how do you identify those interpreters most frequently and persistently received ecumenically, who have held and taught what has generally been received as the mind of the believing church? This is a judgment not of the quantity of historic witnesses but of their quality, as assessed by the centuries of accumulated comment. Which interpreters of scripture are considered historically as being most reliable?

THE LEADING CONSENSUAL EXEGETES

As a matter of fact, the conciliar process has already identified its most noteworthy consensual interpreters. They are frequently specified in the documents of the Ecumenical Councils and their faithful descendants. Those most generally recognized are: four great doctors of the East: Athanasius, Basil, Gregory of Nazianzus, and John Chrysostom; and of the West, Ambrose, Augustine, Jerome, and Gregory the Great. Virtually all who have thought seriously about any question of faith and morals would include these "doctors of the church" in an effort to identify classic consensus on questions not decided by official conciliar actions.

Classic Christian teaching listens most often and most intently to those voices most generally received by the whole church for the longest period of time as trustworthy interpreters of the apostles.[156] These are teachers of scripture whose names have been widely respected not for a few decades or centuries but throughout most of the history of Christianity. These are widely attested as best representing the broadest consent of the believers of all cultures and periods in rightly dividing the word of truth.

These are with few exceptions consensually reliable voices of the mind of the believing church. Most were writing just after the earliest ecumenical councils had winnowed away many digressions, when the vitality of the church of martyrdom had not waned, and when the disciplined spirit was most alive. We listen to them because the more we know scripture, the more we realize that they understood well and early just how the consenting community reads and compares the texts of scripture and the gist of the history of salvation.

In classic Christian teaching the resolution is not merely a matter of individual opinion. It is a documentable historic fact that these great doctors have repeatedly been more widely received than any others as perennial consensus bearers.[157] That does not imply that they never made any missteps or that they possessed infallible judgment. They themselves warn against making that assumption. It is not that there

---

156. The fact that Vincent omitted Augustine's name in speaking of "eminent men" does not imply that Vincent disapproved of Augustine's teaching. Too much has been made of the argument from silence on this matter.

157. A fact that can be easily validated by counting references in the history of exegesis.

are only eight. Rather it is that there are at least eight that are on virtually everyone's list of consensual teachers.

The tradition of identifying key teachers of the Christian consensus established itself early. One example: by 495 AD, the Gelasian decretal commended to all as consensual teaching not only the canons of Nicea, Ephesus, and Chalcedon "to be received *after* those of the Old or New Testament, which we regularly accept. Likewise the works of blessed Caecilius Cyprian . . . *and in the same way* the works of Gregory of Nazianzus, Basil, Athanasius, John Chrysostom, Theophilus, Cyril of Alexandria, Hilary, Ambrose, Augustine, Jerome and Prosper."[158] Another: the fifth ecumenical council (Constantinople II, 553 AD) urged believers to "hold fast to the decrees of the four councils, and in every way follow the holy Fathers, Athanasius, Hilary, Basil, Gregory the Theologian, Gregory of Nyssa, Ambrose, Theophilus, John Chrysostom of Constantinople, Cyril, Augustine, Proclus, Leo, and their writings on the true faith."[159] The most widely quoted Patriarchs of Alexandria are Peter I, Athanasius, Theophilus, and Cyril, as seen in the catenae.[160]

Again and again the faithful have returned to the proximate consensus of those interpreters of scripture who displayed the best habits of mind, the highest competencies, and the greatest faithfulness. Their durability is sufficient evidence of their faithfulness. Orthodoxy has learned not to be afraid of any of these voices. It has learned to listen trustingly to all and view them in a complementary way so that each deepens the wisdom of the others. The champions of African orthodoxy are Cyprian, Anthony, Athanasius, Augustine, and Cyril the Great. They are worthy of being trusted.

Orthodox writers reference key precedents and keep their own thoughts in the background. Vincent: "Everything [should] be transferred to the sons in the same spirit of faith in which it was accepted by the fathers; . . . it is proper to Christian modesty and earnestness not to transfer to posterity one's own ideas, but to preserve those received from one's ancestors."[161] In worship we transfer not our own ideas but the testimony of the body of Christ.

Summarizing: There are four filters through which to sift Christian truth claims: (a) the universal prevails over the particular (the whole is preferred to the part), (b) the older apostolic witness prevails over the newer alleged general consent, and (c) conciliar actions and decisions prevail over those as yet untested by conciliar acts. Finally (d) in special cases where no conciliar rule avails, the most reliable consensual ancient authorities prevail over those less consensual across the generations.

The Holy Spirit has in fact led the consenting community to unity and consensus through an actually lived history supported by an abundance of consistent

---

158. SCD 165, p. 69. This list includes all the Ecumenical Councils and the great Doctors of the Church except Gregory the Great, who had not yet been born.

159. Session I, NPNF 2 14:303.

160. See also the canons of the Council of Ephesus, 431 AD.

161. Vincent, *Commonitory*, FC 7:277.

C. THE APOSTOLIC MODEL OF RIGHT REMEMBERING

THE APOSTLE PAUL AS CHIEF MODEL OF ORTHODOX REMEMBERING

The biblical prototype for right remembering is the Apostle Paul. He shows how right remembering has been a concern of the apostolic tradition from the outset.[162] Vincent demonstrates that the apostolic way of remembering is not a method that emerged incrementally generations after Paul. Rather it is repeatedly found in the earliest Pauline letters themselves.

Paul showed that the gospel can move from culture to culture without itself changing. The gospel addresses different audiences with the same truth. It flows within an immense continuous wave of historical flux, but does not itself change. It enters freely into new language structures but in doing so remains faithful to the same word as that received from the events that revealed God's love to humanity.[163]

Paul's gospel was not bound to a single culture. He likely read and spoke in Hebrew, Aramaic, and Greek before he went to Galatia, Bithynia, and Athens, and Latin in Rome where he spent his last two years. His whole mission was dedicated to showing the universal significance of life in Christ. Otherwise his letters would not have been found circulating so quickly among all the diverse churches around the known world. The gospel is offered to all cultures, and remains at all times transgenerational.

In Colossians the author gives greetings to the "brothers and sisters in Laodicea, along with Nympha and the church that meets in her house. After this letter has been read to you publicly, make sure that the church in Laodicea reads it and that you read the one from Laodicea" (Col 4:15-16 CEB). Paul assumed that his letters would be passed from church to church where different cultural assumptions prevailed. In Galatians 1:6-7 Paul rebuffs those who have deserted to another gospel, following their own desires, having turned away from the truth they have originally received, forgetting their loyalty to the first faith, the earliest teaching of the earliest witnesses to the good news.

---

162. Ibid., ch. 8, FC 7:281–82.

163. John Henry Newman, *An Essay on the Development of Christian Doctrine*, 5.1.1 (London: Sheed and Ward, 1960), p. 125, translating *Commonitory*, 29. "Let the soul's religion imitate the law of the body, which, as years go on, develops indeed and opens out its due proportions, and yet remains identically what it was. Small are a baby's limbs, a youth's are larger, yet they are the same."

When Paul speaks of the first witnesses to the resurrected Lord, he points to a shared testimony: "He appeared to Cephas, then to the Twelve, and then he appeared to more than five hundred brothers and sisters at once—most of them are still alive to this day, though some have died. Then he appeared to James, then to all the apostles, and last of all he appeared to me, as if I were born at the wrong time" (1 Cor 15:5-8 CEB). This became the common faith of a global worshipping community. If someone should preach some idea contrary to that which you have received, even if it seems to come from a heavenly messenger, if it goes against the gospel you first heard, do not trust it.[164]

Against the frogs, gnats, and dayflies who imagine that they have an improved gospel, different from and better than the received testimony, Paul exhorts his readers to hold fast to the gospel "we preached to you," which is validated by living it out.[165]

Paul writes to Timothy and Titus, warning them not to make void their first faith,[166] warning them to "watch out for people who create divisions and problems against the teaching that you learned" (Rom 16:17 CEB). Such innovators will cause the shipwreck of faith,[167] subverting whole houses for the sake of passing short-lived values,[168] confusing gain with godliness,[169] and their infections spread like cancer.[170] They are busybodies who go from house to house blabbering about what would be better left unsaid,[171] causing dissension and offence, always chasing after the latest fad, while never attaining knowledge of the truth.[172]

THE SPIRIT GUIDES AND PROTECTS THE CHURCH'S REMEMBERING

Individualistic Christians who judge individually without apostolic memory cannot avoid eventual review by those who remember accurately the salvation event. Every generation is subject to being reminded where the center is when necessary.[173]

Only right remembering can remedy our persistent tendencies to self-righteousness. Since believers as well as unbelievers remain tempted to sin, all may

---

164. Vincent, *Commonitory*, ch. 8; cf. Gal. 1:8.
165. Gal 1:8-9 CEB; Vincent, *Commonitory*, ch. 9, FC 7:282-83.
166. 1 Tim 5:12 KJV.
167. 1 Tim 1:19 NIV.
168. Titus 1:10, 11 KJV.
169. 1 Tim 6:4, 5 KJV.
170. 2 Tim 2:16-17 NKJV.
171. 1 Tim 5:13 CEB.
172. 2 Tim 3:6-7 NKJV.
173. Vincent, *Commonitory*, ch. 21, FC 7:305–307.

tend toward an "insatiable lust for error."[174] Human nature, created good but fallen into sin, is "possessed by a permanent desire to change religion, to add something and to take something away."[175]

But through the guidance of the Holy Spirit the apostles remembered events accurately and transmitted them reliably in the written tradition. The faithful can entirely trust the received apostolic teaching that emerges out of that memory. I personally have made no theological decision more important than to trust the consensus. The Christian community is not merely a human institution that needs constantly to be protected by human guarantees. It stands under the protection of God the Spirit, who helps the faithful to remember rightly. One who pushes through a hedge is more likely to get bitten by a snake.[176]

Paul urged Timothy to avoid an excessive interest in "the profane novelties of words."[177] Paul's words strike like a hammer: Keep away from empty discussions. Avoid futile phrases. Novelty is fleeting while apostolic truth endures. These innovators promise a great deal but deliver little of durable value.

THE SHORT-LIVED HERESIES

Four metaphors used by Vincent reveal the instability of heresy:

Chaff. In the harvest the chaff is blown away from the wheat. The faith (the wheat) is separated by its gravity, its weightiness. For lack of weight the heresies are cast away to the wind. Those wafted away by this sifting process are like the furling sails of puffed-up minds.

Shipwreck. Such lightweight notions are pushed around by the winds of change. Like ships amid the storms of history, they have left the secure harbor, the traditional wisdom of the apostolic faith. They are now exposed to every gust of the sea and to potential shipwreck. They are never sure of their direction.

The Wayward Child. They do well if somehow, by some providence, they are brought back to the harbor of the faith once for all delivered to the saints. There they find a gentle and kindly mother, a community of faith, where they might again drink streams of living water, and disgorge the errors they have learned. When they come under this mother's care, they may have to unlearn much of what they had been erroneously learning.[178]

Toxicity. Swallowing heresy is like ingesting poison, not enough to kill but too much to be painlessly digested. Many who have fallen from faith suffer in a miserable situation in which they cannot die and cannot live in good health.

---

174. Ibid., FC 7:305.

175. Ibid.

176. Eccl 10:8.

177. *kenophonias*, 1 Tim 6:20 Douay-Rheims.

178. Vincent, *Commonitory*, ch. 20, FC 7:303-05.

D. TREASURES OLD AND NEW

"Have you understood all these things?" asked Jesus. They answered, "Yes." And he taught them that every teacher "who has been trained as a disciple for the kingdom of heaven is like the head of a household who brings old and new things out of their treasure chest" (Matt 13:51-52 CEB). The old treasures are the gifts of God. The new treasures consist in currently receiving once again God's gifts in the present. The new is the active claiming of the inheritance of the old. The old reforms itself once again in the new.

The power to transform societies and to redeem the human condition finds its most prolific roots in the stored wisdom of the human past. Classic Christianity conserves this long memory.

THE WORD MADE FLESH

In his personal coming, God truly assumed, rather than just appeared to assume, humanity. His manner of life was not artificial or synthetic. This personal coming was not an impersonation. Unlike an actor on a stage, the triune God does not change roles, at one time playing a king, at another time a priest, at another time a prophet, so that at the end of the play the persons being impersonated cease to exist.[179]

In Jesus Christ we have truly God become truly human—in person. Unlike an actor, he became that which he embodied. He was just like us—we who are precisely who we are, not players on a stage.

Each of us exists as a person of flesh and spirit, soul and body. We do not imitate ourselves; rather we are ourselves.[180] God the Word does not mimic dying or pretend to be suffering on the cross. God the Son suffers in the flesh. He truly assumed humanity without ceasing to be God the Son. In the person we meet God and man, one who is at once created and uncreated, unchangeable and suffering, co-equal and voluntarily submissive to the Father, begotten of the Father before time and born of a human mother in time. Fully human, his flesh like our flesh comes from his mother, having a soul endowed with intelligence, mind, and reason. The incarnation remains a mystery even when it is rationally described.

Athanasius was reminded of an incident reported by Mark, when Jesus drove out of the Temple courts the unfair money-changers.[181] When it comes to speech about the "Word made flesh," there is a need for fair exchange agents,[182] especially among those who speak rightly of the human and divine nature of Christ in the same breath:

---

179. Ibid., ch. 14, FC 7:293-95.
180. Ibid., ch. 13, FC 7:290-93.
181. Mark 11:15.
182. Athanasius, *On the Incarnation*, 10.

He who is indicated by both statements is one Person, for "the Word was made flesh." But the expressions used about his Godhead, and his becoming man, are to be interpreted with discrimination and suitably to the particular context. And he that writes of the human attributes of the Word knows also what concerns His Godhead: and he who expounds concerning His Godhead is not ignorant of what belongs to His coming in the flesh: but discerning each as a skilled and "approved money-changer," he will walk in the straight way of piety; when therefore he speaks of His weeping, he knows that the Lord, having become man, . . . exhibits his human character in weeping.[183]

The reality of one person, truly human and truly God, had to be tested out in every possible way to show that the incarnation was not an imitation or a fiction. Thus the consenting community had to say no to Arius, Nestorius, Photinus, and Apollinaris, and the others, since they all departed from the baptism into which we were all baptized.[184] The challenges to the orthodox consensus required faith to become explicitly accountable. Even the brightest teachers like Tertullian and Origen left ambiguities which led to them occasionally misreading the consensus.

VINCENT MARKED THE TENTH GENERATION FROM THE APOSTLES

Think of this transition metaphorically in terms of roughly ten generations. Note the swift succession of generations of blessed witnesses from the apostle John to Vincent—only about ten generations:[185] John knew[186] about Polycarp in Asia Minor, who met Irenaeus as a boy, who knew Callistus (d. 222), who knew Dionysius of Alexandria (fl. ca. 200–265), who knew Anthony of the Desert (d. 355), who knew Athanasius (d. 373), who knew Damasus (d. 384), who knew John Cassian (d. 432), who knew Honoratus, who was the abbot of Lérins at the time of Vincent. Only ten generations separated John and Vincent. In these generations the guardianship of the apostolic witness was taken with absolute seriousness and defended to death.

Vincent was the first to bring to clear statement the long-established procedure for how one discerns Christian truth when disputed. He was writing shortly after

---

183. Athanasius, Letter on the Opinion of Dionysius, 9.

184. Vincent, *Commonitory*, ch. 14, FC 7:293–95.

185. Ten generations are not calculated here numerically in terms of years, but personally by known or inferred person to person knowledge or interaction. Many of those listed lived very long, (Polycarp over eighty, Anthony over a hundred; Athanasius and John Cassiam over seventy-five), so the years between personal links were stretched to an average of thirty-year generations, much longer among ascetics on average than the norm.

186. "Knew" here implies "knew of" or "could have known of" in a metaphorical or extended sense. The purpose is not to prove disputed human interactions, but to show how the generations flowed from Paul to Vincent. These estimated links are conjectural rather than historically demonstrable.

the death of Augustine and Jerome, during the time of Cyril of Alexandria (412–444), less than eighty years after the death of Anthony of the Desert, less than three hundred years following Polycarp (ca. 69–155) and Justin Martyr (d. ca. 167). Ten generations is only one-tenth of the one hundred generations of apostolic consensus since the first century.[187] Those first ten generations of consensus provided a vast accumulation of valuable consensual experience prior to the Council of Ephesus out of which to assess the best method of deciding contested Christian truth.

Over a century before Vincent wrote on right remembering, the council of Nicea had met in 325 AD to engage in a major debate and make a crucial decision about the inadequate Christology of the Arians. The kernel of the method of classical consensual thinking already existed by that time. The unpretentious method that Vincent explicitly described around 432 AD was fully operational at the time of Nicea, and Vincent thinks embryonically in Paul, even if it had not been explicitly articulated and systematically explained.

What part did Africa play in these first three hundred years from 30 AD to 330 AD? Mark of Alexandria wrote the first Gospel. Tertullian, Cyprian, Clement, and Origen all preceded Nicea by a century. Athanasius wrote the *Life of Anthony* and was a major mentor of the language of Nicea. Following these, Augustine provided the most thorough expression of the consensus in the years before Vincent. Through the influential Councuncils of Carthage and Alexandria, these Africans before Nicea were taken with great seriousness in the decisions made at Nicea and following. Origen provided the most sophisticated approach to scripture, and Athanasius provided the classic language for the mystery of the incarnation.

The council fathers of Nicea repeatedly said of their own decision-making that it was not new but that they were only confirming what had been believed by the community of faith since the apostles. They insisted that their way of settling the Arian dispute was the same way that the worshipping Christian community had always decided cases of contested doctrine. This process became further refined in the crucible of the Council of Constantinople in 381, and especially at Ephesus in 431. This is the very method that Vincent would describe around 432. Augustine, before Vincent, used much the same method for discerning the truth, but it remained to Vincent to state it in a detailed systematic form and defend it as an historical hypothesis.[188]

By the time Vincent provided its classic expression, this method had already had three centuries of testing. By negotiating many contested issues it had by then proved

---

187. Assuming a generation as about twenty years, or five generations per century, twenty centuries of Christian consensus would embrace about one hundred generations since Jesus.

188. It has been argued that Vincent himself was uneasy with some of Augustine's views, but there can be no doubt that Vincent and the community at Lérins read Augustine thoroughly, viewed him as authoritative, and quarreled with him only on specific points, not with respect to his method or legitimacy as exegete. From the fact that an Augustinian defender, Prosper of Aquitaine, wrote an essay resisting certain points made by Vincent, one cannot conclude necessarily that Vincent was generally opposed to Augustine. Such a conclusion requires much speculation.

its durability. It is entirely mistaken to assume that Vincent is the inventor of the Vincentian rule. He only gave it expression, according to his own testimony, after it had been rigorously tested for these generations.

THE TRANSFORMING POWER OF FAITH

This stubborn fact remains: a single cohesive deposit of faith, formed and shaped by the Spirit, and confirmed by free mutual consent of generations, persisted for many centuries before Vincent described its method. Translated into many tongues, this consensus has formed many cultures without losing its core identity. The Spirit has enabled mutual general consent on key points of interpretation of canonically received holy writ in ways that are sufficient not only for salvation but also for better life in this world. In this ancient teaching lies special power to renew and transform societies, as the history of orthodoxy makes clear.

Laypersons are quite capable of understanding and assessing the fairness of this process of consensus discernment. They have a right to understand how the great consensual teachers have gained repeated consent from generation to generation over two millennia, so that Orthodox, Catholics, and Protestants can, despite diverse liturgical and cultural memories, find unexpected common ground ecumenically by returning to classic interpreters of scripture texts that still stand as reliable Christian teaching today.

REPRISE

There are reliable evidences for the rebirth of orthodoxy, most notably in Africa. These evidences include personal narratives, as seen in accounts of conversions. They are academic, as seen in the study of the history of scripture interpretation. They are open to cross-cultural discernment, as seen in the multicultural nature of orthodoxy. Yet they are capable of transforming cultures, as seen both in Africa and in global Christianity. They are embodying a new African Christian unity based on the faith of ancient consensual teaching.

E. CONCLUDING IMPERATIVES

We have seen how orthodoxy persists despite all contrary predictions, and how worshipping communities are now moving confidently beyond the constricted future of modern disappointments. Amid the modern gridlock the classic religious traditions are being rediscovered by believers today. African Catholics, Copts, Pentecostals, and charismatics, and many traditional Protestants, have received and continue to guard the African memory of God's revelation in history.

African Orthodoxy has all the advantages of long-term memory spurned by modern consciousness. Those who are willing to suffer for truth are still witnessing with their blood to the unique revelation of God in Jesus Christ. They are opening doors for wider intellectual freedom than is available within modern assumptions.

These are signs of the new birth of African Orthodoxy. They point to the gift of regeneration. To rightly lay hold of the power of this gift will require more than description or argument. It requires an act of willing and the risk of obedience, the risk of making behavioral changes. In sum, six imperatives follow:

1. Do not withhold the true story of your own rediscovery of early Christian teaching.

2. Study the classic African religious writers.

3. Enjoy and respect the cross-cultural, intergenerational nature of the African Christian community.

4. Live within doctrinal and moral boundaries firmly established for millennia.

5. Reclaim wayward religious and educational institutions and initiate transformed ones.

6. Apply the ancient ecumenical method of discernment to contested questions.

BIBLIOGRAPHY OF ORTHODOX AFRICAN WRITERS: CLASSIC AND CONTEMPORARY

INTRODUCTION

I have not yet seen a bibliography of African-born theologians[189] that includes Coptic, Catholic, Protestant, Pentecostal/charismatic, and Africa Instituted Churches, and both women and men, so I have tried to supply one. All these traditions are embraced under the general heading of early African orthodoxy, since all confess the core of the classic consensus, even if they differ on questions of ecclesiology, church order, and sacramental life. The only qualification for inclusion is that these African theologians and writers, however diverse, have a heart for classic Christianity in the early centuries in which it was formed on the African continent. Since African American Theology has been much studied, and since the theologians of the continent of Africa have not always been included in these studies, this bibliography supplements other excellent bibliographies of African American Theology (Charles Bellinger, James H. Evans Jr., Peter T. Vogt, Herbert V. Klem, and Robert V. Rakestraw).

This bibliography is divided into four parts:

A. PRIMARY SOURCES: CLASSIC AFRICAN CHRISTIAN THEOLOGIANS AND KEY TEXTS BEFORE 700 AD

B. THE AFRICAN DESERT MOTHERS

C. THE AFRICAN DESERT FATHERS

---

189. Those not African-born are marked with an asterisk.

D. CONTEMPORARY ORTHODOX AFRICAN THEOLOGIANS AND WRITERS (with an addendum on the future of African Christianity)

A. PRIMARY SOURCES: CLASSIC AFRICAN CHRISTIAN THEOLOGIANS AND KEY TEXTS BEFORE 700 AD

Since this bibliography focuses on ancient Christian texts written in African before 700 AD, and since there are many versions of translations and critical editions, I cite only standard titles in English.

Athanasius: *On the Incarnation*

Athanasius: *Life of Antony*

Athanasius: *The Festal Epistles*

Athanasius: *Against the Arians*

Augustine: *The Confessions*

Augustine: *Enchiridion on Faith, Hope, and Love*

Augustine: *On the Spirit and the Letter*

Augustine: *The City of God*

Augustine: *On the Trinity*

Augustine: *On Nature and Grace*

Augustine: *On Faith and Works*

Clement of Alexandria: *Exhortation to the Greeks (Protrepticus)*

Clement of Alexandria: *Christ the Educator (Paedagogus)*

Clement of Alexandria: *Miscellanies (Stromata)*

Cyprian of Carthage: *On the Unity of the Church*

Cyprian of Carthage: *On the Lord's Prayer*

Cyprian of Carthage: *On the Advantage of Patience*

Cyprian of Carthage: *On the Vanity of Idols*

Cyprian of Carthage: *On Works and Alms*

Cyprian of Carthage: *The Epistles*

Cyril the Great, Patriarch of Alexandria: *Festal Letters*

Cyril of Alexandria: *Commentary on Luke*

Cyril of Alexandria: *Commentary on John*

Cyril of Alexandria: *Commentaries on Pentateuch, Isaiah, Minor Prophets, Songs, Proverbs, and the Pauline Epistles*

Cyril of Alexandria: *Against Julian*

Cyril of Alexandria: *Against Nestorius*

Didymus the Blind: Citations from *Catenae Fragments* of Lost Writings from Commentaries on Job, Zechariah, Psalms XX–XLXI, Genesis and Ecclesiastes, and the Catholic Epistles, three books on the Trinity, *On the Holy Spirit, Against the Manichaeans, On Dogmas, On the Death of Young Children, Against the Arians, First Word*, and fragments from the *Papyri of Tura*

Fulgentius (Fulgence), bishop of Ruspe: *The Rule of Faith, Synodal Letter*

Fulgentius, Fabius Planciades: *On the Ages of the World and of Man*

Fulgentius, Fabius Planciades: *The Explanation of Ancient Words*

Fulgentius, Fabius Planciades: *Mythologies*

Julius Africanus: *Epistle to Aristides*

Lactantius: *The Divine Institutes*

Lactantius: *On the Manner in which the Persecutors Died*

Marius Victorinus: *Commentaries on Cicero, Aristotle, and Porphyry*

Marius Victorinus: *On the Trinity*

Marius Victorinus: *Against the Arians*

Marius Victorinus: *The Son of the Same Substance*

Marius Victorinus: Fragments of commentaries on Galatians, Ephesians, and Philippians

Minucius Felix, the Octavius

Optatus: *Against the Donatists*

Origen: *On First Principles*

Origen: *On Prayer*

Origen: *Contra Celsum*

Origen: *Hexapla, Six Versions of the Bible* (from texts in Hebrew, Hebrew transliterated into Greek, Aquila of Sinope, Symmachus the Ebionite, the Septuagint, and Theodotion)

Perpetua, Felicity, and companions, Saints. *Calendarium Romanum*. Libreria Editrice Vaticana, 1969.

Peter I, the Great, Patriarch of Alexandria: *Life and Martyrdom*

Peter I, the Great, Vivian, Tim. *St. Peter of Alexandria, Bishop and Martyr*. Philadelphia: Fortress, 1988.

Peter I, the Great, Saint, Patriarch of Alexandria: *On the Canons of the Holy Fathers*

Pontius: *The Life and Passion of Cyprian*

Posidius: *Life of Augustine*

Primasius, Bishop of Hadrumetum: *Commentary on the Apocalypse and Letters*

Quodvultdeus of Carthage: *The Creedal Homilies*

Quodvultdeus of Carthage: *The Book of the Promises and Predictions*

Stephen, Bishop of Heracleopolis Magna: *Panegyric on Apollo of the Monastery of Isaac*

Tertullian: *Against Marcion*

Tertullian: To the Nations (*Ad Nationes*)

Tertullian: To An Address to the Martyrs (*Ad Martyrs*)

Tertullian: *Against Praxeas*

Tertullian: *On the Spectacles*

Tertullian: *On Baptism*

Tertullian: *On Prayer*

Tertullian: *On Patience*

Tertullian: *On the Testimony of the Soul*

Victor of Vita: *History of the Persecution in the Province of Africa*

Vigilius, Bishop of Thapsus: *Dialogues against the Arians and Eutychians*

B. THE AFRICAN DESERT MOTHERS

1. COLLECTIONS

Sister Benedicta Ward. "Apophthegmata Matrum," *Studia Patristica*. Berlin: Akademie Verlag. 16 (2): 63–66, 1985.

Sister Benedicta Ward. *Lives of the Desert Fathers,* Monastic Studies Series, LDF, 4, Gorgias Press and Cistertian Publications.

Selections from the Sayings of the Desert Fathers. Cistercian Publication, 1975, orthodoxebooks.org.

Apophthegmata Patrum, or *The Sayings of the Fathers*, newadvent.org.

Vitae Patrum, vitae-patrum.org.uk.

2. AFRICAN DESERT MOTHERS AND SAINTS

Amma Syncletica of Alexandria: *Sayings*

Amma Sarah of the Desert: *Sayings*

Catherine of Alexandria: *Martyrologium Romanum*

Desert Mothers and Fathers: abbeyofthearts.com

Mary of Egypt: *Vita of Saint Mary of Egypt* by St. Sophronius

Mary of Egypt: Saint Mary the Egyptian from the *Prologue from Ohrid*

Theodora of Alexandria: *Sayings*

3. ABOUT THE AFRICAN DESERT MOTHERS

Chryssavgis, John. *In the Heart of the Desert: Revised Edition: The Spirituality of the Desert Fathers and Mothers (Treasures of the World's Religions)*. Bloomington, IN: World Wisdom, 2008, pp. 29–32.

Earle, Mary C. *The Desert Mothers: Spiritual Practices from the Women of the Wilderness*. Church Publishing, 2007.

Forman, Mary. *Praying with the Desert Mothers*, Liturgical Press, 2005.

Johnston, William M. "Desert Mothers", *Encyclopedia of Monasticism* 1, Fitzroy Dearborn Publishers, 2000, pp. 373–74.

King, Margot. *The Desert Mothers*, Peregrina Publishing, 1989.

Puttick, Elizabeth. *Women as Teachers and Disciples in Traditional and New Religions*, Lewiston: The Edwin Millen Press, 1993, pp. 11–24.

Swan, Laura. *The Forgotten Desert Mothers: Sayings, Lives, and Stories of Early Christian Women*. Paulist Press, 2001.

4. AFRICAN WOMEN TODAY: THEOLOGY AND NARRATIVE

Burke, Joan F. *The Sisters of Notre Dame de Namur in Lower Zaire: A Social and Historical Study*. University of Oxford: DPhil. thesis, 1990.

Burke, Joan F. *These Catholic Sisters Are All Mamas!: Towards the Inculturation of the Sisterhood in Africa, an Ethnographic Study*. Leiden: Brill, 2001.

Burke, Joan F. "Becoming an 'Inside-Outsider,'" *JASO*, Vol. XX, no. 3, pp. 219–27, 1989.

Ilibagiza, Immaculée (with Steve Erwin). *Led by Faith: Rising from the Ashes of the Rwandan Genocide*. Carlsbad, CA: Hay House, 2008.

Mbugua, Judy, ed. *Our Time Has Come*. Association of Evangelicals of Africa and Madagascar. World Evangelical Fellowship by Baker Book House, 1994.

Ngunjiri, Faith Wambura. *Women's Spiritual Leadership in Africa: Tempered Radicals and Critical Servant Leaders*. SUNY Press, 2010.

Oduyoye, Mercy Amba. *Hearing and Knowing: Theological reflections on Christianity in Africa*. Maryknoll, NY: Orbis Books, 1986.

Oduyoye, Mercy Amba. "The Christ for African Women," in Fabella, V & Oduyoye, M A (eds), *With passion and compassion: Third world women doing theology. Reflections from the Women's Commission of the Ecumenical Association of Third World Theologians*, 35–46. Maryknoll, NY: Orbis Books, 1988.

Oduyoye, Mercy Amba. *The Wesleyan presence in Nigeria*. Ibadan: Sefer, 1992.

Oduyoye, Mercy Amba. *Daughters of Anowa*. Maryknoll, NY: Orbis Books, 1995.

Oduyoye, Mercy Amba, ed. *Transforming power: women in the household of God*, 54–65. Ghana: Circle of Concerned African Women Theologians, 1997.

Oduyoye, Mercy Amba. *Introducing African women's theology*. Sheffield: Sheffield Academic Press, 2001.

Oduyoye, Mercy Amba. *Beads and strands: Reflections of an African woman on Christianity in Africa*. Maryknoll, NY: Orbis Books, 2004.

Oduyoye, Mercy Amba. "A letter to my ancestors," in Otieno, N & McCullum, H (eds), *Journey of hope: Towards a new ecumenical Africa*, xv–xxii. Geneva: World Council of Churches, 2005.

Oduyoye, Mercy Amba. "The value of African religious beliefs and practices for Christian theology," in Kofi, A-K & Sergio, T (eds), *African Theology en route*, 109–16. Maryknoll, NY: Orbis Books, 1979.

Stinton, Diane B. *Jesus of Africa: Voices of Contemporary African Christology*, Maryknoll, NY: Orbis Books, 2004.

Tkaczow, Barbara. "Archaeological Sources for the Earliest Churches in Alexandria." In *Coptic Studies*, ed. W. Godlewski, pp. 431–36. Acts of the Third International Congress of Coptic Studies, Warsaw, 20–25 August 1984. Warsaw: PWN, 1990.

Uchem, Rose N. *Overcoming Women's Subordination in the Igbo African Culture and in the Catholic Church: Envisioning an Inclusive theology with Reference to women*, dissertation.com, 2001.

C. THE AFRICAN DESERT FATHERS

1. COLLECTIONS OF SAYINGS

Apophthegmata Patrum, or The Sayings of the Fathers

Vitae Patrum, vitae-patrum.org.uk

Paradise of the Desert Fathers, Coptic.net/articles/paradiseofdesertfathers.txt

Lives of the Desert Fathers, Sister Benedicta Ward, Monastic Studies Series, 4, Gorgias Press and Cistertian Publications.

Arras, Victor. *Collectio monastica: Ethiopic text.* Secrétariat du CorpusSCO, 1963.

Selections from the Sayings of the Desert Fathers. Cistercian Publication, 1975, orthodoxebooks.org.

Rufinus. "The History of the Monks in Egypt," in Norman Russell, *The Lives of the Desert Fathers.*

Palladius, *The Lausiac History,* tertullian.org/fathers/palladius

2. THE AFRICAN DESERT FATHERS TEXTS

Amoun (Amun) of Nitria, Palladius: *The Lausaic History; Lives of the Desert Fathers,* 4:90

Anthony the Great: *Life of Antony* by Athanasius; "Saint Anthony Father of the Monks." www.coptic.net.

Arsenius the Great: in *The Sayings of the Fathers*

Isidore of Alexandria, Damascius: *Life of Isidore*

Isidore of Pelusium: *Lives of the Desert Fathers,* 4:111

John of Lycopolis: *Lives of the Desert Fathers,* 4:62

Kaleb of Axum: *Blessed Elesbaan, the King of Ethiopia*

Macarius of Alexandria: *Lives of the Desert Fathers,* 4:123

Macarius the Egyptian: *Fifty Spiritual Homilies*

Moses the Black: in *The Sayings of the Fathers*

Pachomius: *The Rule of Pachomius,* seanmultimedia.com/Pie_Pachomius_Rule_1.html

Palladius: *The Lausiac History,* Tertullian.org

Paphnutius of Thebes: *Lives of the Desert Fathers,* 4:105

Paul of Thebes: *Lives of the Desert Fathers,* 4:124

Piammonas: *Lives of the Desert Fathers,* 4:126

Poemen: in *The Sayings of the Fathers*

Sarapion, *Lives of the Desert Fathers*, 4:112

Shenouda the Archimandrite, Emmel, Stephen. *Shenoute's Literary Corpus*. 2 vols. Corpus Scriptorum Christianorum Orientalium.

Sisoes the Great: in *The Sayings of the Fathers*

D. CONTEMPORARY ORTHODOX AFRICAN THEOLOGIANS AND WRITERS

[Since we are focusing on African theologians, those not African-born are marked with an asterisk.*]

Adamo, David Tuesday. *Africa and Africans in the New Testament*. London: Oxford University Press, 2006.

Adeyamo, Tokunboh. *Salvation in African Tradition*. Nairobi: Evangel, 1979.

Alberigo, Giuseppe and Ngindu Mushete. *Toward the African Synod*. London: SCM Press, 1992.

Asheia, Coptic Bp., Isaac of El Eskeet (Sketis). *His Life, Teaching and Writing*, orthodoxebooks.org.

Attia, Father Matthew. *The Coptic Orthodox Church and the Ecumenical Movement*, orthodoxebooks.org.

Atiya, Aziz S, ed. *The Coptic Encyclopedia*. 8 vols. New York: Maxwell Macmillan International, 1991.

Bediako, Kwame. *Theology and Identity: The Impact of Culture upon Christian Thought in the Second Century and in Modern Africa*. Oxford: Regnum Books, 1992.

Bediako, Kwame. *Christianity in Africa: The Renewal of a Non-Western Religion*. Edinburgh: Edinburgh Univ. Press, 1995.

Bediako, Kwame. "Cry Jesus! Christian Theology and Presence in Modern Africa." *Vox Evangelica* 23 (1993): 7–25.

Bimwenyi-Kweshi, Oscar. *Discours théologique négro-africain - Problème des fondements (Black African Theological Discourse)*. Maryknoll, NY: Orbis Books, 1995.

Bujo, Bénezet. *African Christian Morality at the Age of Inculturation.* Nairobi: Paulines Publications, 1990.

Bujo, Bénezet. *Foundations of an African Ethic: Beyond the Universal Claims of Western Morality.* Translated from German by Brian McNeil. New York: Crossroad Publishing, 2011.

Bishoy of Damiette, Kafr El-Sheikh, Coptic Bishop, Barary and the Monastery of Saint Demiana. *Deification of Man and the Interpretation of "Partakers of the Divine Nature,"* http://www.metroplit-bishoy.org/english/index.htm.

*Clark, Jawanza Eric. *Indigenous Black Theology: Toward An African-Centered Theology of the African-American Religious Experience.* Palgrave-Macmillan, 2012.

De Gruchy, John W. and Villa-Vicencio. *Apartheid Is a Heresy.* Grand Rapids: Eerdmans, 1983.

Dickson, Kwesi. *Theology in Africa.* Maryknoll, NY: Orbis Books, 1984.

Dickson, Kwesi. *Story of the early Church as found in the Acts of the Apostles.* Darton, Longman & Todd Ltd. 1976.

Dickson, Kwesi, and Paul Ellingworth. *Biblical Revelation and African Beliefs.* Lutterworth, 1969.

Dickson, Kwesi. *From Abraham to the Early Days of Israel in the Promised Land (History & Religions of Israel).* Darton, Longman & Todd Ltd., 1970.

Dickson, Kwesi. *Uncompleted Mission: Christianity and Exclusivism*, Maryknoll, NY: Orbis Books, 1991.

Ezeogu, Ernest Munachi, Nigerian Holy Ghost Father. *Jesu Onye Afrika: Ozioma Maka uwa Nile* (Jesus the African: Good News for the Whole World, Ibgo Odenigbo Lectures, Nwangele) 2009.

Gœrgen, Donald J., O.P. "The Quest for the Christ of Africa," *The Journal of the Faculty of Theology,* Catholic University of Eastern Africa, vol. 17, # 1 (September 2001).

Hanciles, Jehu. *Beyond Christendom: Globalization, African Migration and the Transformation of the West.* Maryknoll, NY: Orbis Books, 2009.

Hanna, Amir, Deacon. *Doctrinal Theology,* orthodoxebooks.org.

*Harmless, William. *Desert Christians: an introduction to the literature of early monasticism.* London: Oxford University Press, 2004.

Idowu, Bolaji. *Towards an Indigenous Church*. London: Oxford University Press, 1965.

Idowu, Bolaji. *African Traditional Religion: a Definition*. Maryknoll, NY: Orbis Books, 1973.

Idowu, Bolaji. *Olódùmarè: God in Yoruba Belief*. New York: Wazobia, 1994.

Kalu, Ogbu U., ed. *African Christianity: An African Story*. Perspectives on Christianity 5.3. Pretoria: Department of Church History, University of Pretoria, 2005.

Kalu, Obgo. *African Pentecostalism: An Introduction*. Oxford University Press, 2008.

Kamil, Jill. *Christianity in the Land of the Pharaohs: The Coptic Orthodox Church*. New York: Routledge, 2002.

Katabole, Emanuel. *Stories from Bethany: On the Faces of the Church in Africa*. Nairobi: Paulines Publications, 2013.

Katabole, Emanuel. *Reconciling All Things*. Downers Grove, IL: IVP, 2008.

Kato, Byang H. *Theological Pitfalls in Africa*. Kisumu, Kenya: Evangel, 1975.

Kirwen, Michael C. *African Cultural Knowledge: Themes and Embedded Beliefs*. Nairobi: Maryknoll Institute of African Studies, 2005.

Kurewa, John Wesley Zwomunondiita. *Biblical Proclamation for Africa Today*. Nashville: Abingdon, 1995.

Magesa, Laurenti. *Anatomy of Inculturation: Transforming the Church in Africa*. Nairobi: Paulines Africa, 2004.

Majawa, Clement Chinkambako Abenguni. *Integrated Approach to African Christian Theology of Inculturation*. Nairobi: Creations Enterprises, 2005.

Malaty, Fr. Tadros Y. *The Gospel According to St. Mark*. Translated by George Botros. Revised by Samy Anis and Dr. Nora El-Agamy. Orange, CA: Coptic Orthodox Christian Center, 2003.

Malaty, Fr. Tadros Y. *The School of Alexandria*. 2 vols. Jersey City, NJ: St. Mark's Coptic Orthodox Church, 1995.

Malaty, Father Tadros Jacoub. *The Unity of the Church and Orthodoxy*, orthodoxebooks.org.

Malaty, Father Tadros Jacoub. *Preaching in the Post-Apostolic Era*, orthodoxebooks.org.

Malaty, Father Tadros Jacoub. *Man and Redemption*, orthodoxebooks.org.

Malaty, Father Tadros Jacoub. *Origen: The Deans of the School of Alexandria*, orthodoxebooks.org.

Malaty, Father Tadros Jacoub. *Orthodoxy and the Contemporary Believer*, orthodoxebooks.org.

Malaty, Father Tadros Jacoub. *Introduction to the Coptic Orthodox Church*, orthodoxebooks.org.

Malaty, Father Tadros Jacoub. *Is There a Divine Justice?* orthodoxebooks.org.

Malaty, Father Tadros Jacoub. *Patristic Commentary on the Book of Genesis*, orthodoxebooks.org.

Malaty, Father Tadros Jacoub. *Patristic Commentary on the Book of Exodus*, orthodoxebooks.org.

Malaty, Father Tadros Jacoub. *Patristic Commentary on First Samuel*, orthodoxebooks.org.

Malaty, Father Tadros Jacoub. *Before Origen*, orthodoxebooks.org.

Malaty, Father Tadros Jacoub. *Evangelism and the Church of Alexandria*, orthodoxebooks.org.

Malaty, Father Tadros Jacoub. *The Coptic Orthodox Church and the Dogmas*, orthodoxebooks.org.

Malaty, Father Tadros Jacoub. *The Epistle of Paul to Titus*, orthodoxebooks.org.

Malaty, Father Tadros Jacoub. *The Gospel According to St. Mark*, orthodoxebooks.org.

Mana, Kä. *Christians and Churches of Africa: Envisioning the Future: Salvation in Jesus Christ and the Building of a New African Society*. Theological Reflections from the South. Akropong-Akuapem, Ghana: Regnum Africa, 2002; Maryknoll, NY: Orbis Books, 2004.

Manus, Ukachukwu Chris. *Christ, the African King: New Testament Christology*. Frankfurt-am-Main, Germany: Peter Lang, 1993.

"Martyrium Marci." In *New Testament Apocrypha*, edited by W. Schneemelcher, 2:461-464. Translated by R. M. Wilson. 6th ed. Louisville: Westminster/John Knox Press, 1989.

Maviiri, John Chrysostom. *African Christian Studies*, CUEA Publications, Catholic University of East Africa, http://www.slideshare.net/IAU_Past_Conferences/utrecht-sb-john-c-maviiri.

Mbiti, John. *Bible and Theology in African Christianity*. Nairobi: Oxford University Press (April 1987).

Mbiti, John S. *Bible and Theology in African Christianity*. Nairobi: Oxford University Press, 1986.

Mettaous, Coptic Bp. *The Perfect Worship*, orthodoxebooks.org.

Mettaous, Coptic Bp. *The Characteristics of Orthodox Teaching*, orthodoxebooks.org.

Moussa, Coptic Bp. *Born Crucified*, orthodoxebooks.org.

Moussa, Coptic Bp. *Dimensions of Human Sexuality*, orthodoxebooks.org.

Mpagi, Peter Wasswa. *African Christian Theology in the Contemporary Context*. Nairobi, Kenya: Marianum Publishing, 2002.

*McCray, Walter Arthur. *The Black Presence in the Bible: Discovering the Black and African Identity of Biblical Persons and Nations*. Chicago: Black Light Fellowship, 1990.

Mofokeng, Takatso Alfred. *The Crucified Among the Crossbearers: Towards a Black Christology*. Kampen: Kok, 1983.

Mudimbe, V. Y. *The Idea of Africa*. Bloomington: Indiana University Press, 1994.

Mugambi, J. N. K. *The African Heritage and Contemporary Christianity*. Nairobi: Longman Kenya, 1989.

Muschete, Alphonse Ngindu. *Les thèmes majeurs de la théologie africaine*. Paris: L'Harmattan, 1989.

Nicoliello, Dominic A. *Our Ancestors in the Faith*. Nairobi, Kenya: Paulines Publications Africa, 1995.

Nkansah-Obrempong, James. "The Contemporary Theological Situation in Africa: An Overview." *Evangelical Review of Theology* 31, no. 2 (2007): 140–49.

Noshy, Ibrahim. *The Coptic Church: Christianity in Egypt*. Washington, D.C.: Coptic Diocese, 1955.

Nyamiti, Charles. *Christ Our Ancestor: Christology from an African Perspective*. Mambo Occasional Papers. Missio Pastoral 11. Gweru, Zimbabwe: Mambo, 1984.

Oduro, Thomas. *Christ Holy Church International*. Perfect Paperback, 2007.

Ogbo, Keno and Joe Aldred, eds. *The Black Church in the 21st Century*. London: Darton, Longman and Todd, 2010.

*O'Leary, De Lacy. *The Saints of Egypt in the Coptic Calendar*. New York: SPCK, 1937.

Olofinjana, Israel. *Twenty Pentecostal Pioneers in Nigeria: Their Lives, Their Legacies*. Xlibris Corporation, 2011.

*Orlandi, Tito. "La patrologia copta." In *Complementi interdisciplinari di patrologia*, edited by Antonio Quacquarelli, pp. 457–502. Rome: Città Nuova, 1989.

*Osborn, Eric. *Clement of Alexandria*. Cambridge: Cambridge University Press, 2005.

Oshitelu, G. A. *The African Fathers of the Early Church*. Ibadan, Nigeria: Sefer, 2002.

Pearson, Birger A. *Gnosticism and Christianity in Roman and Coptic Egypt*. Studies in Antiquity and Christianity. New York: T & T Clark, 2004.

Pearson, Birger A. *Gnosticism, Judaism, and Egyptian Christianity*. Philadelphia: Fortress Press, 1990.

Pearson, Birger A. and James E. Goehring, eds. *The Roots of Egyptian Christianity*. Studies in Antiquity and Christianity. Minneapolis: Fortress Press, 1986.

Philopos, Father Anba Bishoy. *Flight of the Holy family to Egypt*, orthodoxebooks.org.

Pobee, John S. *Toward an African Theology*. Nashville: Abingdon, 1979.

Riad, Henri, Youssef Hanna Shehatta and Youssef al-Gheriani. *Alexandria: An Archeological Guide to the City*. 2nd ed. Alexandria: Regional Authority for Tourism, 1996.

Riad, Zaher. *The Church of Alexandria in Africa*. Cairo: Coptic Orthodox Patriarchate, 1962.

*Russell, Norman. *Cyril of Alexandria*. New York: Routledge, 2000.

Samaan el Suriany, Father. *The Hermit Fathers*, orthodoxebooks.org.

Samuel, Bishop Habib Badie. *Ancient Coptic Churches and Monasteries in the Delta, Sinai, and Cairo*. Cairo: Institute of Coptic Studies, Amba Reweis Abbasiya, 1996.

Sanneh, Lamin. *Disciples of All Nations: Pillars of World Christianity*. Studies in World Christianity. London: Oxford University Press, 2007.

Sanneh, Lamin. *Whose Religion Is Christianity? The Gospel Beyond the West*. Grand Rapids: Eerdmans, 2003.

Sanneh, Lamin. *Abolitionists Abroad: American Blacks and the Making of Modern West Africa*. Harvard University Press, 2000.

Sanneh, Lamin. *The Crown and the Turban: Muslims and West African Pluralism.* Westview Press, 1997.

Sanneh, Lamin. *Piety and Power: Muslims and Christians in West Africa.* Maryknoll, NY: Orbis Books, 1996.

Sanneh, Lamin. *Religion and the Variety of Culture: A Study in Origin and Practice.* Trinity Press International, 1996.

Sanneh, Lamin. *Encountering the West: Christianity and the Global Cultural Process: The African Dimension.* Maryknoll, NY: Orbis Books, 1993.

Sanneh, Lamin. *Translating the Message: The Missionary Impact on Culture.* Maryknoll, NY: Orbis Books, 1989.

Sanneh, Lamin. *West African Christianity: The Religious Impact.* Maryknoll, NY: Orbis Books, 1983.

Sanneh, Lamin. *Summoned from the Margin: Homecoming of an African.* Grand Rapids: Eerdmans, 2012.

Sawirus (Severus) Ibn al-Mukaffa'. *History of the Patriarchs of the Coptic Church of Alexandria.* Patrologia Orientalis 1:101–124 and 381–518. Arabic text edited and translated by B. T. Evetts. Paris: Firmin-Didot, 1906, 1948; Cairo: Society of Coptic Archeology, 1943–1959.

*Scobie, Edward. "African Popes." In *African Presence in Early Europe,* edited by Ivan Van Sertima, pp. 96–107. New Brunswick: Transaction Books, 1985.

*Shaw, Mark. *The Kingdom of God in Africa: A Short History of African Christianity.* Grand Rapids: Baker, 1996.

Shenuda III, Pope. *The Nature of Christ,* orthodoxebooks.org.

Shenuda III, Pope. *What is Man?,* orthodoxebooks.org.

Shenuda III, Pope. *Comparative Theology,* orthodoxebooks.org.

Shenuda III, Pope. *Calmness,* orthodoxebooks.org.

Shenuda III, Pope. *Beholder of God, The Life of St. Mark,* orthodoxebooks.org.

Shenuda III, Pope. *The Life of Repentance and Purity,* orthodoxebooks.org.

Shenuda III, Pope. *Homosexuality and the Ordination of Women,* orthodoxebooks.org.

Shenuda III, Pope. *Words of Spiritual Benefit* (4 volumes), orthodoxebooks.org.

Shenuda III, Pope. *The Transfiguration,* orthodoxebooks.org.

Sleman, Abraam, Father. *The Meaning of the Holy Trinity,* orthodoxebooks.org.

Tawadros, Maurice. *Commentary on the Epistle to the Romans*, orthodoxebooks.org.

Tite Tiénou. *Theological Task of the Church in Africa, Theological Perspectives in Africa*. Africa Christian Press, 1996.

Tite Tiénou. *Tâche théologique en Afrique (Theological Task in Africa)*, Institute of Theological Studies—African Theology and Religions, 2006, Audio CD.

Verstraelen, Frans J. *History of Christianity in Africa in the Context of African History: A Comparative Assessment of Four Recent Historiographical Contributions.* Gweru, Zimbabwe: Mambo Press, 2002.

Villa-Vicencio, Charles, Verwoerd, Wilhelm, eds. *Looking Back, Reaching Forward: Reflections on the Truth and Reconciliation Commission of South Africa.* Zed Books, 2000.

*Wilhite, David E. *Tertullian the African: An Anthropological Reading of Tertullian's Context and Identities.* New York: Walter de Gruyter, 2007.

Zokoué, Isaac. Curriculum, "M.A. Program in Early African Christianity," Bangui, Central African Republic: Bangui Evangelical Theological Seminary.

ADDENDUM: THE FUTURE OF AFRICAN CHRISTIANITY

Bosch, David. *Transforming Mission: Paradigm Shifts in Theology of Mission.* New York, 1991.

Burrows, William R. and Mark R. Gornik. *Understanding World Christianity: The Vision and Work of Andrew F. Walls.* Maryknoll, NY: Orbis Books, 2011.

Dyrness, William A. *Emerging Voices in Global Christian Theology.* Grand Rapids: Zondervan, 1994.

Dyrness, William A. *Learning about Theology from the Third World.* Grand Rapids: Academie Books, 1990.

Jenkins, Philip. *The New Faces of Christianity: Believing the Bible in the Global South.* New York: Oxford, 2006.

Jenkins, Philip. *The Next Christendom: The Coming of Global Christianity.* 3rd edition. Oxford University Press, 2011.

Walls, Andrew. *The Missionary Movement in Christian History: Studies in the Transmission of Faith.* Maryknoll, NY: Orbis Books, 1996.

Walls, Andrew F. *The Cross-Cultural Process in Christian History: Studies in the Transmission and Appropriation of Faith.* Maryknoll, NY: Orbis Books, 2002.

www.ingramcontent.com/pod-product-compliance
Lightning Source LLC
Chambersburg PA
CBHW011751220426
43670CB00021B/2937